Praise for *The New N*

"Dr. Helen Caldicott has the rare ability to combine science with passion, logic with love, and urgency with humor. . . . At the dark dawn of another war without end, it is once again time to listen up as she sounds the global alarm."   —NAOMI KLEIN, author of *No Logo*

"What a contribution to the planet! Helen Caldicott's . . . untiring commitment to the public's health is hastening the end of the nuclear madness."   —BEN COHEN, co-founder of Ben & Jerry's

"Helen Caldicott has done it again. Now, more than ever, her voice is crucial. . . . Read this."   —ROBIN MORGAN

"Helen Caldicott reminds us that the world still possesses thousands of warheads, enough to blow up the world many times over, and that policy remains inordinately influenced by the manufacturers of weapons rather than the makers of peace."
     —DANIEL HIRSCH, President, Committee to Bridge the Gap

"No one has worked harder and longer to prevent human extinction than Helen Caldicott."   —PATCH ADAMS, M.D.

"Dr. Helen Caldicott speaks the truth . . . and her command of the medical consequences of nuclear warfare communicates with visceral force the ultimate madness of those leaders who seek security and safety with nuclear weapons." —ADMIRAL GENE CARROLL

For May

Helen Caldicott

THE
NEW NUCLEAR
DANGER

George W. Bush's
Military-Industrial Complex

HELEN CALDICOTT

THE NEW PRESS
NEW YORK

This book is dedicated to Scott Jeffrey Powell, without whose unswerving perseverance it would never have been written.

Published in the United States by The New Press, New York, 2002
Distributed by W. W. Norton & Company, Inc., New York

LIBRARY OF CONGRESS CATALOGING-IN-PUBLICATION DATA
Caldicott, Helen.
   The new nuclear danger : George W. Bush's military-industrial complex / Helen Caldicott.
       p. cm.
   Includes bibliographical references and index.
   ISBN 1-56584-740-7 (pbk.)
   1. Nuclear weapons—United States.   2. United States—Military policy.
3. Arms race—History—21st century.   4. Nuclear warfare.   5. World politics—21st century.   6. Military-industrial complex—United States.   I. Title.
UA23.C18 2002
627.1'747—dc21   2001055806

The New Press was established in 1990 as a not-for-profit alternative to the large, commercial publishing houses currently dominating the book publishing industry. The New Press operates in the public interest rather than for private gain, and is committed to publishing, in innovative ways, works of educational, cultural, and community value that are often deemed insufficiently profitable.

The New Press, 450 West 41st Street, 6th floor, New York, NY 10036
www.thenewpress.com

Printed in the United States of America

10 9 8 7 6 5 4 3 2 1

CONTENTS

ACKNOWLEDGMENTS

WITH GRATEFUL THANKS to all who helped to assemble and organize the information for this book: Bruce Gagnon, whose prophetic work first inspired the notion of this project; Mary Cunnane whose support and advice was ever present; Diane Wachtell, my excellent editor; Faith Hamlin, my wonderful and persistent agent; Scott Powell, whose meticulous research provided some of the data and all the reference lists; Karl Grossman, Bob Alveraz, and Jacqui Cabasso at Western States Legal Foundation; Hugh Gusterson, MIT; Robert Aldridge, Pacific Life Research Center; Admiral Eugene Carroll, Center for Defense Information; William Hartung and Frida Berrigan, World Policy Institute; Richard Marek and Bonnie Urfer, Nukewatch; Gregory Talmadge, The Center for Responsive Politics; Stephen Schwartz, Bulletin of the Atomic Scientists; Bill Sulzman, Katya Komisaruk, and Jack Cohen-Joppa, The Nuclear Resister; and Maria Gilardin, TUC Radio.

Discretionary Budget, Fiscal Year 2001

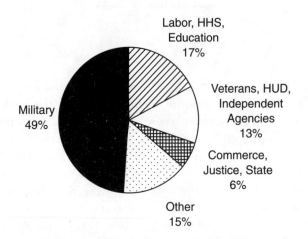

The pie chart shows discretionary spending for Fiscal Year 2001, which runs from October 1, 2000 to September 30, 2001. This is the last discretionary budget settled under the Clinton presidency. Discretionary spending refers to the part of the federal budget that is up to the discretion of Congress. Entitlement programs such as Social Security and Food Stamps are non-discretionary; Congress can restrict or expand eligibility, but cannot directly determine the level of spending. Pentagon spending still consumes almost half of discretionary spending while education takes up only about 7%. (*Source:* © 2001 National Priorities Project, Inc.)

INTRODUCTION

O N S E P T E M B E R 1 1 , before much of the world was even aware of what had happened in New York, Washington, and Pennsylvania, the Bush administration had raised the country's nuclear alert codes from defcon 6 to defcon 2—the highest state of alert before the launch code is operable.* Russia, the country with the second largest nuclear arsenal in the world, almost certainly responded in kind. As a result, thousands of nuclear weapons stood poised on hair-trigger alert, ready to be launched by the president of either country with a decision time of just three minutes. The intercontinental nuclear-armed ballistic missiles controlled by these codes have a thirty-minute transit time from Russia to America or vice versa. They cannot be recalled. And they pose an ever-present threat of global nuclear holocaust.

In the months since the terrorist attacks, Secretary of Defense Donald Rumsfeld and others in the administration have also used September 11 to justify everything from pursuit of a missile-defense shield (even though such a shield would be utterly useless against suicidal men armed with boxcutters and plane tickets) and abandonment of long-standing weapon-control treaties, to massive increases in defense spending. While most Americans desire an increased sense of security in a newly destabilized world, many do not realize that the new "security" measures and the "conventional" war the United States has waged against Afghanistan are intimately connected to the enormous nuclear threat posed by the current American posture. Aggressive militarization under the rubric of defense against terrorism threatens to provoke a chain reaction among nuclear nations, big and small, that, once set in motion, may prove impossible to control. No

* It is not known how long this situation was maintained.[1]

military confrontation anywhere in the world is free from this ominous and ever-present danger.

The U.S.'s own behavior in Afghanistan has veered frighteningly close to deployment of nuclear weapons, which could easily have engendered a nuclear response. In addition to deploying the most horrific conventional weapons known to man (even though there were very few targets of military significance), the defense department recommended the use of tactical nuclear weapons,[2] while some members of Congress strongly advised the use of small nuclear "bunker busters."[3] Bush advisors, including Stephen Hadley, Deputy National Security Advisor Stephen Cambone, and William Schneider, also advocated the use of nuclear weapons.[4] The founder of the neutron bomb, Samuel Cohen, even postulated that his weapon might be appropriate for Afghanistan.[5] (The neutron bomb has a relatively small blast effect compared with its radiation, hence it tends to kill large numbers of people with horrendous radiation illness while leaving buildings intact.) Although the U.S. has previously been clear that it would attack only nuclear-armed countries with nuclear weapons, Secretary of Defense Rumsfeld consistently refused to rule out the use of nuclear weapons in Afghanistan, which is not nuclear-armed.[6]

Some of the conventional weapons America used to support the Northern Alliance during their advances on the Taliban were so powerful that they are described by the Pentagon as "near nuclear" weapons. They are as follows:

15,000-POUND FUEL AIR EXPLOSIVES (FAEs): In military jargon these are referred to as "Daisy Cutters." The Foreign Military Studies Office at Fort Leavenworth says "A fuel air explosive can have the effect of a tactical nuclear weapon without the radiation."[7] There are many different varieties of FAEs, but they typically consist of a container of fuel and two separate explosive charges. Dropped by parachute from a huge MC-130 Combat Talon plane, they detonate just above the ground, creating a wide area of destruction.[8] The first explosion bursts the container at a predetermined height, disbursing the fuel, which mixes with atmospheric oxygen. The second charge then detonates this fuel-air cloud, creating a massive blast that kills people and destroys unreinforced buildings. Near the ignition point people are obliterated, crushed to death with overpressures of 427 pounds per square inch, and incinerated at temperatures of 2500 to 3000 degrees centigrade. Another wave of low pressure—a vacuum effect—then ensues. People in the second zone of destruction are severely burned and suffer massive internal organ injuries before they die. In the third zone, eyes are extruded from their orbits, lungs and ear drums rupture, and severe concussion ensues. The fuel itself—ethylene oxide and propylene oxide—is highly toxic.[9] Up to 200 civilians died 20 miles away from the cave complex in Afghanistan where Osama bin Laden was thought to be hiding at Tora Bora when U.S. planes attacked. They suffered blast trauma—ruptured lungs, blindness, arms and hands blown off, almost certainly from FAEs.[10]

CLUSTER BOMBS: These have been used extensively in Afghanistan by the U.S. Terrifying and deadly, each bomb is composed of 202 bomblets, which are packed with razor-sharp shrapnel dispersed at super-high speed over an area of 22 football fields, ripping into human bodies. These weapons are prohibited by the Geneva Protocol.[11] Civilians were inevitably killed throughout Afghanistan by these illegal and dreadful weapons. On one documented occasion, the U.S. bombed a mosque in Jalabad during prayer and while neighbors were digging out 17 victims, additional bombs killed more than 120 people.[12]

Historically, between 5 and 30 percent of these bomblets fail to explode initially, lying around the countryside as mines that explode with violent force if touched, tearing their victims to pieces. Tragically, the bomblets are colored yellow and shaped like a can of soft drink, and therefore attractive to children.[13] The food parcels containing peanut butter, Pop Tarts, rice, and potatoes dropped throughout Afghanistan by the U.S. are also yellow and the same size and shape as the munitions. (Some of these food drops themselves went astray, destroying houses and killing more people.[14]) Human Rights Watch estimates that over 5000 unexploded cluster bomblets may be littered across Afghanistan, adding to the hundreds of thousands of mines left after the Russian–American war of 1979 to 1989.[15] Afghanistan is currently the most heavily mined country in the world.

GUN SHIPS: These lumbering C-130 planes built by Lockheed Martin have been converted to airborne gunships, capable of firing a fearsome array of weapons, inflicting the most devastating damage, and leveling an area of several football fields, with up to 2000 rounds per minute. They are armed with 25mm Gattling guns, which fire 1800 rounds per minute; 40mm Bofors cannons, which fire 120 rounds per minute; and 105mm Howitzer cannons, which fire 8 to 10 rounds per minute.[16] Secretary of Defense Rumsfeld said Afghanistan is not a "target rich" area, and many analysts felt that these attacks far exceeded their expectations. On October 22nd, in the village of Chowkar-Karez, scores of civilians were mown down by these gunships. CNN quoted an "unnamed" Pentagon official as saying "The people are dead because we wanted them dead."[17] Almost certainly, many civilians therefore were wounded and killed. [18, 19]

BUNKER BUSTERS: Dropped from B-1 or B-2 planes, these 5000-pound behemoths are made from the gun barrels of retired naval ships and are so heavy that they burrow 20 to 100 feet into the ground before their high explosive materials detonate. Most are laser guided, but some use Global Positioning satellites for guidance.[20]

CARPET BOMBING: This means dropping tons of bombs from B-52 planes at a 40,000-foot altitude: high enough to protect pilots but too high to protect civilians. This is indiscriminate bombing, and the pilots have no idea on whom their bombs are landing. In 1969 carpet bombing used in Cambodia by Kissinger and Nixon during the Vietnam War induced the total destruction of the ancient irrigation system and water supply and most of the rice-growing areas of the country and, as a secondary effect, caused the absolute disintegration of Cambodia's culture. The bombing runs were called "breakfast," "lunch," and "supper."[21]

UNMANNED DRONES. These are pilotless planes armed with Hellfire missiles, guided by the Global Positioning System, allowing the military to reduce the time between "identification and destruction of a target."[22] Clearly these planes pose no threats to pilots but terrible threats to civilians on the ground, who may live next to or within a certain "military target," which could be a factory, an electricity generator, or a railway station.

The U.S. has not announced whether or not it used depleted uranium weapons in Afghanistan (as it has done elsewhere in recent wars), but it is quite possible that it did. We will not know for sure until independent sources can enter the war zones and test for this radioactive element.

During the first four weeks of the war, half a million tons of bombs were dropped on Afghanistan, 20 kilos for every man, woman, and child.[23] During eight and a half weeks of U.S. bombing, a documented 3,763 civilians were killed.[24]

WHAT ARE THE INTERNATIONAL RAMIFICATIONS OF THIS BEHAVIOR LIKELY TO BE?

Pakistan has been deeply involved in Afghanistan since the 1979–1989 U.S.–Russian war, when America channeled weapons, training, and funding through the Pakistani military and intelligence services to the mujahadeen, the Taliban, and Osama bin Laden to fight the Russians. After September 11, America changed sides, pressuring Pakistan to ally with the U.S. against their previous friends and allies, the Taliban, bin Laden, and al-Qaeda, because the U.S. needed Pakistani airports to fight their war—a move that was anathema to thousands of Pakistani supporters of bin Laden and the Taliban. These supporters include many members of the Pakistani military, who could well rebel and gain control of the army and its 20 to 50 nuclear weapons, passing these on to the Taliban and al-Qaeda in Afghanistan or to their global networks.

The use of Pakistani nuclear weapons could trigger a chain reaction. Nuclear-armed India, an ancient enemy, could respond in kind. China, India's hated foe, could react if India used her nuclear weapons, triggering a nuclear holocaust on the subcontinent. If any of either Russia or America's 2,250 strategic weapons on hair-trigger alert were launched either accidentally or purposefully in response, nuclear winter would ensue, meaning the end of most life on earth.

OTHER NUCLEAR THREATS

TERRORIST NUCLEAR WEAPONS

Up to 100 small suitcase Russian nuclear weapons have been lost over some years. Al-Qaeda network may now possess several of these, which could well be smuggled into America on a small boat or overland, from Canada or Mexico, in a truck. Nuclear Oklahoma Cities are not beyond question. Immediate deaths would number in the tens of thousands, while tens of thousands of cancers would incubate quietly among the survivors over decades. Britain, Europe, and Australia, among other places, will not remain immune.

DIRTY NUCLEAR DEVICES

Hundreds of tons of highly carcinogenic plutonium and enriched uranium stand unguarded in Russia. From 1993 to 2000, the UN International Atomic Energy Agency—which monitors nuclear security—documented 153 confirmed cases of theft of nuclear materials.[25] Some of this material could be obtained by terrorists to make primitive nuclear weapons, or "dirty" bombs. There would be no nuclear explosion, but conventional explosives would be used to scatter plutonium or uranium across a wide area, contaminating all in the pathway with these carcinogenic elements. Other radioactive elements from reprocessed nuclear fuel, such as cesium-137, strontium-90, and cobalt-60, could also be deployed.[26]

Terrorists could, with some difficulty, manufacture their own nuclear devices from stolen plutonium or uranium. The design for a primitive weapon can be found on the internet. The possibilities for nuclear terrorism seem endless.

NUCLEAR MELTDOWNS

Terrorists do not actually need nuclear weapons. They have been conveniently supplied with 103 nuclear power plants scattered throughout the United States (438 of these deadly facilities exist throughout the world).[27] A planned meltdown at one of these facilities would make the World Trade Center attacks seem like child's play. The massive concrete containers protecting the reactors are not strong enough to withstand the impact of a jumbo jet.

Alternatively, an infiltrator working as an operator could engineer a meltdown by taking over the control room, as the hijackers on September 11 took over the planes. They could also disrupt the water supply (one million gallons a minute is needed to cool a reactor core) or the external electricity supply. Either event would induce a meltdown within hours. The spent-fuel cooling pools adjacent to the reactor contain 20 to 30 times more long-lived radiation than the actual reactor core.[28] (A 1000 megawatt nuclear reactor contains as much long-lived radiation as that released by the explosion of 1000 Hiroshima-sized bombs).

Here is the medical description of the meltdown of a 1000-megawatt nuclear power plant near New York City (there are two reactors at Indian Point, 35 miles north of Manhattan):

With ten million people at risk, 3300 people would die from severe radiation damage within several days; 10,000 to 100,000 would develop lethal acute radiation sickness within 2 to 6 weeks of exposure; 45,000 would become short of breath from lung damage caused by inhalation of intensely radioactive gases; 240,000 would become hypothyroid, with accompanying symptoms of weight gain, lassitude, slow mental functions, loss of appetite, constipation, and absent menstruation; 350,000 males would be rendered temporarily sterile, while the remaining sperm would be genetically mutated; 40,000 to 100,000 women would stop menstruating, many permanently. Up to 100,000 babies would be born as cretins, mentally retarded, as radioactive iodine destroys their thyroid glands (imperative for neurological development), and there would be 3000 deaths in utero. Five to sixty years later, 270,000 people would develop cancers of various organs, and there would be an estimated 28,800 cases of thyroid malignancy.[29]

Apart from the nuclear power plants, there are many military-related nuclear facilities in the United States with massive quantities of nuclear waste, all vulnerable to terrorist attacks.

Since September 11, the FAA banned all aircraft flying within 12 miles of any nuclear facility. The Nuclear Regulatory Commission (NRC) advised all reactors to go on the highest state of alert,[30] and for the first time, the NRC is investing 800,000 dollars to stockpile massive quantities of potassium iodide tablets to be made available to the public in case of a meltdown. Specific states will need to request the

tablets, and this medicine must be taken within hours of a meltdown
to block the uptake of radio-iodine by the thyroid gland. (This measure may not be adequate, however, because over one hundred different deadly radioactive elements are also released during a meltdown,
and these concentrate in other bodily organs.[31])

POLITICAL IMPLICATIONS

The scope of U.S. retaliation for September 11 may be as important a
factor in international response as the nature of the weapons the U.S.
employs. In Washington, the Bush administration is experiencing its
own internecine warfare around this topic. On the one hand, Secretary of State Colin Powell and the state department put together a
harmonious if tenuous international coalition with Europe, Russia,
China, and the Arab nations to "battle" terrorism in Afghanistan
only. But the defense department has been taken over by unrecon-
structed, Reagan-era Cold War warriors, intent on moving the war
from Afghanistan to other states.[32]

This policy is extremely dangerous. Vice President Cheney has
listed fifty states or countries that could be targeted by the U.S. for
military, financial, or diplomatic action, including North Korea, Somalia, Yemen, Iran, the Sudan, Libya, Syria, Lebanon, Indonesia, the
Philippines, Saudi Arabia, and countries in South America. Victoria
Clarke, a Pentagon spokeswoman, warned, "The war on terrorism
neither begins nor ends with Afghanistan. The president will decide
the next target." [33]

Iraq tops the list. Ever since the U.S.–Iraqi war in 1991, when
America "failed to eliminate Hussein," a right-wing putsch has been
eager to finish the job. The excuse: Iraq will not allow weapons in-
spectors to enter the country, barring them since December 1998
from checking for nuclear, biological, or chemical weapons activities.
(However, Iraq's foreign minister, Naji Sabri, said in late November
2001, "We will consider a return of monitoring [of weapons] after
the lifting of sanctions." [34]) Deputy Secretary of Defense Paul Wolfowitz is spearheading the Iraqi attack movement along with his
close colleague Richard Perle, who was Reagan's undersecretary of
defense.

Perle chairs an unofficial bipartisan group called the Defense Policy Board, which is vigorously promoting the overthrow of Hussein, even though there is no evidence linking him to the September 11 attacks.[35,36] (The Defense Policy Board meets in a room adjacent to the secretary of defense's office, and includes such luminaries as Henry Kissinger, former secretary of state; Harold Brown, former secretary of defense; Newt Gingrich, former house majority leader; and R. James Woolsey, former director of the CIA. The group has assumed a quasi-official status with the imprimatur of Secretary Rumsfeld.) This attitude seems to be prevailing within the administration, and Powell appears to be losing his authority, although the international community is outraged by these proposals.

An attack on Iraq would infuriate Arab populations, the U.S.-led alliance against al-Qaeda[37] would dissolve, and the world would descend into a terrorist-ruled chaos. A veteran of the CIA's Directorate of Operations said "The agency as an institution would never offer up a view of these people [Perle, et al.], but if you ask individuals, they think these guys are more than a little nuts." Another longtime case officer at the CIA said, "Attack these places and there will be consequences that we simply will not be able to deal with. But Perle and Wolfowitz are absolutists, and they're stupid."[38]

Meanwhile, other destabilizing plans are afoot in the Bush administration:

- The administration will aggressively pursue testing of its missile defense system, a.k.a. Star Wars, even though Russia and China are adamantly opposed. After the cordial Bush-Putin meeting at Crawford Ranch in Texas in November 2001, National Security Advisor Condoleezza Rice said, "The timeline has not really changed. The president continues to believe that he has got to move forward with the testing program in a robust way, so that we can really begin to evaluate the potential for missile defenses." What she means is that the U.S. will withdraw from the seminal Anti Ballistic Missile Treaty (ABM) with six months notice.[39] Such a move will destabilize global arms control and the associated treaties, and induce a massive new nuclear arms race.
- The Bush administration boycotted the Comprehensive Test-Ban Treaty Conference (CTBT) at the United Nations in November

2001 and had the audacity to remove its nameplate from its seat in the conference room. A week before, at a General Assembly meeting, the U.S. was the only country to vote against placing the CTBT on the General Assembly's agenda for 2002. Washington has signed, but the Senate has not ratified the treaty, which would ban all above- and below-ground nuclear testing. As a group of non-government organizations said, "Failure to act may lead to a cascade of proliferation events that will enable future terrorists to use nuclear weapons." [40]

- There is a strong move by Bush's people to resume nuclear testing at the Nevada Test site because, as Secretary of Defense Rumsfeld said, "we may need to develop new nuclear weapons." This could stimulate Russia, China, India, and Pakistan, among others, to resume nuclear testing, leading to a new nuclear arms race. [41]

- In July 2001, the U.S. prevented the UN conference on curbing small-arms exports from convening by insisting that it was a threat to the Second Amendment.

- Also in July 2001, after ten years of negotiations, the U.S. refused to endorse a protocol on a compliance to ban biological weapons, saying it would put at risk national security and confidential business information.

- In February 2001, the U.S. delegate at a UN debate to combat terrorism said such a conference would have no practical benefits. [42]

- In November 2001, Congress cut 69 million dollars from a program designed to safeguard Russian nuclear materials in order to prevent terrorists stealing plutonium and enriched uranium to build their own nuclear bombs. Bush wanted to reduce the program still further by 29 million dollars. [43]

- Simultaneously, Congress increased the funding for U.S. nuclear weapons by 300 million dollars and granted 8.3 billion dollars for missile defense. [44] As Joseph Cirincione of the Carnegie Endowment for International Peace said, "Tragically some are using the terrible tragedy [September 11] to justify their existing programs, slapping an 'anti-terrorist' label on missile defense and military budget increases." [45]

- The terrorist attack has provided a great fillip for the military-industrial complex. The military budget is expected to reach 375 billion dollars in 2001, a 66 billion dollar increase from 2001, and

Deputy Secretary of Defense Paul Wolfowitz said that these appropriations will "just be a down-payment" toward the major long-term increases the Pentagon will need to fight its new kind of war [46] which Vice President Cheney says "may not end in our lifetimes." [47]

- The war in Afghanistan is costing 1 billion dollars a month,[48] while two thirds of the world's children are malnourished and starving.

Loren Thompson, defense analyst from the Lexington Institute said "The whole mind set of military spending changed on September 11. The most fundamental thing about defense spending is that threats drive defense spending. It's now going to be easier to fund almost anything." Indeed, Lockheed Martin stocks rose from $39.39 on September 11 to $48.11 by November 12, 2001. The Pentagon is to receive 20 billion dollars of the 40 billion dollars allocated by congress for antiterrorist activities, an amount to be added to 343.2 billion dollars for fiscal 2001, already the largest military budget since Reagan's at the height of the cold war—greater than 50% of all discretionary funding for domestic needs. Among the firms already benefitting from this extraordinarily extravagant and unnecessary largess are Lockheed Martin, Grumman, Raytheon, and Boeing. Most of this money will not be used for the war in Afghanistan, but for new fighter planes like the F/A-18E/F, the F-22, and the Joint Strike fighter, for a new Virginia class submarine designed to trail now-extinct Soviet subs around the globe, and for 12 more Trident D5 submarine ballistic missiles. In this context it is interesting to note that the Afghanis had very few planes to speak of, and that these were destroyed by massive U.S. bombing within the first few days of the war. Paul Nisbet, another defense analyst said, "With the [Bush] administration, we will see a rebuilding of the military to bring it back to where it was eight years ago. We will see a considerable appreciation in defense stocks as we saw in the Reagan years." [49, 50]

RECENT INTERNATIONAL WEAPONS DEVELOPMENTS

People may feel reassured that President Bush, meeting in Texas in November 2001 with President Putin, offered to reduce America's stockpile of strategic weapons from some 7000 down to 2220–1700 over the next ten years. But this offer was made without the guarantee of any formal written treaty and can therefore be abandoned or reversed at any time. Without verification, it will be impossible to confirm that cuts are actually carried out, while the ten-year duration gives much latitude for reversal and change.

In fact, although the cuts look good on paper, they mean nothing. The U.S. will still have plenty of weapons to maintain its first-strike winnable nuclear war policy, and none of the weapons will be dismantled, but will be stored, awaiting possible future use. The reductions do not include the removal of multiple warheads on missiles required by the START II Treaty (the Russians have a monstrous ten-warheaded SS-18 missile, code named "Satan"). And the U.S. Trident submarine fleet, with their invulnerable first-strike arsenal, will be exempt, as will weapons on long-distance bombers being overhauled, and all tactical nuclear weapons.[51]

In truth, if Russia comes to the party, such bilateral reductions will make it easier for the U.S. to win a nuclear war against Russia, because there will be fewer targets, and the missile-defense system now under construction will mop up any Russian missiles that escape the initial surprise attack. U.S. antisatellite weapons under construction will also be necessary to destroy the "eyes and ears" of the Russian early-warning system. This is a terrifying but realistic scenario, a logical extension of the Pentagon's current policy to "fight and win" a nuclear war.

So Bush's unilateral reductions proposal is a ploy to divert the world's attention away from his Star Wars project, which Simon Tisdall of the London *Guardian* called "a reckless act of weapons proliferation," which will provoke an international arms race, entangle third parties such as Britain and Australia, and, as this book makes clear, lead directly to the militarization of space if it does not cause nuclear winter first.

Tisdall warns that "the highly contentious military and geostrategic foundations of the 21st century are being laid—and hardly anybody is watching."[52]

That is why I wrote this book.

THE NEW NUCLEAR DANGER

Chapter One

THE TRAGEDY OF WASTED OPPORTUNITIES

*The hidden hand of the market will never work without a hidden fist.
McDonald's cannot flourish without McDonnell Douglas, the
designer of the F-15. And the hidden fist that keeps the world safe for
Silicon Valley's technologies is called the United States Army, Air
Force, Navy, and Marine Corps.*
                    —Thomas Friedman, *New York Times Magazine,*
                                                March 28, 1999

IMAGINE THIS: The cold war is over. A wise and visionary young American president, elected in 1992, decides that now is the time to rid the world of nuclear weapons. Six months into his first term he flies to Moscow to meet with a pliable Russian president, who agrees to sign a treaty to eliminate Russian and American nuclear weapons within five years. The governments of France, China, England, and Israel follow suit. India and Pakistan choose not to pursue the development of nuclear armaments, a path they were about to take. The United Nations is vested by the international community with the authority and funding to prevent lateral proliferation of nuclear weapons. Hundreds of tons of deadly plutonium are removed over the next five years from the world's total of 52,972 nuclear weapons.[1] The overwhelming relief that the world will soon be free from the threat of instant annihilation catalyzes effective international planning and cooperation to solve the problem of where and how to store the plutonium.

American tax dollars are diverted from massive Pentagon and corporate military budgets into projects designed to take care of the nation's people. A government-funded system of universal health care is instituted, and free, state-of-the-art education from kinder-garten through college gradually becomes available throughout the nation. Congress passes a law mandating that all cars be built to oper-ate at 80 miles per gallon and appropriates funding for public-transportation initiatives in every state. Legislation is enacted requiring that most buildings be retrofitted to collect solar energy, and that every new building be powered, heated, and cooled by solar energy. Generous safety nets are put in place, providing for the old, the poor, the sick, and the indigent, and the Social Security system re-mains immune to the work of "market forces." Every American child will be fully immunized, and no child will live below the poverty line.

Almost five decades since the dawn of the atomic age, the United States of America is on the way to becoming truly secure, no longer dependent on a nuclear barricade for its safety. The nation becomes an inspirational example to all other countries as we enter the twenty-first century.

Now blink and reenter reality.

A newly elected young president—touched paradoxically with both hubris and timidity—who had never acquired an in-depth knowledge of matters military or nuclear was handicapped by a se-vere leadership impediment: He had evaded the Vietnam draft. In his own mind he never overcame this apparent character deficit, and the military that he allegedly commanded made sure that he never forgot it. To exacerbate this situation, several acute personal prob-lems of a deeply embarrassing—not to mention compromising—nature occupied this president, to the point where he contemplated possible resignation and faced actual impeachment.

Partly to compensate for these "deficiencies," Clinton used U.S. military force overseas—in Bosnia, Iraq, and Kosovo, among other places—more frequently than any other U.S. president of the last twenty years. Further, his was the only administration since Eisen-hower's that did not negotiate a single significant nuclear arms con-trol treaty.[2]

Bill Clinton's basic disinterest, distraction, draft handicap, and lack of vision allowed the military—Pentagon, nuclear scientists, and military corporations—to move into this presidential vacuum.[3] They wooed, seduced, and bought Congress and the administrative staff, and the opportunity for nuclear disarmament was tragically lost. Ironically, as we enter the twenty-first century, after eight years of a Democratic administration, the world is in a position even more dangerous than it was at the height of Reagan's buildup of nuclear weapons and Star Wars dreams. It is against this unfortunate backdrop that the events of September 11, 2001, took place, adding ominously to the possibility of international nuclear war or nuclear accidents, as the U.S. nuclear arsenal was placed on the highest state of alert and international tensions rose. U.S. nuclear policy and weaponry has never been more aggressive:

- The U.S. currently has 2000 intercontinental land-based hydrogen bombs, 3456 nuclear weapons on submarines roaming the seas 15 minutes from their targets, and 1750 nuclear weapons on intercontinental planes ready for delivery. Of these 7206 weapons, roughly 2500 remain on hair-trigger alert, ready to be launched at the press of a button.[4] Russia has a similar number of strategic weapons, with approximately 2000 on hair-trigger alert.[5, 6] In total there is now enough explosive power in the combined nuclear arsenals of the world to "overkill" every person on earth 32 times.[7]

- The U.S. currently has in place plans to fight and win a nuclear war, and is prepared to use nuclear weapons first if necessary. Winning a nuclear war with Russia, for example, requires the use of anti-satellite weapons to destroy Russian early warning systems, a secret preemptive first strike attack to destroy Russian missiles before they can be launched from their silos, and preemptive destruction of Russian nuclear subs in port and at sea, all of which capabilities are currently in place. (Any Russian missiles escaping the initial attack would have to be destroyed en route to the U.S. in space, using a newly developed U.S. ballistic missile defense system.)

- The Pentagon's official targeting plan, the single integrated operational plan (SIOP), has been upgraded since 1989: Instead of a total of 2500 targets there are now 3000. These include 2260 Russian sites, 1100 of which are ostensibly "nuclear facilities," 160 of which are "leadership" targets—government offices and military command centers (in a country almost devoid of leadership)—and 500 of which are disintegrating factories that produced almost no arms last year.[8]

- China is now included in SIOP for the first time in twenty years, despite the fact that the U.S. Senate moved to normalize relations with China by granting it permanent normal trading relations status (PNTR) in September 2000. (This country of 1.3 billion people, potentially a huge market for the U.S., has only twenty nuclear missiles capable of reaching America.)

- Non-nuclear nations such as Iran, Iraq, and North Korea are also targeted with nuclear weapons for the first time.[9] (Before the nineties, the U.S. had targeted only other countries with nuclear weapons.)

- The U.S. department of energy's nuclear laboratories—Los Alamos and Sandia in New Mexico, and Lawrence Livermore in California—are embarked on a second "Manhattan Project"—a massive scientific undertaking costing 5 to 6 billion dollars annually for the next ten to fifteen years, to design, test, and develop new nuclear weapons under the guise of ensuring the safety and reliability of the U.S.'s current stockpile of nuclear weapons.[10] This is twice the cost of the original Manhattan Project, which developed the first three atom bombs in the early forties, and significantly more than the annual average of 3.8 billion dollars spent on nuclear weapons during the cold war.[11]

- The Bush administration is pledged to fast-track plans for a new national missile defense system. This runs the risk of destabilizing the many arms-control treaties already negotiated between Russia and America.

Who are the enemies that America is so frantically and expensively arming against at the dawn of the twenty-first century? Until September 11, 2001, America had no enemies with the potential to wreak real harm on its land or people. It has friendly countries to the north and south, and vast oceans to the east and west. Under the current configuration, no foreign nation would ever think of invading the U.S. But it is now apparent that America has terrorist enemies—amorphous, difficult to track and locate, and almost impossible to extinguish by firepower or enormous arsenals of weapons.

The Pentagon and State Department justify the extraordinary U.S. military expenditure—now 310 billion dollars annually—with potential threats from North Korea, Iraq, Iran, China, Russia, and possibly Libya. But of these, only the 5000 strategic nuclear weapons in Russia—half of which could hit U.S. cities thirty minutes after launching—pose a major threat to American security. More relevantly, as recent events have made all too clear, the largest nuclear stockpile in the world can accomplish little in the face of terrorists armed with box cutters, except, possibly, offering the potential for terrifying escalation of any ensuing conflict between nations. America currently spends 22 times as much on its military forces as all the other so-called rogue states or "states of concern"—Iraq, Iran, Syria, North Korea, Cuba, and Libya—put together, when nullification of any threat they might pose could be achieved for a fraction of that amount.[12, 13]

Other possible explanations for America's immense military expenditure include:

- It fattens the coffers of weapons makers.
- It is a direct result of the rivalry between the air force, the army, the navy, and the marines, each of whom want their own weapons systems.
- It elevates the prestige of top lawmakers within Congress and the White House who are the recipients of huge donations from weapons manufacturers as they legislate for more weapons.
- A huge conventional and nuclear arsenal allows America to do what it will around the world with impunity—it is the iron hand in the velvet glove of U.S. corporate globalization.

All of this is why Clinton's failure to seize the opportunity to eliminate or pare down the number of nuclear weapons in the world through rapid and realistic negotiation with Russia—at a time when this was possible—is so deeply tragic. Ironically, it may well be the very fact of the September 11 attack, and the U.S.'s resulting need to adopt a more conciliatory stance toward Russia, that leads George W. Bush to enact the stockpile reductions that eluded Clinton in calmer times.

The nuclear weapons establishment has four arms—the nuclear scientists, the military corporations, Congress plus the White House, and the Pentagon. Subsequent chapters look at each of these in turn. But first, let's set the stage by imagining what nuclear war might really be like.

Chapter Two

THE REALITY OF NUCLEAR WAR

W HAT WILL LIKELY BE the final conclusion to in-
cessant nuclear-war planning? The destruction of the
planet. And such an event could be triggered tonight
or tomorrow by human or computer error, or even by a terrorist
attack.

What would nuclear war be like?

MEDICAL CONSEQUENCES OF NUCLEAR WAR

If launched from Russia, nuclear weapons would explode over American cities thirty minutes after takeoff. (China's twenty missiles are
liquid-fueled, not solid-fueled. They take many hours to fuel and
could not be used in a surprise attack, but they would produce similar
damage if launched. Other nuclear-armed nations, such as India and
Pakistan, do not have the missile technology to attack the U.S.) It is
assumed that most cities with a population over 100,000 people are
targeted by Russia. During these thirty minutes, the U.S. early-
warning infrared satellite detectors signal the attack to the strategic
air command in Colorado. They in turn notify the president, who has
approximately three minutes to decide whether or not to launch a
counterattack. In the counterforce scenario the U.S. government currently embraces, he does launch, the missiles pass mid-space, and the
whole operation is over within one hour.

Landing at 20 times the speed of sound, nuclear weapons explode
over cities, with heat equal to that inside the center of the sun. There
is practically no warning, except the emergency broadcast system on

radio or TV, which gives the public only minutes to reach the nearest fallout shelter, assuming there is one. There is no time to collect children or immediate family members.

The bomb, or bombs—because most major cities will be hit with more than one explosion—will gouge out craters 200 feet deep and 1000 feet in diameter if they explode at ground level. Most, however, are programmed to produce an air burst, which increases the diameter of destruction, but creates a shallower crater. Half a mile from the epicenter all buildings will be destroyed, and at 1.7 miles only reinforced concrete buildings will remain.

At 2.7 miles bare skeletons of buildings still stand, single-family residences have disappeared, 50 percent are dead and 40 percent severely injured.[1] Bricks and mortar are converted to missiles traveling at hundreds of miles an hour. Bodies have been sucked out of buildings and converted to missiles themselves, flying through the air at 100 miles per hour. Severe overpressures (pressure many times greater than normal atmospheric pressure) have popcorned windows, producing millions of shards of flying glass, causing decapitations and shocking lacerations. Overpressures have also entered the nose, mouth, and ears, inducing rupture of lungs and rupture of the tympanic membranes or eardrums.

Most people will suffer severe burns. In Hiroshima, which was devastated by a very small bomb—13 kilotons compared to the current 1000 kilotons—a child actually disappeared, vaporized, leaving his shadow on the concrete pavement behind him. A mother was running, holding her baby, and both she and the baby were converted to a charcoal statue. The heat will be so intense that dry objects—furniture, clothes, and dry wood—will spontaneously ignite. Humans will become walking, flaming torches.

Forty or fifty miles from the explosion people will instantly be blinded from retinal burns if they glance at the flash. Huge firestorms will engulf thousands of square miles, fanned by winds from the explosion that transiently exceed 1000 miles per hour. People in fallout shelters will be asphyxiated as fire sucks oxygen from the shelters. (This happened in Hamburg after the Allied bombing in WWII when temperatures within the shelters, caused by conventional bombs, reached 1472 degrees Fahrenheit.)[2]

FALLOUT

Most of the city and its people will be converted to radioactive dust shot up in the mushroom cloud. The area of lethal fallout from this cloud will depend upon the prevailing wind and weather conditions; it could cover thousands of square miles. Doses of 5000 rads (a rad is a measure of radiation dose) or more experienced by people close to the explosion—if they are still alive—will produce acute encephalopathic syndrome. The cells of the brain will become so damaged that they would swell. Because the brain is enclosed in a fixed bony space, there is no room for swelling, so the pressure inside the skull rises, inducing symptoms of excitability, acute nausea, vomiting, diarrhea, severe headache, and seizures, followed by coma and death within twenty-four hours.

A lower dose of 1000 rads causes death from gastrointestinal symptoms. The lining cells of the gut die, as do the cells in the bone marrow that fight infection and that cause blood clotting. Mouth ulcers, loss of appetite, severe colicky abdominal pain, nausea, vomiting, and bloody diarrhea occur within seven to fourteen days. Death follows severe fluid loss, infection, hemorrhage, and starvation.

At 450 rads, 50 percent of the population dies. Hair drops out, vomiting and bloody diarrhea occurs, accompanied by bleeding under the skin and from the gums. Death occurs from internal hemorrhage, generalized septicemia, and infection. Severe trauma and injuries exacerbate the fallout symptoms, so patients die more readily from lower doses of radiation. Infants, children, and old people are more sensitive to radiation than healthy adults. Within bombed areas, fatalities will occur from a combination of trauma, burns, radiation sickness, and starvation. There will be virtually no medical care, even for the relief of pain, because most physicians work within targeted areas.

NUCLEAR POWER PLANTS

The United States owns 103 nuclear power plants, plus many other dangerous radioactive facilities related to past activities of the cold war. A 1000-kiloton bomb (1 megaton) landing on a standard 1000-

megawatt reactor and its cooling pools, which contain intensely radioactive spent nuclear fuel, would permanently contaminate an
area the size of western Germany.[3] The International Atomic Energy
Agency now considers these facilities to be attractive terrorist targets,
post–September 11, 2001.

DISEASE

Millions of decaying bodies—human and animal alike—will rot, infected with viruses and bacteria that will mutate in the radioactive
environment to become more lethal. Trillions of insects, naturally
resistant to radiation—flies, fleas, cockroaches, and lice—will trans-
mit disease from the dead to the living, to people whose immune
mechanisms have been severely compromised by the high levels of
background radiation. Rodents will multiply by the millions among
the corpses and shattered sewerage systems. Epidemics of diseases
now controlled by immunization and good hygiene will reappear:
such as measles, polio, typhoid, cholera, whooping cough, diphtheria,
smallpox, plague, tuberculosis, meningitis, malaria, and hepatitis.

Anyone who makes it to a fallout shelter and is not asphyxiated in
it, will need to stay there for at least six months until the radiation de-
cays sufficiently so outside survival is possible. It has been postulated
that perhaps older people should be sent outside to scavenge for food
because they will not live long enough to develop malignancies from
the fallout (cancer and leukemia have long incubation periods ranging from five to sixty years). But any food that manages to grow will
be toxic because plants concentrate radioactive elements.[4]

NUCLEAR WINTER

Finally, we must examine the systemic global effects of a nuclear
war. Firestorms will consume oil wells, chemical facilities, cities, and
forests, covering the earth with a blanket of thick, black, radioactive
smoke, reducing sunlight to 17 percent of normal. One year or more
will be required for light and temperature to return to normal—perhaps supranormal values, as sunlight would return to more than its
usual intensity, enhanced in the ultraviolet spectrum by depletion of
the stratospheric ozone layer. Subfreezing temperatures could de-

stroy the biological support system for civilization, resulting in massive starvation, thirst, and hypothermia.[5]

To quote a 1985 SCOPE document published by the White House
Office of Science and Technology Policy, "the total loss of human
agricultural and societal support systems would result in the loss of
almost all humans on Earth, essentially equally among combatant
and noncombatant countries alike . . . this vulnerability is an aspect
not currently a part of the understanding of nuclear war; not only are
the major combatant countries in danger, but virtually the entire
human population is being held hostage to the large-scale use of nuclear weapons. . . ."

The proposed START III treaty between Russia and America,
even if it were implemented, would still allow 3000 to 5000 hydrogen bombs to be maintained on alert.[6] The threshold for nuclear
winter? One thousand 100-kiloton bombs blowing up 100 cities[7]—a
distinct possibility given current capabilities and targeting plans.

ACCIDENTAL NUCLEAR WAR

On January 25, 1995, military technicians at radar stations in northern Russia detected signals from an American missile that had just
been launched off the coast of Norway carrying a U.S. scientific
probe. Although the Russians had been previously notified of this
launch, the alert had been forgotten or ignored. Aware that U.S. submarines could launch a missile containing eight deadly hydrogen
bombs fifteen minutes from Moscow, Russian officials assumed
that America had initiated a nuclear war. For the first time in history, the Russian computer containing nuclear launch codes was
opened.

President Boris Yeltsin, sitting at that computer being advised on
how to launch a nuclear war by his military officers, had only a three-
minute interval to make a decision. At the last moment, the U.S. missile veered off course. He realized that Russia was not under attack.[8]

If Russia had launched its missiles, the U.S. early-warning satellites would immediately have detected them, and radioed back to
Cheyenne Mountain. This would have led to the notification of the
president, who also would have had three minutes to make his launch
decision, and America's missiles would then have been fired from

their silos. We were thus within minutes of global annihilation that day.

Today, Russia's early-warning and nuclear command systems are deteriorating. Russia's early-warning system fails to operate up to seven hours a day because only one-third of its radars are functional, and two of the nine global geographical areas covered by its missile-warning satellites are *not under surveillance for missile detection.*[9] To make matters worse, the equipment controlling nuclear weapons malfunctions frequently, and critical electronic devices and computers sometimes switch to combat mode for no apparent reason. According to the CIA, seven times during the fall of 1996 operations at some Russian nuclear weapons facilities were severely disrupted when robbers tried to "mine" critical communications cables for their copper![10] This vulnerable Russian system could easily be stressed by an internal or international political crisis, when the danger of accidental or indeed intentional nuclear war would become very real.

And the U.S. itself is not invulnerable to error. In August 1999, for example, when the National Imagery and Mapping Agency was installing a new computer system to deal with potential Y2K problems, this operation triggered a computer malfunction which rendered the agency "blind" for days; it took more than eight months for the defect to be fully repaired. As the *New York Times* reported, part of America's nuclear early-warning system was rendered incompetent for almost a year.[11] (At that time I was sitting at a meeting in the west wing of the White House discussing potentially dangerous Y2K nuclear weapons glitches. Several Pentagon officials blithely reassured me that everything would function normally during the roll-over. But in fact, their intelligence system had already been disabled.)

Such a situation has the potential for catastrophe. If America cannot observe what the Russians are doing with their nuclear weapons—or vice versa—especially during a serious international crisis they are likely to err on the side of "caution," which could mean that something as benign as the launch of a weather satellite could actually trigger annihilation of the planet. This situation became even more significant after the September 11 attack.

Chapter Three

IT'S A MAD, MAD WORLD:
NUCLEAR SCIENTISTS AND THE PENTAGON
PLAY WITH DEADLY GADGETS

We were fascinated by abstract violence on a huge scale. I became addicted to nuclear weapons work. It gave me a sense of great power. I remember dreams about a weapons design that I'd been working on— when it failed it was a nightmare. When it succeeded it was a high—that sense of: I'm good at this. It's my bomb. Except we never called them bombs. We called them gadgets.

—Ted Taylor, former bomb designer

NUCLEAR SCIENTISTS have been called priests or monks by a media and public in awe of their inventions.[1] Most journalists and policy-makers therefore assume that the scientific activities within the weapons labs are sacrosanct and beyond question.[2] Because of the almost-mystical power these individuals are granted, they have dominated the national security scene since the Manhattan Project began in 1942. Virtually unimpeded and uncontrolled, over a period of fifty years they designed sixty-five different types of nuclear weapons, exploded 1030 bombs at the testing site in Nevada, and directed the manufacture of over 70,000 bombs.[3] (As noted above, 1000 bombs exploding over 100 cities could induce "nuclear winter" and the end of most life on the earth.)[4]

These scientists have always operated in absolute secrecy, which gave them the anonymity they needed to pursue their work. They used a language that was incomprehensible to all but the most educated, and, like physicians, they hid behind an arcane scientific complexity, never emerging to inform the world what they were doing.

They still operate the three major nuclear weapons labs—Los Alamos and Sandia in New Mexico, and Lawrence Livermore in California. All are currently run by the department of energy (DOE) and overseen by the University of California. (While most Americans know that the DOE supervises U.S. energy policy, few are aware that the same department also oversees all nuclear weapons research.)

At the end of the cold war, nuclear scientists saw their future slipping away from them. The euphemistically named the Stockpile Stewardship and Management Program (SS & M), was a way to ensure their continued employment. Ostensibly created to ensure that old weapons will still explode if necessary, the labs are actually designing, testing, and building a variety of new nuclear weapons, many in violation of existing treaties and bans. (See Chapter Five for a full discussion of the SS & M charade.)

At a political level the scientists have been able to associate their work with nationalism and the preservation and protection of the United States. Yet it is doubtful that any of the individuals involved—from the politicians mandated to guide and direct these scientists on our behalf to the scientists themselves, the military personnel, or the businessmen who profit from the nuclear weapons enterprise—understand the philosophical, moral, spiritual, or biological problems engendered by capturing gigantic extraterrestrial forces manifested only in the sun and the stars.

Let us begin with the nuclear scientists: thousands of physicists, chemists, and engineers—the cream of the crop, recruited from U.S. colleges over a period of sixty years—brilliant, rational, careful, strictly scientific, engaged in exploring the very elements of creation, and all committed to the design, construction, and testing of nuclear weapons.

Surprisingly, while many are to the right of the political spectrum, others are liberal in their views. They do not believe that designing bombs is an act of patriotism as the right-wingers do, but are drawn to the culture of low-key "rational-speak" (their term for strictly rational discussion, bereft of emotional overtones) and find joy in scientific problem-solving.[5]

The Lawrence Livermore Lab has a policy that if an employee expresses any concern about the ultimate result of the use of nuclear weapons (i.e., the possible destruction of the world), they are advised—and sometimes required—to see a counselor. In a scenario right out of *1984* (and a classic sign of a cult mentality), anyone giving voice to the stark truth must be counseled to accept the lie of the labs.[6]

Cults also typically withhold information from potential recruits to conceal the true nature of the group or the work with which it is involved.[7] Thus, when Dr. Andreas Toupadakis, a chemist, became an employee of the Lawrence Livermore nuclear weapons lab in 1988, he was led to believe that he would be working on environmental cleanup and nuclear disarmament. In fact, as he gradually realized, he was participating in an ongoing nuclear arms race, and he became agitated and deeply concerned. Toupadakis was advised to see a counselor shortly before he left Livermore Lab in January 2000.[8]

Since the 1940s, the scientific bomb cult has allowed individual scientists to design and test their very own bombs. If the testing proved successful, it was a rite-of-passage for the newcomer. More experienced members have attested to gaining a sense of power over the forces of nature while renewing their stature.[9] Bomb designers often slept alone in a room above the Nevada Test Site with the control mechanisms that would trigger the explosion the next day,[10] like a racing-car driver flirting with death—in this case, not just individual death, but the death of millions, the death of life.

At a more fundamental level, these scientists felt that their technical mastery over the bomb implied that they would then be able to control the impending annihilation that their work signified. But in psychological terms the mastery they had acquired actually implied that they had intense fear of the bomb and of death.[11] Interestingly, the language of the scientists reflects the imagery of birth and new life, denoting more profound psychological dynamics. The first nuclear bomb ever tested in 1945, code-named Trinity (after the Father, Son, and Holy Ghost), was called "Oppenheimer's baby" in honor of the scientific director of the Manhattan Project. The telegram Edward Teller sent to Los Alamos after the first successful A-bomb test in 1945 read "it's a boy."[12] The bomb gets "married" to the diagnostic canister, and as it explodes it "couples" with the ground, making "daughter fission products" that pass through "generations."[13] One of the scientists described the test as "like having a baby" and compared the tenseness he experienced during the test to "whether to push or not."[14] Another bomb designer compared his post-test feelings to a state of "postnatal depression."[15]

The anthropologist Hugh Gusterson, in his book *Nuclear Rites,* surmises that to the scientists, nuclear weapons tests "symbolize not despair, destruction, and death but hope, renewal, and life" and therefore nuclear weapons must be part of the natural order. Perhaps at a subliminal level these scientists—almost exclusively men—are seeking an archetypal understanding of the experience of conception and delivery, otherwise unavailable to them. The ultimate destruction of the creation is, in their minds, analogous to creation itself. Oppenheimer quoted the *Bhagavad Gita* upon witnessing Trinity, the first nuclear explosion: "I am become death, the shatterer of worlds."

On the other hand, unlike the nurturing instincts of a new mother, much of their language reflects their profound dehumanization of people. To them, people are "human resources" and "components" within a system. They describe human communication as "interfacing" and miscommunications as "disconnects." The pain of human injuries is referred to as "damage," and when a human being is killed she is "disassembled."[16] The Pentagon echoes this language, calling targeting of cities "countervalue targeting." People are dubbed "soft targets" (missile silos are hard targets). The 15 million civilians who would initially be killed in a counterforce attack on Russian hard targets are "collateral damage."[17]

As Gusterson writes, "Techno-strategic discourse is characterized by its lack of emotion, its game-theoretical models of human motivation, its fondness for abstraction and for passive sentence constructions, its focus on hardware rather than people. And its fundamental unquestioned and unquestionable assumption that weapons development must continue."[18] As they remove pain and fear from their vocabulary, presumably the scientists are protecting their psyches from the human consequences of their work. At the same time, however, they wax lyrical about their weapons, describing nuclear equipment as beautiful, and their relationships to technology as Zen. Weapons are arms, bombs are warheads, a nuclear attack is a decapitating strike, the strategic nuclear forces have three legs, early-warning satellites are eyes and ears, missiles are covered with skins, and aging weapons grow "whiskers" that can interfere with their "health."[19]

Superimposed upon the humanization of nuclear weapons and the mechanization of human bodies is the culture of careful expert rationalism, very similar to the rational language used by physicians to distance themselves from the almost unbearable human pain and suffering they deal with on a daily basis. One obvious difference, however, is that, while physicians deal with pain already existing in their patients, these scientists create the source of their pain. The psychological pain these scientists must then confront is self-imposed.[20]

MILITARY MADNESS AND THE PENTAGON CULT[21]

You start talking about targeting or strategic command and control and, baby, that's the family jewels.

—General Jack Merritt, former director of the Joint Chiefs of Staff

According to retired admiral Eugene Carroll, interservice rivalry is the real engine of the nuclear arms race—the three services under the direction of the Pentagon, each competing for the nuclear dollar. It's about power building, each wanting and demanding more planes, bombs, and ships.[22]

This competition among the services—a dynamic centered at the mental and psychological age of my grandchildren, aged eight, seven, and five years, who argue continuously and competitively about toys, all wanting their very own and never having enough— may have been socially and politically acceptable during World Wars I and II, in a prenuclear era. In a world bristling with nuclear weapons, such rivalry is calamitous. Any military skirmish in an interdependent world involving the navy, the army, or the air force, could escalate and trigger a thermonuclear holocaust. Indeed, all nuclear war games "played" by the Pentagon end up obliterating both the victors and the vanquished. In this context it is interesting to examine the powerful political role that the Pentagon has played since the cold war ended.

The new international scenario, in which the Pentagon was left without a major national enemy at the end of the cold war in 1989, came as a shock to the entrenched military establishment, which was faced with a kind of post-traumatic stress syndrome. Indeed, many individuals overtly mourned the loss of their once-predictable former enemy.[23]

To the contrary, in the face of newfound opportunity President George Bush displayed commendable leadership, defying Pentagonian pressure and moving decisively and unilaterally to eliminate all ground-based tactical missile bombs, all tactical nuclear weapons from naval vessels, and all hydrogen bombs from long-range bombers. He also cancelled certain land-based missile programs. He de-escalated both as a gesture of goodwill and as a strategic defense maneuver; as he explained to one of his aides at the time: "I want tactical nuclear weapons out of Europe. Gorbachev needs U.S. cover to get their nukes out of the republics before they collapse."[24] At the same time, then–Secretary of Defense Dick Cheney and Chairman of the Joint Chiefs of Staff Colin Powell instigated a full-scale review of the single integrated operational plan (SIOP)—the U.S. nuclear targeting strategy that was the guiding light of the Pentagon, but that had now been rendered obsolete.[25]

Both men were appalled by the subsequent report. Not only was SIOP arcane and hopelessly out of date, it also lacked clear logic and objectives. According to one account, "Cheney concluded that SIOP was not a nuclear war plan . . . it seemed like a jumble of processed data. . . . Every time the Pentagon had bought a new nuclear weapons system to match the Soviets' . . . Omaha [the Strategic Command Headquarters in Omaha, Nebraska] had simply found targets for the added warheads and rearranged the SIOP math formulas. This had gone on for years, as captains and majors who wrote the SIOP plan rotated in and out."[26] This dynamic was so out of control that by 1986, SIOP had targeted 16,000 "nuclear facilities" in the So-viet Union[27] (as a point of comparison, there are only 240 major cities in the entire northern hemisphere). Following the Cheney-Powell review, thousands of targets in the former Soviet republics were re-moved from the SIOP plans, and all focused targets were now located in Russia,[28] which was fast becoming an ally. The targets still in-cluded command and control centers, conventional forces, all war-supporting industries including such things as shoe factories, most other factories, oil and gas facilities, power plants, railroad stations, schools, and universities, in addition to actual nuclear forces—so there was overkill, but less overkill.[29]

Bush continued to take command of nuclear weapons policies, never allowing the military bureaucracy to prevail in decision-making. He counted on his main advisors, who were astute inside players, to carry out his objectives, and they received powerful presi-dential support in the face of Pentagon opposition.[30]

Prior to the Bush administration, no president, presidential aide, or official from the office of the secretary of defense had been in-volved in directing or even trying to understand the logic of the SIOP planners in the Pentagon. Indeed, one military official from the Joint Strategic Planning Service charged that officials in prior administra-tions "were criminally negligent" for their lack of oversight for SIOP, all the details of nuclear targeting strategy having been left to junior officers in the Pentagon.[31]

In *An Elusive Consensus*, Janne Nolan describes the years before the first Bush administration as follows:

> Briefings to senior officials about the SIOP typically were perfunc-tory and often unintelligible. The thousands of pages of SIOP data and computer codes contained in the plans would be translated into an hour-long briefing and presented in several dozen view graphs. "Generally no one at the briefings wanted to ask questions because they didn't want to embarrass themselves," according to one ac-count, in reference to both military and political authorities. "We would cut deals as junior officers [of the different services] in al-locating weapons . . . sometimes this resulted in remarkable changes in the guidance, which should have been reviewed at the highest levels."[32]

Once, while being briefed on the SIOP, then–Secretary of Defense Cheney began squirming uncomfortably in his chair as he watched Moscow—which had been targeted with 200 separate hydrogen bombs, entailing an enormous excess of megatonnage—turn slowly into a solid red mass covered over and again with ludicrous targets.[33]

The Pentagon thinks about nuclear strategy in a strange and pathological way. (One could readily diagnose the attitudes of the Pentagon as clinically sick and suggest that all people who subscribe to these theories need urgent counseling and therapy.) "Aggression" by an enemy will be "deterred" with a threat to vaporize millions of people as Joanne Nolan comments in her book. The rationale is as follows: Officers responsible for nuclear weapons must have the ability to hold "at risk" anything that an adversary would "value most." But because those doing the targeting cannot know what is most valued, almost everything is held "at risk." As one military official was heard to say, "If he values his grandma, we have to target grandmas."[34]

While the Bush administration bequeathed an activist legacy of potent arms control and unilateral disarmament programs to the next president, this tradition was not perpetuated by President Clinton. Clinton vacillated and was ever reluctant to engage himself directly in nuclear issues. And Clinton simply never took command of the Pentagon. As one of Bush's aides said, "Clinton debates objectives with his subordinates. Bush debated tactics but never objectives."[35]

Clinton's first secretary of defense, Les Aspin, the former chairman of the House Armed Services Committee, was highly experienced in the area of nuclear weapons strategies. Aspin had doubts about the relevance of nuclear deterrence in the post–cold war era, noting, "A world without nuclear weapons would actually be better. . . . Nuclear weapons are still the big equalizer, but the United States is not the equalizer but the equalizee."[36]

To this end, Aspin initiated a nuclear posture review, based upon the concepts of "mutual assured safety" and "cooperative de-nuclearization." The review was to encompass and incorporate policies, doctrines, force structure, operations, safety, security, and arms control and was to include a critique by an outside panel of experts. Aspin specifically planned the review to emphasize the fundamentally political character of nuclear policy. However, there was strong opposition from Pentagon officials who decided that outside participation would not be necessary or desirable. As one commented, "We certainly weren't about to invite any weirdos from ACDA [the Arms Control and Disarmament Agency]." [37]

Aspin resigned in 1994 shortly before he died, and responsibility for the review passed on to Deputy Secretary of Defense John Deutch, a relatively inexperienced man who had recently been appointed from the private military sector. (He was later appointed head of the CIA.) Operational responsibility for the review was shared by Ashton Carter, assistant secretary of defense for national security and counterproliferation, and Lieutenant General Barry McCaffrey [38] (who later became Clinton's drug czar).

Aspin's instruction to the nuclear posture review had been to extricate the entrenched nuclear establishment—including the Pentagon—from its obsolete cold war preoccupations and to foster more appropriate understandings of the post–cold war reality. The military establishment, Aspin believed, needed to accept and understand the enormous dangers of the U.S. nuclear strategy. But in the absence of senior oversight and disciplined leadership once Aspin resigned, the review process failed. President Clinton declined to become involved, Secretary of State Warren Christopher was disengaged, and National Security Advisor Anthony Lake was uninterested. So the job was left essentially to Deutch and Carter. [39]

Carter, who was well intentioned, sincerely believed that a process of logical analysis could alter orthodox military thinking about nuclear weapons strategy. To this end, he established six working groups, staffed by midranking and junior military officers plus career bureaucrats. Most had little background in nuclear strategy, and all met in closed-door meetings within the Pentagon. Their attitude was derisive to any "outsider analysis" and new ideas were given polite but frosty receptions. [40]

The Pentagon personnel overwhelmingly opposed any changes to their triad of nuclear forces, and to the concept of de-alerting their strategic nuclear weapons. The air force also strenuously resisted eliminating their land-based ICBM weapons. The others charged that any change in their strategy of employing a variety of launch options threatened America's ability to respond to nuclear attacks effectively. Some military officials also sensed an assault on their nuclear procedures and their lines of authority. As one midlevel officer asserted: "We know how to produce nuclear war plans. We have the methodology, we can analyze damage expectancies." [41]

The vice chair of the Joint Chiefs of Staff, Admiral William Owens, who oversaw the committees was a potent critic of nuclear weapons, but unfortunately he did not challenge his colleagues when they vigorously opposed the mandate of the review. (Even had consensus been reached by the Pentagon however, the White House never at any stage attempted to engage or educate the Congress about these extraordinarily important issues.) Eventually, after ten months of review process, the working groups sabotaged Aspin's original concept, opposing even minor changes or innovations. Instead they produced analyses and a series of view graphs totally supporting the structure, doctrine, and force levels implicit in the current nuclear doctrine. [42]

Carter became so frustrated that he bypassed the working groups and appointed two outsiders to rescue the process—Steve Fetter, a physicist and professor from the University of Maryland, and Lieutenant Commander Leo Mackay, who wrote his Harvard doctoral dissertation on nuclear strategy. He organized high-level clearances in order to give them full access to the necessary documents. This "counter-review" was specifically structured to analyze the possible removal of land-based ICBMs vulnerable to a first strike, de-alerting of strategic weapons, removal of the remaining U.S. nuclear weapons in Europe (there are still 200), and alteration of nuclear targeting doctrines. Post–cold war, it was obvious, to Carter at least, that America could operate with a much smaller strategic nuclear arsenal, if indeed it needed one at all. [43]

Deutch expressed sympathy with these proposals, but when the Joint Chiefs of Staff got wind of the briefing charts, a revolt was triggered in the Pentagon. Although Carter had been appointed to oversee the nuclear posture review by the office of the secretary of defense, in the end he was abandoned to do solitary battle against the power and might of the Pentagon. A meeting called by regional commanders "to call Ash on the carpet" progressed to a brutal showdown. Carter had no authority to present options to the secretary of defense they said, unless the options had been approved by the "working groups." [44]

Though Carter defended himself, saying that it was not appropriate for colonels and lower-level Pentagon personnel to craft U.S. national policies, the policy that was finally given approval by a disengaged president was a complete triumph for the Pentagon. It called for a "lead and hedge" strategy in which the U.S. would publicly pursue nuclear arms control while at the same time hedging "against . . . a return to an authoritarian military regime in Russia hostile to the United States." In the end, this new policy allowed America to retain its nuclear weapons should the cold war reemerge, to double the number of strategic intercontinental weapons allowed under the START II treaty—from 3000 to 6000—and there were to be no limits on nondeployed warheads (nuclear weapons in storage) or tactical nuclear weapons (tactical nuclear weapons are not delivered by intercontinental missiles or intercontinental planes, but are launched from short-range missiles, cruise missiles, or short-range planes). Finally the policy reinforced the triad of land-, air-, and sea-based weapons. Ashton Carter has since disclaimed that there was really any genuine attempt to alter the U.S. force structure or the overall nuclear policy. [45]

The Pentagon had prevailed. There was no change in nuclear policy, and the status quo of nuclear comfort returned.

When the review was released, one Russian commentator observed, regarding the lack of leadership displayed in the face of the Pentagon's post-review tantrum: "Clinton's foreign policy is determined by immediate reactions to internal, and to a lesser degree, external factors." [46]

Chapter Four

CORPORATE MADNESS
AND THE DEATH MERCHANTS

*I see in the near future a crisis approaching that unnerves me and
causes me to tremble for the sake of my country. . . . Corporations
have been enthroned and an era of corruption in high places will
follow, and the money power of the country will endeavor to prolong
its reign by working upon the prejudices of the people until all wealth
is aggregated in a few hands and the Republic is destroyed.*

—Abraham Lincoln, November 21, 1864

W H O R U N S T H E Congress all these years later? The
transnational corporations whose executives wine and
dine, woo, bribe, and corrupt the officeholders of the
White House and Congress—from the president and vice president
to almost all the elected congressional officials. These all-powerful
corporations manipulate and control most of the federal legislation,
foreign and domestic, that passes through Congress. They do it
through a variety of mechanisms: think tanks, corporate mergers,
lobbying, and political donations.

THINK TANKS

In the seventies leading international corporations jointly organized
and endowed a series of think tanks—their own "battle management organizations"—whose primary purpose was to sway popular
and political opinion in directions useful to the think tanks' corporate

sponsors. These think tanks are staffed by erudite researchers who produce editorials, TV news pieces, papers, media releases, and legislative material, which are well-conceived, well-researched, well-written, easy to understand, and very acceptable to the media and Congress.[1] Production of this material is orchestrated in a timely fashion to guide specific pieces of legislation. Mostly Washington based, these think tanks also have a pervasive presence in the media, their spokespeople being regular political commentators on the Sunday-morning talk shows and in print.

TREE TOPS PROPAGANDA

If the mass will be free of the chains of iron, it must obey the chains of silver. . . . If it will not love, honor and obey, it must not expect to escape seduction.

—Harold Lasswell, leading American scholar of propaganda, 1939[2]

This broad-reaching, sophisticated, high-level manipulation of the so-called free, democratic media and legislature is known as "tree tops" propaganda, and it has been extraordinarily successful for the sponsoring corporations and the points of view they espouse. Such an approach effectively controls government agendas in many countries—certainly including the United States—and is more effective by far than grassroots organizing, for all but the very few issues around which millions of concerned citizens can be mobilized. The right-wing think tanks almost alone created the new conservative movement of the 1970s.

But these think tanks are neither free nor democratic. They are nonelected, private bodies controlled by wealthy and powerful corporations. In effect they are advertising agencies acting for the corporations that founded and fund them. They represent the corporate philosophy of "economic rationalism," which favors the corporate takeover of all public enterprises, from health care and education to water and electricity, and an agenda that includes decreasing or abolishing government regulation of big business, decreasing corporate taxes and taxes for the rich, destroying the unions, and increasing corporate profits.[3] The IMF, the World Bank, GATT,

NAFTA, APEC, FTAA, and WTO have all taken their cues from these think tanks.*

One of the most influential think tanks is the Heritage Foundation. Funded by transnational corporations and wealthy individuals including Amway, Hyundai, Exxon, Phillip Morris, United Parcel Service Foundation, Joseph Coors, Timothy Mellon and the Sarah Scaife Foundation, the Heritage Foundation's income for 1999 was 43.6 million dollars.[5] The Heritage Foundation established a comprehensive list of agenda items for the Reagan presidency, which they titled "Mandate for Leadership—Policy Management in a Conservative Administration." Items included arming America to fight and win a nuclear war, and to develop "superiority over the Soviet Union." Most of these agenda items became policy.[6] (They followed up by issuing another Mandate for Leadership in Reagan's second term.)

THINK TANKS AND THE MILITARY-INDUSTRIAL COMPLEX

The think tanks exert a huge amount of influence on behalf of the military-industrial complex. The Heritage Foundation is still very much involved in promoting the nuclear arms race in all arenas, and actively lobbying for Star Wars.[7] Other powerful right-wing think tanks that involve themselves in American "nuclear security" include the American Enterprise Institute and the CATO Institute.[8] Yet another think tank, the Center for Security Policy (CSP), serves as the nerve center of the Star Wars lobby. It was organized by Frank Gaffney, a Pentagon official under Reagan and a high priest of mis-

---

* In January 1998, a chief World Bank economist, Joseph Stiglitz, attracted worldwide attention during a lecture he gave in Helsinki when he criticized this so-called "Washington consensus." Stiglitz pointed out that Washington-inspired austerity, privatization, and deregulation—which has become the standard policy prescription for much of the world—was misguided and often disastrous. He said that market ideologues were using economic crises in various countries as excuses to discredit government intervention and to promote more market liberalization. He argued, contrary to the economic rationalist line, that moderate inflation is fairly harmless, budget deficits are not necessarily evil, privatization is not a panacea, and deregulation of domestic and international financial markets can do serious harm. Not surprisingly, he was fired from the World Bank at the end of 1999.[4]

sile defense. (Gaffney also heads the Coalition to Protect Americans Now, a group that organizes TV ads to promote missile defense and all-out Star Wars. One ad depicts visions of babies in their cradles and children playing baseball, interspersed with missiles falling from the sky, and a caption reading, *Where will you be when the missiles are launched?*).[9]

CSP is funded by military contractors including Lockheed Martin, Boeing, TRW, General Dynamics, Rockwell International, and Northrop Grumman. CSP's board includes six Lockheed Martin executives; members of the Heritage Foundation;[10] President Reagan's science advisor George Keyworth; two staunch Republican supporters of missile defense, Senator John Kyl of Arizona and Representative Kurt Weldon of Pennsylvania; and the notorious—and now elderly—Edward Teller, the inventor of the hydrogen bomb. (Teller calls Star Wars the "third generation" of nuclear weapons, the atomic bomb being the first and the hydrogen bomb the second. For thirty-two years he has urged the nuclear weapons labs to conduct more research on "defensive weapons.") The CSP packs a powerful corporate punch, publishing over 200 press releases a year, euphemistically called national security decision briefs.[11] (In 1998, the Center for Security Policy gave its Keeper of the Flame award to Donald Rumsfeld, former defense secretary under Ford and now secretary of defense in the present Bush administration; other notable recipients of the award have included Ronald Reagan and Newt Gingrich.)

But even as early as 1983, when Reagan—under Edward Teller's guidance—gave his speech advocating Star Wars, most credible scientists knew that the scientific hypothesis upon which the theory was based—that a comprehensive and effective missile shield could be built—was simply unworkable. Seventy billion dollars and a string of uninterrupted technical failures later, the Center for Security Policy, the Heritage Foundation, Lockheed Martin, TRW, Raytheon, and Boeing remain committed to the Star Wars concept and the country is still trying to build a missile shield.

HOW THE THINK TANKS RESUSCITATED STAR WARS

When the Soviet Union collapsed in 1991 it became necessary for the corporations, their think tanks, the State Department, and the Pentagon to invent new excuses to justify this unworkable, enormously expensive military-scientific adventure.

First, a new arch-enemy had to be found, and North Korea (a country unable to feed its own people) was the propaganda machine's number-one choice. Originally labeled (along with Iraq) a "rogue state" by the State Department, and now called a "state of concern," [12] North Korea does not have a single missile that could hit the U.S., nor any nuclear weapons. John Pike, then with the Federation of American Scientists, commenting on the North Korean missile test site, said, "This facility was not intended to support and in many respects is incapable of supporting the extensive test program that would be needed to develop a reliable missile program." The site has no transportation links, no paved roads, no storage facility for propellant, and no staff housing. [13]

Nevertheless, the ongoing demoniacal representation of North Korea is important to the Pentagon because it has been and is used to justify the only U.S. military deployment on mainland Asia (the U.S. maintains 37,000 troops in South Korea). Adherence to this policy is essential because it gives the U.S. a reason to maintain a military presence and a belligerent policy in an Asian country while it is currently positioning itself to cast China as the next major enemy on the horizon. Though recently Afghanistan has, on an acute basis, replaced China as a major Pentagon focus.

Consequently the Pentagon, State Department, and military industry have worked with the leading think tanks to make the public case for the need to defend the U.S. from this "rogue state." So important has the North Korean "threat" been to U.S. military policy that William Cohen's first question to policy officials when he became Secretary of Defense in 1994 was "How can we change the assumption that U.S. troops will be withdrawn after peace comes to the Korean Peninsula?" [14]

Unfortunately this "enemy" is not behaving according to plan. For one thing, North Korean President Kim Chong-il and South Korean President Kim Dae Jung signed a peace treaty on June 15, 2000, agreeing that they needed reconciliation and the establishment of peace. (A military officer who closely follows the situation noted that "The U.S., in my opinion, is obsessed with the status quo," and said the Pentagon was underestimating the potential for a peace breakthrough and resisting changes in its forces in South Korea that could ease tensions further.)[15] North Korea even informed Russian President Putin that it would abandon its fledgling missile program in exchange for Western aid in building scientific satellites.

But the State Department remains less than convinced. As one department spokesman insisted, "The threat of war is still there. In terms of the [North Korean] military capability, they still have over one million troops ready to go."[16] And in the spring of 1999, despite the "problems" brought on by Korean peacemaking, the Star Wars partisans claimed success. Their prodigious lobbying efforts, corporate political donations, and propaganda exercises persuaded the House and Senate to pass legislation stating that the official policy of the United States government is to deploy a national missile defense as soon as is "technically feasible."[17] A Pentagon intelligence report quoted in the *New York Times* in September 2000 concluded that "North Korea remains a dangerous military threat." And when Kim Dae Jung, a Nobel Peace Prize laureate, visited George W. Bush soon after Bush's inauguration, he was essentially snubbed by the president and his staff.[18]

CORPORATE MERGERS AND NUCLEAR POLICY

The most powerful military corporation on earth, Lockheed Martin, was created in 1993 by a series of corporate mergers. During the eighties and early nineties there were ten to fifteen major U.S. weapons firms. However, in 1993, Secretary of Defense Les Aspin concluded that the Pentagon could no longer sustain the enormous weapons procurement budgets of the lavish Reagan years,[19] and, in an early-1993 meeting, Undersecretary of Defense William Perry bluntly informed industry executives of the new Pentagon policy of encouraging corporate mergers.

That seminal meeting was triumphantly dubbed "the last supper" by Norman Augustine, at that time CEO of Martin Marietta and subsequently the guiding hand behind the mergers. Martin Marietta merged with Lockheed, to become Lockheed Martin, a 35-billion-dollar behemoth, and the number-one contractor for the Pentagon, NASA, and the Department of Energy.[20] Boeing absorbed McDonnell Douglas, and Raytheon bought the military units of Hughes Aircraft and Texas Instruments to become numbers two and three, respectively. Other smaller firms survived, including TRW, Northrop Grumman, and United Defense, but their earnings were significantly lower than those of the big three's.[21] (Ironically, the Pentagon has not closed a single major weapons production line since the mergers were instituted. With a smaller number of corporations now bidding competitively for military contracts, prices have gone up, not down, and, in the end, no actual savings have been passed on to taxpayers.)

Two government officials, William Perry and his Pentagon colleague John Deutch, both of whom were past paid consultants to Martin Marietta, shepherded the mergers through the government bureaucracy. Officially it was against the law for Perry and Deutch to act on behalf of their former employer, but they obtained "conflict of interest waivers" from Defense Secretary Aspin. Perry and Deutch even went so far as to change the Pentagon's contracting rules, thus allowing merging companies to be compensated for costs involved in moving factories, for legal fees, and for executive bonuses (a policy memorably dubbed "payoffs for layoffs" by Congressman Bernie Sanders from Vermont). This type of corporate-orchestrated merger and payoff operation is a classic example of the "revolving-door syndrome": Corporate employment leads to a Pentagon position, where one is then able to featherbed the nest of one's corporate colleagues. Then, when the government term of office expires, some return to private industry equipped with invaluable Pentagon connections.

Lockheed Martin realized a taxpayer-financed windfall from the merger amounting to 1.2 billion dollars. The company also became the single largest advocate of aggressive nuclear development in the country, in a quest to protect its *billions of dollars* worth of government arms contracts (18 billion dollars in 1997).*

---

* Less than two months after the September 11 attacks, the Pentagon awarded Lockheed Martin a mammoth contract of 200 billion dollars over the next several decades to build 3000 F-35 joint strike fighter planes.[22]

BIRTH OF A DEATH MERCHANT

As Lockheed Martin came to power, so did Norman Augustine, CEO of the newly merged company and perhaps the key player on the corporate side of the military-industrial equation. Augustine personally received 8.2 million dollars in government payouts stemming from the merger. As one Pentagon source noted, "If you're concerned about corporate welfare, the one you should look out for is St. Norman Augustine."[23] (Former Tennessee governor Lamar Alexander also got 250,000 dollars for the "hardship" he endured when asked to leave the board of the newly merged company!)

Who is the man who has come to play such a key role in the defense industry?

Originally a forest ranger, Augustine majored in geological engineering. As a first-year graduate student, however, he was "utterly shocked" when the Soviet Union launched *Sputnik*—"I couldn't imagine how we could be number two," he said—and within months he took a job at the Douglas Aircraft Corporation. He has stayed in the weapons industry ever since.[24] He sees weapon production as a patriotic duty, and he refers to the military corporations as "the fourth armed service," noting that increased spending on weapons is a national imperative, not merely a means to increase corporate profits.[25]

While he led the nation's largest corporate military contractor, Augustine was also influential in other areas. As chairman of the Defense Science Board (DSB), a Pentagon panel, he helped to decide for or against multibillion-dollar weapons projects. He was president of the Association of the United States Army, a politically influential group of retired army personnel, and he served as chairman of the Defense Policy Advisory Committee on Trade, a committee that gives confidential guidance on arms exports to the secretary of defense.[26] (Beyond his military credentials, Augustine was also the chairman of the American Red Cross and president of the Boy Scouts of America.)

A hard-driving man conversant with all the major policy and technical issues affecting Lockheed Martin, Augustine was a high-stakes lobbyist and became an unofficial—and intimidating—policy maker, successfully advocating initiatives that yielded billions of dollars in government funding for his corporation.[27] Former govern-

ment officials declined the opportunity to testify on Pentagon procurement recommendations because "Norman Augustine really
wants this." During the summer of 1994, he had become such a presence on the Hill that one staff member referred to him sarcastically
as "the secretary of defense." [28] (Augustine continued in his dynami-
cally influential role as CEO of Lockheed Martin until 1998, when
he was replaced by Vance Coffman. But Augustine remains on the
board, an effective lobbyist for his company, and he continues to participate in military-related activities. He sat on a congressionally
mandated bipartisan committee to investigate increasing terrorist
threats to the United States. He also participated in a committee in
2001 to assess the efficacy of the ill-fated Osprey helicopter.) [29]

WHAT NORMAN WANTS . . .

One of the ways military corporations curry favor with lawmakers is
by employing people in multiple political districts. The legislators
express gratitude for increased employment in their districts by en-
acting legislation that forces the Pentagon to spend money on
weapons that it doesn't necessarily want or need.

Lockheed Martin, headquartered in Bethesda, Maryland, has
major military research and production centers in eight other states:
Moorestown, New Jersey; Marietta, Georgia; Oak Ridge, Tennessee;
Colorado Springs, Colorado; Fort Worth, Texas; Albuquerque, New
Mexico; Vandenberg Air Force Base and Sunnyvale, California; and
at the Nuclear Test Site in Nevada. But actually the corporation
maintains facilities in fifty states.[30] As John Pike, formerly of the
Federation of American Scientists, said, Lockheed Martin carries a
"big political footprint." [31]

Since 1994, when the Republicans gained control of both houses of
Congress, billions of dollars beyond Pentagon requests have been
added each year to the military budget. For instance, in the years
1996–98, 20 billion dollars extra was added, three-quarters of which
was earmarked for weapons that benefited only their corporate pro-
ducers.[32] Dozens of unnecessary weapons systems were crammed
into the Pentagon budget during the Gingrich era in an add-on game
called "the waste that keeps on wasting." [33]

An egregious example is the huge C-130 military transport plane, manufactured by Lockheed Martin just outside Newt Gingrich's congressional district in Georgia. Since 1978, the air force has requested only five of these planes, yet Congress built 256—a ratio of fifty for each plane requested! Republican Senator John McCain of Arizona was heard to say that there were so many surplus C-130s that "we could use them to house the homeless." Indeed, the air force was forced to retire more than a dozen C-130s because they had no use for them. (And Congress doesn't even budget for the actual operation of the planes—said to be 1 billion dollars over the next six years.) These C-130s are deployed as trophies with national guard units in the states of key congressional members—for example, more than a dozen C-130s sit at Kessler Air Force Base in Trent Lott's home state of Mississippi.

MERGED MONEY TALKS

Political donations represent even more overt efforts by the huge new military corporations to affect policy. In 1997, for example, the military corporations spent more than 2.4 million dollars contributing to political campaigns and parties. From 1991 to 1997 they surpassed even the tobacco companies in political donations by a margin of 32.3 to 26.9 million dollars. Lockheed Martin led the pack.[34] One Lockheed operator, Bernard Schwartz, a former company board member who owned Loral Industries before it merged with Lockheed in 1996, gave 601,000 dollars to the 1996 Democratic war chest and more than 1.1 million dollars to committees of the Democratic party in 2000.[35] And in just two years—1997 and 1998—America's six biggest weapons makers spent 51 million dollars actively lobbying for their killing weapons. Lockheed Martin alone spent 10.2 million dollars lobbying in 1997 and 1998.[36] (Of course most lobbying activities are tax deductible.)

Lockheed Martin has even installed company people in key positions in Democratic and Republican presidential campaigns. For example, Lockheed's vice president Bruce Jackson served as vice-chair for the Dole fundraising campaign in 1996; he subsequently occupied the same position for Governor George W. Bush in 2000. Lockheed

Martin shared the limelight at the 2000 Republican convention with other notable U.S. corporations, including the United States Tobacco Company, AT&T, Freddie Mac, and Southern Co. Each of these firms contributed 60,000 dollars to Senate Majority Leader Trent Lott for a fifties-style sock hop titled the "Lott Hop." Lockheed then cemented this political connection by pledging 1 million dollars to the "Trent Lott Leadership Institute." [37] Lott, it turns out, had helped to bail out Lockheed's multimillion-dollar F-22 fighter plane project in the late nineties, when it experienced huge cost overruns and was not performing according to specifications. He also helped to fund the construction of many superfluous C-130 planes, and he vigorously supported the theater high altitude area defense project (THAAD), for which Lockheed received 4 billion dollars. (THAAD has failed six of eight tests.) [38]

Lott's generosity did not stop there. In September 2000, he steered a bill through the Senate to provide 4 to 6 billion dollars in tax subsidies to the tobacco, arms, and pharmaceutical industries over the next decade. As William Hartung, a senior fellow at the World Policy Institute, writes, "The provision of the bill that would give double tax breaks to weapons exporters like Boeing, Raytheon, and Lockheed Martin is particularly outrageous. These companies already benefit from over seven billion dollars per year in government grants, loans, and promotional activities designed to promote U.S. weapons exports. . . . If there was ever an example of an industry that emphatically does not need more government subsidies, the U.S. weapons industry is it." [39]

Other corporate-influenced people at the Republican convention included House Majority Whip Tom DeLay, who received the Boeing-Lockheed award with no apparent embarrassment. When DeLay was later questioned about ubiquitous corporate donations, he said, "We're raising money left and right, we'll leave this convention with a significant amount of resources." Then he added "It's cynical for the media to make it like it's bad: it's better to raise money than to have the government pay for elections." [40] While 97 percent of Americans do not contribute to any political party, [41] Lockheed Martin, TRW, Raytheon, and Boeing collectively gave 6 million dollars in campaign contributions during the election year of 2000. (These weapons firms have consistently contributed more to Republicans than Democrats by a 2:1 margin since the Republicans took control of Congress in 1994.)[42]

And the connections don't stop there. George W. Bush attempted to award a contract to Lockheed Martin to run the Texas welfare system! Bush relented in the face of strong public opposition.[43] Lynne Cheney, the wife of the vice president, for years served on Lockheed's board, for which she received 120,000 dollars annually in compensation.

Dick Cheney himself served as secretary of defense under George Bush and was a fellow at the American Enterprise Institute from 1993 to 1995.[44] He scored a 100 percent rating from the American Conservative Union and zero percent from Americans for Democratic Action during the eighties.[45] Appointed chief executive of Halliburton corporation in 1995, he doubled the size of the company both through a series of mergers and through business deals with the Pentagon. Under Cheney's reign, Halliburton became one of the nation's largest weapons contractors, ranking twenty-second in prime Pentagon contracts by January 2001.[46] Cheney organized a 1.1-billion-dollar Pentagon contract for Halliburton to support military operations in the Balkans,[47] and 2.3 billion dollars in government loans, an increase from 1.2 billion dollars received over the previous five years. The company donated a total of 1.2 million dollars to both political parties and congress over five years, and in 1999 it spent 600,000 dollars on lobbying—up from 280,000 dollars in 1996. When Cheney retired to run for vice president, he left with a "package" of 20 million dollars in stock options and an overall worth of 50 million dollars.[48]

His Democratic opponent in the vice presidential race, Joseph Lieberman, is not without corporate taint either. Both Gore and Lieberman were avid solicitors of campaign funds from Lockheed Martin and Raytheon. Lieberman was one of the first Senate Democrats to join Senate Majority Leader Trent Lott and Senator Thad Cochran to support Star Wars. He lobbied extensively for the troubled Lockheed Martin F-22 plane (at 200 million dollars per plane it is the most expensive ever built); the engines are constructed by a branch of United Technologies in his home state of Connecticut. He received over 96,000 dollars in political donations from military corporations in 2000.[49]

Lieberman also supported loan-guarantee programs for countries buying American weapons, and he voted against the arms sale code of conduct—legislation that prevents weapons from being sold to countries with a poor human-rights record or countries that may be working on developing nuclear weapons. He voted consistently against initiatives to reduce the U.S. military budget, and supported programs to prevent transfer of money from military to domestic programs.[50] For the past five years he has served as chairman of the pro-military Democratic Leadership Council with a corporation-friendly, pro-military, fiscally conservative agenda. Although Lieberman was vocal about religion and personal behavior during the campaign, as William Hartung commented, the Democratic ticket demonstrated "a failure of public ethics, not private morality."[51]

TO THE VICTOR GO THE SPOILS

To give some feel for how Lockheed Martin has benefited through lobbying, revolving-door policies, political donations, etc., here is a short list of some of the company's nuclear weapons related contracts:

Lockheed Martin currently produces the Trident 11 submarine-launched ballistic missile, armed with eight 100- kiloton or 475- kiloton hydrogen bombs. (As a reference, the Hiroshima bomb was equivalent to 13 kilotons of TNT.) Each Trident submarine is equipped with 24 of these missiles. (Eighteen Trident subs, together containing killing power three times the threshold for nuclear winter, glide silently beneath the oceans of the world, invisible to all: a subliminal global holocaust machine.)

But this is not all.

Lockheed Martin has government contracts, all together worth billions of dollars, for:

- The payload launch vehicle for the interceptor system
- The space-based infrared system (SBIRS) "high" component
- The theater high altitude area defense (THAAD)

- The airborne laser (ABL), in partnership with Boeing and TRW
- The navy theater-wide system
- The medium extended air defense system (MEADS), in partnership with Alenia of Italy and Daimler Chrysler of Germany

On the side, Lockheed Martin is also developing the capability to conduct simulated nuclear tests at the Nevada Test Site with the Bechtel Corporation and receives 2 billion dollars a year to run the department of energy's Sandia National Laboratory in New Mexico.[52]

TWO CASE STUDIES

I once naively believed that the administration in power and Congress determined U.S. foreign policy. I was wrong. Here are but two examples of recent foreign policy deals orchestrated by the weapons industry.

NATO EXPANSION

During the cold war years, the North Atlantic Treaty Organization (NATO), was the military bulwark in Western Europe against invasion by the Soviet Union. Western European countries enjoyed "protection" under the American nuclear umbrella: If the Soviets invaded, America would use nuclear weapons to fend off the attack. If necessary, the U.S. would be prepared to absorb a nuclear attack on its own territory to defend its NATO allies. (The U.S. has always controlled the NATO alliance.)

When the Berlin Wall fell, the Bush administration promised Gorbachev that NATO would not expand into Eastern Europe if Russia did not oppose the admission of a unified Germany into the alliance. But when Clinton was elected, he decided to enlarge NATO, in violation of President Bush's agreement. By welcoming the Czech Republic, Hungary, and Poland into NATO, and arming these former Eastern Bloc countries—two of which directly adjoined the Russian border—America reestablished a hostile situation with Russia. The reason given was that free-market democratic reforms would be consolidated, and an expansion of the market into former Eastern Bloc

countries would benefit trade and the U.S. economy. But the truth
was different. U.S. military corporations knew that NATO expansion
presented a huge marketing opportunity—any new NATO country
would be forced to upgrade its weapons systems to NATO standards.

Lockheed Martin was well represented among the lobbyists.
Bruce Jackson, a vice president, volunteered to become president
of the U.S. Committee to Expand NATO, a lobbying and public
education organization operating out of the offices of the American
Enterprise Institute. This committee ran a series of ads in the congressional magazine *Roll Call*, stating that "Americans agree" on
NATO expansion. (The "Americans" they chose were "Stormin'"
Norman Schwarzkopf and three former secretaries of state, including Henry Kissinger.) The Committee to Expand NATO delivered
speeches, gave congressional briefings, published articles, produced
white papers, and sponsored ad campaigns within the U.S., all promoting the "widest possible expansion of NATO."

In 1997, Norman Augustine toured prospective NATO countries
and enthusiastically supported the entry of Romania into the club—
a country that shares a long contiguous border with Russia and to
which his company had already sold 82 million dollars in radar
equipment. Lockheed Martin, Textron, and McDonnell Douglas
funded organizations such as American Friends of the Czech Republic, and foundations promoting Romania's entry into NATO. They
also bankrolled a public referendum in 1997 in Hungary on NATO
expansion and vigorously worked with the top leadership in Poland,
the Czech Republic, Romania, and Hungary to convince them that
the best way to gain U.S. support for entry into NATO was to buy
American weapons.

Despite official rhetoric to the contrary, the expansion of NATO
was entirely about weapons sales, the bill for which will run in the
range of 500 billion dollars over twelve to fifteen years—2500 dollars for every American household, since America ends up
bankrolling much of this military expenditure. Sales to foreign governments are particularly lucrative for weapons manufacturers, since
by the time the weapons are ready for export, all research, development, and initial production problems have been covered by the U.S.
taxpayer. But forcing the impoverished nations of the former Soviet
bloc to buy sophisticated weapons as they experienced freedom was

an act of cynicism and exploitation. Furthermore, it is unethical for any foreign corporation or government to interfere with the domestic politics of other countries. (Remember the furor created when China was said to have contributed to Clinton's reelection campaign in 1996?)

In 1998 the Senate voted 81 to 19 to expand NATO, adding Poland, Hungary, and the Czech Republic (Romania did not make it on this round). Russia was understandably furious, regarding the U.S. as hostile and dishonest, and backed away from talks to reduce nuclear weapons. In April 1999 a lavish event was thrown in Washington, D.C. to celebrate NATO's fiftieth anniversary. International politicians and weapons makers mingled at the party that was funded by Boeing, Lockheed Martin, and United Technologies, each of whom donated 250,000 dollars.

And there was an added cause for celebration: the war in Yugoslavia was at its zenith. Although it would cost U.S. taxpayers about 1 billion dollars per month, it was good for corporate business. Replacement of lost Raytheon-made Tomahawk cruise missiles used in battle (each lost cruise missile costs 1 million dollars to replace) and Lockheed Martin F-16 and F-22 fighter planes would provide billions in new contracts for the weapons makers.[53]

When Bush visited Europe in June 2001, he continued actively to promote NATO expansion.

LIFTING THE ARMS BAN ON LATIN AMERICA AND OTHER FOREIGN MILITARY SALES

For twenty years the United States had a policy banning arms sales to Latin America because it was populated by brutal dictators. However, when the Reagan years ended and the domestic weapons spending bonanza faded, foreign markets were seen as a way to increase corporate profits. Lockheed Martin, Boeing, and others decided to eliminate restrictions based on human rights or the possible nuclear weapon proliferation record of a particular country in order to avail themselves of new weapons "markets." They also decided to organize new government subsidies so that U.S. taxpayer dollars would supply cash to foreign countries to buy weapons.

Clinton's defense secretary, William Perry (formerly Norman Augustine's paid consultant), joined Lockheed Martin to become an advocate within the administration to lift the Latin American weapons ban despite strenuous resistance by the state department. To this end, the air force performed demonstration flights of the F-16 fighter plane at the 1996 air show in Santiago, Chile, and Brazilian generals were invited into the cockpits of F-16 planes to do test flights. Aerospace lobbyists then organized thirty-eight senators and seventy-eight house members to send letters to Secretary of State Warren Christopher (a former director of Lockheed) supporting the abolition of the ban. (This was lucrative work because these legislators subsequently received a total of 1 million dollars in political action committee contributions from the relevant military companies.) A Lockheed Martin brochure was published on their web site and distributed at arms conferences and on the Hill, touting the Latin arms market as a 3- to 15-billion-dollar opportunity over the next ten years.

At the same time, former Costa Rican president and Nobel Peace Prize winner Oscar Arias Sánchez was vigorously promoting a moratorium on sales of advanced weapons to countries in Latin America to promote conflict prevention and force reductions.[54] Yet President Clinton's allegiance was to the weapons industry. (On the contrary, Jimmy Carter displayed moral fortitude in the face of corporate displeasure—one notorious Carter state department cable, which became known as the "leprosy letter," warned its diplomats to shun arms exporters.)[55] In May 1993, Secretary of State Christopher instructed U.S. embassies to assist arms companies in promoting international trade. To consolidate this policy, two years later, in February 1995, President Clinton issued Presidential Directive 41, stating that arms sales were essential for preserving industrial jobs. The directive ordered the diplomatic corps to boost arms sales.[56]

The State Department appointed a semi-official body—the Defense Trade Advisory Group (DTAG) to advise on arms exports. In a direct conflict of interest, its forty members included representatives from Boeing, United Technologies, Hughes, Allied Signal, Litton Industries, Raytheon, General Dynamics, Loral Space Systems, the Electronic Industries Association, and the Aerospace Industries Association.[57] In 1995 the federal government also created the 15-billion-dollar Defense Export Loan Guarantee (DELG) program, together with other financially supportive government programs.

These new weapons export policies are complementary to Article XXI in the General Agreement on Tariffs and Trade (GATT), which directs countries to take any action they consider necessary to protect their essential security interests—actions "relating to the traffic in arms, ammunition and implements of war and such traffic in other goods and materials as is carried on directly for the purpose of supplying a military establishment." [58] The GATT accord was written in 1993 by transnational lawyers, some of whom represented the military-industrial complex.

Lockheed Martin and others benefit hugely from foreign military sales. American firms typically arm both sides in regional conflicts, a practice that is fundamentally good for business. Ancient enemies are armed: Turkey and Greece for their conflict in Cyprus, India and Pakistan, Peru and Ecuador, Taiwan and China, and Israel and every other country in the Middle East—the world's largest arms market. Ironically, if a country previously armed by America—such as Iraq—becomes an "enemy," U.S. troops will be killed by American weapons.

In 1999, America garnered 39 percent of new weapons contracts, deals that netted 11.8 billion dollars—outdoing the sales of Russia, France, Britain, and China combined. [59] Secretary of Defense William Cohen's worldwide travels resembled marketing tours for weapons. He encouraged Chile and Argentina, longtime enemies, to upgrade their arsenals; he pushed weapons in the Persian Gulf states, in Eastern Europe, in Western European countries, in Japan, and in Australia. No country is exempt from the outreach of the United States. [60]

Here is a sampling of weapons sold abroad by Lockheed Martin from 1994 to 2000:

- Advanced gunnery-training systems to Egypt
- Army tactical missiles (ATACMs) and launch assemblies to Greece and South Korea
- C-130 Hercules transport planes and/or associated spare parts to Bangladesh, Brazil, South Korea, Kuwait, Saudi Arabia, and Tai-

wan (Turkey and Zimbabwe also took some spare parts of C-139 airplanes)

- C-130 transport planes to Bolivia, Botswana, Bulgaria, Ethiopia, Greece, the Philippines, Romania, South Africa, Tunisia, and Zimbabwe, and H-30 transport planes to Malaysia
- F-16 fighter jets to South Korea and Taiwan (Turkey and Egypt received upgrades to their F-16s)
- F-16 A/B Fighting Falcons to Bahrain and Jordan; F-16 C/D Falcons and upgrades to Bahrain, Egypt, and Singapore; F-104s to Zimbabwe
- Hellfire II air-to-ground antitank missiles to Egypt, Israel, Kuwait, and Taiwan
- LANTIRN (low-altitude navigation and targeting infrared for night) navigation pods to Egypt, Singapore, and Turkey
- MK-41 vertical-launch system to South Korea
- Multiple-Launch Rocket Systems (MIRSs) to Israel, South Korea, and Turkey
- Multiple-Launch Rocket Systems—Extended Range (MLRS-ER) to South Korea
- P-3B Orion patrol aircraft to Argentina and Greece
- Sharpshooter infantry fighting vehicles to Egypt
- T-33 to Zimbabwe and Turkey
- Walleye missile tube vidicons to Israel [61]

Chapter Five

MANHATTAN II

SS & M is a scientific and technical challenge perhaps as formidable as the Manhattan Project.

—Dr. Victor Reis, assistant secretary
of defense programs at the DOE

IN THE LAST SIX years, the nuclear weapons laboratories—
Los Alamos and Sandia in New Mexico and Lawrence Livermore in California—have embarked upon the largest scientific
endeavor ever attempted. This new project, the Stockpile Stewardship and Management Program, nicknamed Manhattan II, was
ostensibly instituted to ensure the proper functioning of the
U.S. stockpile of nuclear weapons post–cold war. But this benign
description disguises the truth. Nuclear scientists are actually designing, developing, testing, and constructing new nuclear weapons at
an annual cost of 5 billion dollars over the next ten to fifteen
years.

Authorization of Manhattan II was the price the department of
energy exacted in 1995 for nominally agreeing to extend the nuclear
Non Proliferation Treaty (NPT). Officially, the U.S. played a key role
in convincing 180 other nations to sign the extension, which reads in
part:

Each of the Parties to the Treaty undertakes to pursue negotiations in
good faith on effective measures relating to cessation of the nuclear
arms race at an early date and to nuclear disarmament, and on a treaty
on general and complete disarmament under strict and effective international control.[1]

In 1996, five nuclear weapons nations—Russia, France, England, China, and the U.S. (excluding India, Pakistan, and Israel)—and forty-four other countries with the potential to construct nuclear weapons, also agreed to abide by the Comprehensive Test Ban Treaty (CTBT). The CTBT preamble states:

> . . . (T)he cessation of all nuclear weapons test explosions and all other nuclear explosions, by constraining the development and qualitative improvement of nuclear weapons and ending the development of advanced new types of nuclear weapons, constitutes an effective measure of nuclear disarmament and nonproliferation in all its aspects . . .

These were noble ideals on the part of the international community and appropriate in the post–cold war era. However, the treaties provoked a major battle for power and control within the U.S. nuclear establishment. In a seemingly irreconcilable irony, the nuclear labs and their overseer, the department of energy, would allow America to be party to a ban on nuclear testing only if the labs were granted funding to expand their nuclear weapons operations. Thus, violation of both international treaties designed to control the spread of nuclear weapons was built into acceptance.

Technically known as the Stockpile Stewardship and Management Program, the new effort was abbreviated to SS & M (amusingly reminiscent of the acronym for sexual sadomasochism, and thus very much in keeping with all the other sexual language of the nuclear labs). According to the labs, the SS & M program is designed to ensure the safety and reliability of the U.S. nuclear stockpile. But, as a February 1996 publication from the DOE makes clear, the labs' real mandate goes far beyond safety and reliability: "Ability to design new warheads will be retained by DOE at its defense programs (DP) laboratories: Los Alamos National Laboratory (LANL), Lawrence Livermore National Laboratory (LLNL) and Sandia National Laboratory (SNL)." [2]

SS & M's real agenda is as follows:

• To expand the scientific knowledge and understanding of nuclear weapons physics and engineering by creating and outfitting a host of new sophisticated experimental facilities

- To model the behavior of exploding nuclear weapons using the world's fastest computers
- To refurbish and modernize all the weapons in the stockpile by replacing components with updated versions and, in some cases, by designing and manufacturing completely *new* nuclear weapons[3]

At the height of the cold war, the U.S. spent an average of 3.8 billion dollars a year on nuclear weapons design, testing, and manufacture. Now, twelve years after the end of the cold war, it is spending 5 billion dollars annually over a ten- to 15-year period on a project that will violate both the Comprehensive Test Ban Treaty and the nuclear Non Proliferation Treaty.[4]* America is engaged in "vertical proliferation"—building more nuclear weapons—which encourages other nuclear countries to do the same. And America is triggering "lateral proliferation," in which nonnuclear nations, emulating its example, will almost certainly develop their own nuclear weapons. Among the side effects of such a wrongheaded effort are the health problems faced by tens of thousands of nuclear industry workers each year and the environmental hazards created by waste products and abandoned sites, discussed at the end of this chapter.

THE INFRASTRUCTURE OF SS & M

Stockpiled Weapons

Nuclear weapons are extremely complex systems composed of more than 5000 parts. Fundamentally they consist of a primary and a secondary mechanism. The primary is usually a hollow sphere of plutonium or highly enriched uranium in some cases, surrounded by conventional explosives. Tritium is injected into the sphere to boost the explosive yield of the primary. The conventional explosives initiate the chain reaction by compressing the plutonium into a critical mass.

---

* This unstable situation was worsened in 2000 when, to the disquiet of the rest of the world, Jesse Helms, the powerful chairman of the Senate foreign relations committee, convinced the Republican-controlled Senate not to ratify the Comprehensive Test Ban Treaty.

The intense flux of gamma and X rays derived from the explosion of the primary are then reflected and directed into the secondary mechanism composed of uranium, lithium, and deuterium compounds. This induces nuclear fusion. The fusion reaction in the secondary mechanism determines the size of the explosion. Hydrogen bombs are cheap to make—cheaper by far than the cost of deploying troops. They can also be very large—50 megatons or the equivalent of 50 million tons of TNT. (The Hiroshima bomb that destroyed a city was a 13,000-ton equivalent.)

Over the years, the U.S. has built 70,302 nuclear weapons using sixty-five different designs. From 1945 to 1991 the U.S. conducted 1030 tests, while the Soviet Union exploded 715, France 210, China 45, England 45, and India 5.[5]

JUSTIFICATION FOR SS & M

SS & M is ostensibly designed to ensure the safety and reliability of the U.S.'s aging stockpile of nuclear weapons. *Safety* is typically defined as a certified guarantee that a bomb will not inadvertently explode should it be involved in an accident—for example, dropped from a crane, or enveloped in a fire. Safety is not affected by aging of the bomb. In fact, weapons actually become safer as they age because the metals corrode, adhesives degrade, and component parts crack, making them less likely to explode by accident. DOE also found no evidence that aging will make the chemical explosive more sensitive.

Reliability is a guarantee that bombs will explode as programmed.[6] A recent DOE study conducted by the JASONS (a group of distinguished scientists who work for the Mitre Corporation and who advise the DOD and DOE on issues of national security) determined that even if the DOE did nothing to detect and repair defects in bomb components, fewer than 2 percent of the stockpiled warheads would fail to function in the first thirty years after manufacture. They also found no evidence to suggest that the rate of failure would increase for older weapons.[7] In fact, since 1970, no defects have been found in the stockpile of nuclear weapons when they were subjected to underground testing. Since 1991, no U.S. weapon has been retired because of aging.

Many experts concur that 100 hydrogen bombs would suffice to guarantee American deterrence. So even if the present stockpile of over 10,000 bombs were left untouched, only some would degrade, over a long time, and the degradation could easily be detected by physical examination of the weapons. The defective bombs could then be removed from the arsenal.[8]

THE TRUE AGENDA

The Stockpile Stewardship and Management Program is not necessary for reasons of either safety or reliability. Contrary to the DOE's alleged motivations, the scientists involved know that testing has little impact on either of these issues. (Indeed, if weapon designs are altered as a result of SS & M research without the benefit of full-scale testing, safety could actually be *compromised*.[9] So the Manhattan II project stands to endanger the very issue of safety that it is said to protect.) In fact, the real agenda of SS & M is nuclear weapons development, and internal DOE documents make that incontrovertibly clear. According to the Stockpile Stewardship and Management Program released by the DOE's office of defense programs on February 29, 1996, for example, the SS & M program is designed to "maintain a surge capability to rebuild a larger stockpile."

NEW WEAPONS DESIGNS AND MODIFICATIONS

Actually, the scientists have already made a new nuclear weapon, violating the NPT. This is the B61-11 earth-penetrating "bunker buster," the first new weapon produced since 1989, designed to have a variable yield of 300 tons to over 300 kilotons. Twelve feet long and weighing 1200 pounds, this bomb is to replace the old B53, with a 9-megaton yield. It has a casing made of uranium 238 (depleted uranium), which is 1.7 times more dense than lead.[10] Because of its weight it supposedly can burrow 15 to 20 feet into the earth before exploding. It is, the scientists say, "a new way to hold at risk robustly defended, deeply buried targets," [11]—for example, Saddam Hussein's bunker. (This is one glaring example of excess. Any nuclear weapon exploding at ground level will gouge out a huge crater in the earth. It doesn't need to "burrow." Furthermore, the construction of such small nuclear weapons may make their use "thinkable," breaking the traditional fire wall between conventional and nuclear war.)

Two new bombs are on the drawing board. One is another updated version of the B-61 equipped with wings, which flies after being dropped from a plane, allowing the plane itself to escape from the close proximity of the nuclear explosion. This bomb is called BIOS (bomb impact optimization system).[12] The other is a new warhead for the Trident missiles, but this is cloaked in secrecy.

The labs are also designing new weapons for the Mark 5 missile of the Trident submarine. One will utilize an existing plutonium pit and the other will require a new pit design. (New pit manufacturing is a medically dangerous process exposing workers to carcinogenic doses of plutonium.) Los Alamos National Lab plans to manufacture between 80 and 500 new pits annually—which signifies the addition of 80 to 500 new nuclear weapons per year.[13]

These new Trident weapons are designed to foil the intent of START (Strategic Arms Reduction Treaty) II, which was specifically designed to eradicate first-strike weapons capable of destroying missile silos, or "hard targets." Most of America's hard-target weapons are deployed in ground-based intercontinental missiles, as are the Russian weapons. But by upgrading the Trident missiles to extreme accuracy, the U.S. will retain its hard-target capability after seeming to comply with START II. No wonder the rest of the world views America's nuclear policies with cynicism.

In October 2000 Congress passed an authorization bill for research and possible development of a "user friendly" mini-nuke. Designed to be less than 5 kilotons in size, it will exert a one-mile radius of blast destruction. (The Hiroshima bomb at 13 kilotons experienced a blast radius of one and a half miles.)[14] Stephen Younger, associate laboratory director for nuclear weapons at Los Alamos National Laboratory, wrote that these low-yield weapons offer the "advantage" of "reduced collateral damage"—but only by half a mile. Younger enthused in a paper titled "Nuclear Weapons in the Twenty-First Century" that mini-nukes would not require testing because they could use enriched uranium instead of plutonium and be triggered by a well-known "gun assembly" mechanism—which was deployed in Little Boy, the Hiroshima bomb. (Enriched uranium combined with the gun assembly is a tried-and-true design and does not need to be tested.) Like the bunker buster, mini-nukes would most likely be regarded as weapons on the battlefield to be used to "defeat hardened and deeply buried targets," thus again crossing the fire wall between conventional and nuclear weapons.

Years ago, the military used Davy Crocketts, similar tactical nuclear weapons small enough to be carried into the battlefield on the shoulders of soldiers. Congress was so worried about these weapons that they banned them under a 1994 defense authorization act. But in 2000, championed by leading Senate Republicans, mini-nukes were authorized [15] and another new weapon was spawned under the guise of testing for safety and reliability.

Since the September 11 attack, there have been numerous suggestions both from within and without the Bush administration to use nuclear weapons in Afghanistan. Secretary of Defense Donald Rumsfeld has categorically failed to rule out the use of nuclear weapons in this war, and Andrew Card, White House chief of staff, said, when asked about the possible use of nuclear weapons, "I'm not going to talk about the operations that might be considered by the defense department and the president. But we're going to do everything we can to defend the United States." [16] Specific nuclear weapons suggested for use in this war are bunker busters, mini-nukes, and neutron bombs. [17] The latter suggestion, made by Sam Cohen, the inventor of the neutron bomb, was received sympathetically by some in the Washington establishment. [18]

Other nuclear weapon "upgrades" are being contemplated by the labs. DOE has elaborate plans to replace each of the thousands of parts in every nuclear weapon on a regular schedule, including the plutonium pit. Parts will be refurbished and modernized with new components of new design. [19] A large arsenal of a variety of modernized nuclear warheads, many of low to moderate yield, will be fitted to an array of faster, stealthier, long-range delivery platforms (planes and missiles). These "platforms" will be equipped with sophisticated electronics, and fully integrated into the U.S. military's vision of a twenty-first century battlefield—a battlefield dominated by satellite surveillance, remotely deployed sensor arrays, and precision weaponry. [20] All of this seems to lose sight of the fact that when the first nuclear weapons are detonated, the "battlefield" will disappear.

THE FACILITIES

Twenty-five thousand people are employed in nuclear facilities located in seven states, researching, testing, and producing nuclear weapon components under the guise of SS & M. These facilities include Lawrence Livermore and Sandia National Labs in California, Los Alamos and Sandia National Labs in New Mexico, the Pantex plant in Texas, the Kansas City plant, the Y-12 plant in Tennesee, the Savannah River plant in South Carolina, and the Nevada Test Site (NTS). All of these facilities were used in the past during the cold war to design, test, and build nuclear weapons. They are ostensibly used to support SS & M, but most are currently being upgraded for the new surge in sophisticated nuclear weapons production.

Broadly speaking, the facilities are devoted to a number of related endeavors, including:

- Learning more about the behavior of plutonium: stereoscopic views of imploding plutonium pits are being created, and experiments are being conducted to simulate "virtually" the behavior of this critical nuclear element
- Experimenting with fusion: machines such as the X-1, which can induce fusion, are being built; laser-powered fusion is being explored; and different "igniters" are being tested
- Testing nuclear weapons: subcritical tests that are difficult to detect are being conducted; facilities to resume full-scale testing are being built as the U.S. plans to abandon the Comprehensive Test Ban Treaty within months of September 2001; and virtual testing via elaborate computer models is being undertaken
- Building new nuclear weapons: the next generation of upgrades to nuclear weapon components—including the design, integration, prototyping, fabrication, and qualification of microsystems for weapon components—is being manufactured

LEARNING MORE ABOUT THE BEHAVIOR OF PLUTONIUM

Hydrodynamic and High-Explosive Test Facilities

The term *hydrodynamic* applies to the motion of plutonium in the pit just before it reaches critical mass. As we've seen, it is compressed by conventional explosives under extremely high pressures in millionths of a second, and it apparently acts like a liquid under pressure. Now, high-energy X rays are being tested that will penetrate deep inside the imploding pit, produce visual images, and take electrical and optical measurements. The scientists will then produce images of the exploding plutonium.

Six of these hydrodynamic measuring facilities are already operational. Two new highly sophisticated operations are under construction or planned: a dual-axis radiographic hydrodynamic test facility (DARHT), and an advanced hydrotest facility (AHF). One DARHT has recently been completed at the Los Alamos Lab to provide stereoscopic images of imploding plutonium pits. Equipped with separate beam lines, the machine will take pictures from two directions. A second axis will be added to give stereoscopic viewing (3-D) of imploding pits. This will produce four images of the pit over a period of four nanoseconds.

And as a follow-on to the DAHRT, the AHF will utilize proton radiography to penetrate deeper into the pit. Four axes are planned to provide 3-D images from multiple directions, each axis producing twenty images in rapid succession. AHF will be constructed at Los Alamos or the Nevada Test Site.

Pulse-Powered Facilities

Virtual experiments are currently being conducted to simulate the behavior of plutonium without actually using the element. Short, intense bursts of electrical energy are focused onto targets to induce extremely high temperatures and/or pressures approaching conditions within a nuclear explosion—millions of degrees centigrade and pressures many times above atmospheric pressure. These experiments are designed to test the basic physics of matter at high energy density. The data is used to improve and test computer codes which model nuclear weapons behavior. Seven of these plutonium testing facilities are already operational. A new one is planned.

Joint Actinide Shock Physics Experimental Research (JASPER)

This is to be a two-stage gas gun able to shoot projectiles that travel at 8 to 15 kilometers per second onto plutonium and uranium targets. Operated by the Lawrence Livermore Lab and under construction at the NTS, it is designed to examine the properties of these and other such materials at high pressures, temperatures, and strain rates.

EXPERIMENTING WITH FUSION

Machines that can induce fusion are being built, laser-powered fusion is being explored, and different "igniters" are being tested.

X-I Machine

This machine, to be constructed at a Sandia National Labs facility, is expected to produce temperatures greater than 3 million degrees Kelvin and enough X-ray energy and power to implode fusion capsules of deuterium and tritium to achieve high-yield fusion. The Sandia scientists believe that this machine could be built for "just" 1 billion dollars.

Inertial Confinement Fusion (ICF)

A major DOE program is being designed to study and produce laser-powered, inertial confinement fusion. Multiple intense laser beams are to be focused on targets of tritium and deuterium in order to heat and compress these elements until they fuse to induce an enormous amount of energy. Already fusion has been produced in a primitive fashion, but not actual "ignition," which simulates the actual energy released in the sun and stars. Five such facilities are already in operation at the labs, but this seems not to be enough.

National Ignition Facility (NIF)

This stadium-sized facility is presently under construction at Lawrence Livermore Lab. Designed to be the world's most energetic laser, it was initially pegged to cost 1.2 billion dollars, but it has incurred huge cost overruns—and an enormous degree of controversy. Completion is now estimated at 4 billion dollars. The lifetime cost over thirty years, including disassembly and cleanup, could approach 10 billion dollars.

Saddled with a history of technical mismanagement, aborted and inadequate peer reviews, endless R and D requirements, and spiraling costs, this facility is one of the more expensive components of the SS & M program.[21, 22] Diagnostic costs have not yet been included in the cost estimates.[23]

The NIF will consist of 192 separate laser beams. When focused on a single target, the combined energy released in bursts of just three-billionths of a second will be 1.8 million joules (a measurement of energy). The laser beams will be fired simultaneously to converge on a tiny BB-sized pellet containing the thermonuclear fuel of tritium and deuterium. For a brief instant, temperatures will reach 100 million degrees centigrade, and the pressure will be 100 billion times earth's atmosphere—conditions existing in the center of the sun.

But there is work to be done. A suitable material for ignition-capable targets has yet to be found. Also, when each laser beam is converted to ultraviolet light (third harmonic), it severely damages the expensive optic components, causing them to explode after only a few dozen experiments.

If successful, the national ignition facility could stimulate the development of a pure fusion bomb. If there are no fission products involved in the production of nuclear weapons, their construction cannot be detected by satellites or other technical means. This means that arms-control verification will be nullified.

Ted Taylor, a highly regarded physicist and former bomb designer at Los Alamos, believes the NIF laser could provide the scientific "means" to move the U.S. to the next level of weapons development. If successful, he says, the United States will have unleashed an entirely new threat to the planet's safety.

The NIF laser has absolutely nothing to do with safety and reliability of nuclear weapons. According to Bob Puerifoy, a retired vice
president of Sandia National Labs, who for thirty-nine years has
been designing, testing, and evaluating nuclear weapons, "NIF is
worthless . . . [it] can't be used to maintain the stockpile, period."

When Edward Teller was asked what role NIF would have in
maintaining the nuclear stockpile, he said "none whatsoever."

Also, five facilities that are used to *split* atoms—be they nuclear reactors or accelerators—already exist at the nuclear weapons labs; a
sixth is about to be built.

TESTING NUCLEAR WEAPONS

Article 1 of the CTBT states, "each state party undertakes not to carry
out any nuclear weapons test explosion or any other nuclear explosion and to prohibit any such nuclear explosion at any place under its
juristiction or control." Yet subcritical tests that are difficult to detect
are being conducted by the U.S. (and probably by other countries as
well), facilities to resume full-scale testing are being built, and virtual testing via elaborate computer models is being undertaken.

Nevada Test Site (NTS)

In 1995, DOE awarded a five-year 1.5-billion-dollar contract to Bechtel Corporation to manage the Nevada Test Site for the possible resumption of full-scale underground nuclear testing. Lockheed
Martin, as previously noted, has also been involved in the NTS. In the
meantime, DOE conducts four underground nuclear tests a year
using small subcritical quantities of plutonium. High explosives
compress the plutonium and its physical properties are collated and
observed when it is "shocked." This data is then incorporated into
computer models of nuclear weapon performance.

Since 1996, nine subcritical tests have taken place at the NTS,
under DOE code names such as *rebound, oboe, bassoon,* and *holog.*
Clearly these tests violate the letter and the law of the CTBT. Difficult to detect because of their size, they complicate seismic verification of the CTB treaty.[24]

It is known that Russia and France are also conducting subcritical tests. Other countries will inevitably follow suit.

The Nevada Test Site is a huge facility. There are more than 1100 support buildings and labs, dozens of holes ready for future underground tests, and extensive equipment and personnel on the ready for the resumption of full-scale nuclear testing. DOE is in the process of renovating 37 miles of roads, and it is currently replacing an electrical supply substation and other electrical facilities.

Los Alamos National Laboratory

Subcritical tests are also being conducted at the Los Alamos National Lab. This program, code named *appaloosa*, is conducted in utmost secrecy, using an eight-foot diameter, two-inch thick, single-use vessel made of special steel developed for submarine hulls.

According to researcher Greg Mello from the Western States Legal Foundation, these Los Alamos tests probably serve several purposes, but one is the unique capability to conduct detailed implosion studies of full primaries using plutonium 242. According to Mello, the tests are the closest thing to an actual nuclear explosion without an actual nuclear detonation. That seems to be the plan for newly manufactured W-88 pits, and for the W-76 replacement warhead, both of which are newly designed bombs.[25]

BUILDING NEW NUCLEAR WEAPONS AND UPGRADING FACILITIES

Camouflaged by "stockpile management" jargon, the next generation of upgrades to nuclear weapon components—including the design, integration, prototyping, fabrication, and qualification of microsystems for weapon components—is being manufactured, and with it, what amounts to brand-new nuclear weapons.

Accelerated Strategic Computer Initiative (ASCI)

A massive undertaking is underway at all three nuclear weapons labs to develop computers with enormous speed and memory capacities far greater than available today.

The computers will be used to model precisely the behavior of an exploding nuclear weapon through all its stages in order to develop extremely complex nuclear weapons codes for virtual testing of nuclear weapons. They will also be used for weapons design, production and accident analysis, for certification, and for the prototyping of manufacturing techniques.[26]

Existing facilities include the ASCI Red Terascale computer, the world's fastest computer, at Sandia Labs; the ASCI Blue Mountain computer, the third fastest computer in the world, at Los Alamos; and the ASCI Blue Pacific computer at Lawrence Livermore Lab, running at 80,000 times the memory of the average personal computer.

The Red Terascale and Blue Mountain computers recently simulated a 3-D explosion in the secondary component of a hydrogen bomb for the first time, and the Blue Pacific simulated a 3-D explosion in the primary plutonium trigger for the first time.[27] So the nuclear establishment is already well on its way into this series of experiments. And more sophisticated computers are planned.

The ASCI Option White TeraOPS computer is currently being built jointly by IBM and the Lawrence Livermore Lab at a cost of 110 million dollars. This will be the world's fastest, most powerful computer. A 30-TeraOPS computer is planned for Los Alamos Lab and a 100-TeraOPS computer for Lawrence Livermore. Each lab, evidently, must have its own.

All of these supercomputers will be manufactured by Intel Corporation, Silicon Graphics Corporation (and its subsidiary, Cray), and IBM.

Other R and D Test Facilities

There are nine major operational facilities at the nuclear weapons labs that work with and on plutonium, tritium, uranium, beryllium, silicon-based microelectronics devices, chemical facilities, flight-test facilities, and high-explosive facilities. All are related to the development of nuclear weapons.

Two more facilities are planned—the first is a chemistry and metallurgy research building (CMR) at Los Alamos, to be constructed for research and experimentation in analytical chemistry, metallurgy, and plutonium and uranium chemistry. The price? One billion dollars. This building will be equipped with hot-cells and glove boxes to handle and machine the plutonium metal with lathes. In all, Los Alamos plans to manufacture 80 to 500 new plutonium pits per year for the equivalent number of hydrogen bombs.[28]

The second is a microsystems and engineering sciences applications (MESA) facility, destined for construction at Sandia. MESA will be used to manufacture the next generation of upgrades to nuclear weapon components, including the design, integration, prototyping, fabrication, and qualification of microsystems for weapon components. The facility will cost 400 million dollars.

Manufacturing Facilities

There are seven huge nuclear weapons complexes, apart from the nuclear weapons labs, which have been operational for decades.

Over many years these facilities have become extremely polluted. They include the Kansas City plant (KCP); the Y-12 plant in Oak Ridge, Tennessee; the Pantex plant in Texas; the Savannah River plant (SRP) in Aikin, South Carolina; the TA-55 plutonium facility at Los Alamos; the nonnuclear manufacturing facilities at Los Alamos; and the neutron generator facility (NGF) at Sandia Labs.

Seven more facilities are planned for the production of ever more hydrogen bombs. These include a tritium extraction facility (TEF) at Savannah River, new uranium enrichment facilities at Y-12, a storage site for enriched uranium, and two other sites to manufacture plutonium pits for bombs. The largest will be the large-scale-pit production facility at Los Alamos at a cost of 3 billion dollars.

It is hard to pretend that any of these activities, let alone all of them, are being undertaken in the name of safety and reliability of already-existing weapons that have been stockpiled.

HAZARDS OF SS & M

COMPUTER CHAOS

In some cases, work that is taking place at these facilities may actually *jeopardize* the reliability and safety of existing weapons. For many years, for example, computer calculations bridged the gap be-

tween partial experimental measurements gained from actual nuclear tests and incomplete theoretical understanding of the bomb
mechanism. These calculations provided a working predictive capability for the design and production of many generations of nuclear
weapons. Obviously, as computers became increasingly sophisticated,
fewer actual nuclear tests were needed. Computer codes thus became
an integrated compendium of the diverse scientific and engineering knowledge relevant to the construction and function of nuclear
weapons, even becoming the principal design tools for specific
weapons. The goal of the SS & M program is to construct a three-
dimensional, full-physics, full-system computer simulation of the
explosion of a nuclear weapon. The problem is that as more new and
sophisticated data is fed into these supercomputers, the old nuclear
codes derived from nuclear testing become confused. In other words,
new data erodes the predictive capability of the old nuclear weapon
performance codes. Any change in the proven design of a hydrogen
bomb undermines its reliability. Therefore, the greater the number
of changes induced by a massive array of experiments, the greater
will be the incentive to resort to full-scale underground testing.

ACADEMIC STRATEGIC ALLIANCES PROGRAM (ASAP) AND INTERNATIONAL ACCESS TO WEAPON DESIGN

Perhaps the most dangerous aspect of SS & M is its real potential to
put sensitive nuclear weapons data into the hands of nonnuclear nations. By developing alliances with a number of universities and
offering their students and staff access to previously confidential material, this program could give foreign nationals free access to U.S.
nuclear weapons design for the first time. This situation will expedite
the ability of nonnuclear countries to design and build advanced nuclear weapons. (The department of energy actually acknowledges
the problem. A 1995 report titled "The National Ignition Facility and
the Issue of Nonproliferation," states that "a modern, sophisticated
proliferator with access to ICF computer codes and today's computer
workstations would have far more tools for designing a secondary
[the major component of a hydrogen bomb] than the U.S., U.K., or
U.S.S.R. had in the 1950s, or France or China in the 1960s.")[29] This

potentially dangerous situation has been alleviated somewhat since the concern at Los Alamos about a potential Chinese spy, Wen Ho Lee, who in December 1999 was charged with downloading sensitive nuclear weapons codes onto insecure computers. He was later cleared of virtually all charges. Since September 11, however, there will almost certainly be stringent conditions imposed upon the ASAP program to prevent foreign students gaining access to sensitive nuclear weapons data.[30]

On July 31, 1997, the DOE announced the award of multimillion-dollar, multiyear contracts to five universities. The purpose was to study basic science, computer science, mathematics, and engineering research for the U.S. nuclear weapons program.[31] Thus nongovernment academic scientists are to be involved in the development of nuclear weapons for the first time since the Manhattan Project.[32]

The lucky campuses are as follows: the California Institute of Technology, Stanford University, the University of Chicago, the University of Illinois at Urbana-Champaign, and the University of Utah. In all, a total of fourteen universities and colleges are already participating to some degree in the ASAP. Each university is to receive 20 to 30 million dollars over a five-year period, possibly to be extended for another five years at another 20 to 30 million dollars.

The universities are establishing "centers of excellence" operating as partners with the nuclear weapons labs in the accelerated strategic computer initiative. This exercise is classified as "level one" funding. Levels two and three are in the pipeline. The schools will work in close collaboration with Los Alamos, Lawrence Livermore, and Sandia on R and D activities in specific areas related to nuclear weapons development as follows:

- The California Institute of Technology (Caltech) will develop a "virtual shock tube," a computer simulation of the detonation of high explosives and the effect of the ensuing shock waves on specific test materials related to nuclear weapons—plutonium and uranium.

  At this stage it is not clear whether data from this virtual shock tube could be incorporated into the labs' supercomputers as a nuclear weapons code. A bomb code would also need to include—

critically—fission and fusion nuclear processes, plus the energy released in the explosion.

Caltech will investigate the combined simulations of high explosives with shocked materials (including plutonium and other
materials used in nuclear weapons); it will also investigate the
physical dynamics at material interfaces of these metals, plus
shock-induced compressible turbulence and the mixing within
these test materials.

The Caltech program is ambiguous. On the one hand it will be
required to produce unclassified research material and to educate
foreign students; on the other, it must produce data relevant to the
explosion of nuclear weapons. This means that foreign nationals
will have free access to the design of nuclear weapons—previously
a closely guarded secret. This posture will obviously induce a conflict of interest for the university and the labs if lateral proliferation of nuclear weapons is to be avoided.[33]

- The University of Chicago plans to simulate thermonuclear
  processes that operate within the sun and stars. This research could
  be complementary to the Caltech program.

- Stanford University is to research the dynamics of gas turbine engines, specifically examining turbulence within gaseous and solid
  states, with specific reference to materials incorporated in thermonuclear weapons.

- The University of Illinois at Urbana-Champaign will conduct research on solid rocket propellants used in missiles. This program
  will concentrate on broad simulation issues of multicomponent,
  multiphenomena, and multiscale systems for solid rocket boosters.

  Rocket propellants are complex materials that have many innate problems. The new information will therefore be very useful
  in new nuclear war planning as well as for the missile defense
  shield.

- The University of Utah will compile data on fires and explosions
  specifically related to nuclear weapons accidents.

Scientific Goals of the Academic Strategic Alliances Program

Overall the academic strategic alliances program has been allocated
five major goals by the department of energy:

1. Establish and validate the practices of large-scale modeling, simulation, and computation as a viable scientific methodology in key scientific and engineering applications supporting DOE science-based stockpile stewardship goals and objectives
2. Accelerate advances in critical basic sciences, mathematics, and computer science areas, in computational science and engineering, in high-performance computing systems, and in problem-solving environments that support long-term ASCI needs
3. Leverage other basic science, high-performance computing systems, and problem-solving environments research in the academic community
4. Establish technical coupling of academic strategic alliances program efforts with ongoing ASCI projects in DOE laboratories
5. Strengthen training and research in areas of interest to ASCI and SBSS (science-based stockpile stewardship) and strengthen ties among Lawrence Livermore National Lab, Los Alamos National Lab, Sandia National Labs, and universities[34]

This last proviso is specifically meant to recruit a new generation of intelligent young people into the "art" of bomb making. Some programs will be designed so that professors and students may never discover the ultimate applications of their research unless they become intimately involved in classified nuclear weapons work.[35]

The chancellor of the University of Illinois, Michael Aikin, enthusiastically endorsed the notion of SS & M when he wrote, "The national importance of simulation of the science-based stewardship program cannot be overestimated, and it is an area in which we are willing and highly able to contribute. . . . I believe that multidisciplinary research and training partnerships embodied in the DOE academic strategic alliance program and our [Illinois's] proposed center are critical to the development of national defense policy and preparedness, and we are excited about the prospects of working in this enterprise."[36]

The ASAP gives university students unprecedented access to the supercomputers of the weapons labs. It also plans to make available to the public more classified information than ever before. It's worth repeating that although foreign nationals will be prohibited from working in this area, it will not prevent the drift of valuable weapons information into foreign hands, for crucial nuclear design programs will be shared with a wide array of weapon and nonweapon scientists, and the computers will run on standard lines. Therefore information from ASCI will be difficult or impossible to keep secret. This leaky situation will expedite the ability of nonnuclear countries to design and build advanced nuclear weapons.[37]

ENVIRONMENTAL HAZARDS OF SS & M

Plutonium—named after Pluto, the god of hell—remains radioactive and biologically dangerous for 500,000 years. It is acknowledged to be the most carcinogenic substance known to humans—hypothetically one pound, if uniformly distributed, could induce lung cancer in every person on earth. The proliferation of nuclear labs and facilities under the SS & M umbrella poses a relentlessly frightening list of health and environmental issues to human beings working or living near the nuclear plants. Plutonium also causes mutations in the genes of the reproductive cells—the eggs and sperm—posing a genetic risk to all future generations, a kind of random compulsory genetic engineering.

But plutonium is not the only danger. The waste from nuclear weapons production contains other deadly radioactive elements, which bio-accumulate thousands of times at each step in the food chain. Because radioactive elements are tasteless, odorless, and invisible, it is impossible to know whether exposed food is contaminated or not. Cesium 137 concentrates in meat and causes cancers of the muscle; strontium 90 concentrates in milk and induces bone cancer and leukemia; radioactive iodine concentrates in vegetables and milk and migrates to the thyroid gland inducing thyroid tumors and cancer. Tritium combines with water molecules and is incorporated into the actual genetic structure. It is a potent carcinogen. Many of these elements also remain radioactive for hundreds of years, well beyond our lifetimes.

These materials and others compose nuclear waste—the detritus from weapons production and the generation of nuclear power. Vast quantities of concentrated high-level waste in liquid and solid form lie scattered around the weapons facilities. Indeed, all the DOE weapons-manufacturing plants scattered across the nation are superfund sites leaking and leaching the most extraordinarily dangerous radioactive and toxic chemical contaminants into soil, rivers, lakes, seas, and water supplies.

One particularly vivid example of an intensely polluted DOE site is the old Rocky Flats plant, which from 1953 to 1989 manufactured approximately 70,000 plutonium pits—that is, an average of five pits per day. During a 7.7-million-dollar "cleanup," several men were delegated to excavate 171 drums of uranium from a trench in the ground that hadn't been touched for forty years. One of the men was directed to scoop out an unmarked barrel with a backhoe. It had rotted and uranium sludge oozed from the barrel. Suddenly, there was a blue flash and the ooze burst into flame. The fire had to be extinguished by a dump of sand. As the *Denver Post* wrote, "one drum down, 1,099,956 to go."

The government is attempting to detoxify this nuclear bomb plant, the first such attempt in the history of the nuclear age.

Included in the challenges:

1. To find 1100 pounds of plutonium that were "lost" in the ducts of the plant, drum, and glove boxes (used to machine the plutonium). This is enough plutonium to build 150 Nagasaki-sized bombs. It is also more than enough to reach critical mass (10 pounds is critical mass) and produce a large nuclear explosion, thereby obliterating much of Denver and Boulder, either by blast and/or fallout.

2. To "clean" thirteen "infinity" rooms—so radioactive that monitoring instruments went off-scale. One room in the plant is so hot that managers welded the door shut in 1972. Another room was filled with plutonium-fouled machinery and entombed in concrete.

3. To ship 16,000 pounds of plutonium by truck through Denver to South Carolina. On top of the plutonium shipments, three additional truckloads of radioactive waste must be shipped out per day in order to comply with the 2006 cleanup deadline. The cleanup is costing 2 million dollars a day, and it is two years behind schedule. It will cost twice as much to raze Rocky Flats as it cost to construct the new Denver airport.

A recent report by the National Academy of Sciences notes that two thirds of the government sites involved in nuclear weapons production will never be decontaminated. Long-term stewardship will be required for 100 of the 144 sites, and many will remain dangerously radioactive for tens or even hundreds of thousands of years. These areas will become—or are now denoted—"national sacrifice zones."

In fact, the federal government lacks the technology, money, or management techniques to prevent the spread of contamination. Many radioactive-contaminated plumes in underground water streams have already migrated well beyond the plant boundaries and it is impossible to police the waste properly. For instance, the DOE erected *no fishing* signs at a creek near the Oak Ridge National Lab, but children stole the signs. This occurred in this generation. What will happen long after we are forgotten?

The NAS report also said that any known barriers for radioactive waste, such as concrete and steel, would fail, and that most of what is now known about the behavior of contaminants in air, soil, and water might "eventually be proven wrong." [38, 39] Even the department of energy finally agreed in October 2000 with the Institute for Energy and Environmental Research, that official government data on the volume and radioactivity of buried plutonium and similar materials were "inconsistent and contradictory."

The amount of plutonium and other man-made radioactive elements—from the manufacture of nuclear weapons—that has been released into the soil or buried in flimsy containers such as cardboard boxes is 10 times greater than original estimates. [40] The DOE itself admitted that "there is little or no information on volumes of soil potentially contaminated by leaching of buried solid wastes, nor is there information on hazardous waste components known to have been commingled with the radioactive components." Some of these wastes are explosive materials, making retrieval difficult. This buried waste comprises 30 percent of the nation's radioactivity. [41]

The DOE surveyed production and dumping records at only six sites—Hanford, the Idaho National Engineering and Environmental Laboratory near Idaho Falls, Los Alamos National Lab, Oak Ridge National Lab in Tennessee, the Savannah River site in South Carolina, and the Nevada Test Site. [42]

There is new evidence to show that plutonium moves through the soil at a rate much faster than previously predicted. For instance, the Snake River aquifer lies 590 feet below the Idaho facility. Plutonium that was originally buried twenty feet below the surface has now been found at 240 feet. At this rate it will take only twenty-five years to reach the aquifer and enter the Snake River. Americium, a decay product of plutonium but even more deadly, has already entered the river.[43]

The department of energy has admitted for the first time that 4 tons of plutonium were released into the soil at the Nevada Test Site. Vast quantities of fission products were also released, some of which are moving rapidly in water systems toward populated areas nearby.[44]

Fires at Nuclear Weapons Labs

In a freak of nature—possibly related to the phenomenon of global warming—the contaminated grounds of three of the nation's major nuclear weapons facilities caught fire during the year 2000—at Los Alamos, Hanford, and Idaho.

A total of 6.4 million acres burned throughout the U.S., 3.5 million acres above the ten-year average.

LOS ALAMOS NATIONAL LAB. On May 4, 2000, a fire set by park rangers during protective burn-off in forests near the lab swept through a total of 48,000 acres and burned 7500 acres or one-third of the lab facility. At temperatures of 2000 degrees Fahrenheit, the fire consumed decommissioned contaminated buildings dating from the Manhattan Project, the machine shop for the main research and development facility (DARHT), and storage areas. In all, it destroyed or damaged 112 lab structures and disrupted the operation of 237 facilities. It burned more than 600 waste-disposal and contaminated sites, plus several contaminated canyons running through the lab.

Los Alamos waste areas are contaminated with the deadliest materials—plutonium 238 and 239, americium 241, tritium, uranium, strontium 90, cesium 137, beryllium, and organic carcinogenic compounds (PCBs and solvents). For many years the preferred storage container for much of the lab's waste was the cardboard box. Over 2120 potentially radioactively contaminated sites at the lab could now release radiation. During the fire, the department of energy failed to deploy airborne monitoring systems to measure smoke contaminants, nor did it attempt to monitor possible localized "hot spots."

Firefighters were not equipped with radiation monitors, nor were they carefully protected as radiation workers are—in fact, they were mostly unaware of the dangers they faced. Fires at nuclear facilities present special dangers, first because they disrupt safety systems leading to loss of power and important means of ventilation, and second because the contaminated vegetation has been converted to ashes, and strong winds sweep radioactive elements into the air to be carried great distances. Flash floods sweep vast quantities of radioactive elements from the canyons at Los Alamos into watersheds. These water sources drain into the Rio Grande River, where they pollute drinking and irrigation supplies through New Mexico and Mexico.

Three particular Los Alamos canyons are at risk:

1. The Parajito Canyon—code-named *TA-18*. Facilities here include a defunct and contaminated Omega West reactor, nuclear weapons test facilities (Kivas) that contain "high-energy burst assemblies," and a vault containing large amounts of plutonium and highly enriched uranium. The White Rock community lies directly downstream.
2. The Los Alamos Canyon—code-named *TA-41, TA-2*. Dangerous facilities in this canyon include the defunct and contaminated Omega West reactor. Placed at the bottom of the canyon, it is vulnerable to slope instability, mudslides, and rock falls.
3. The Pueblo Canyon, which contains the Diamond Road crossing and utility facilities for the town of Los Alamos.

Other radioactive canyons—recipients of decades of waste-dumping—include: Mortandad Canyon, DP Canyon, and Acid Canyon. Some of these radioactive canyons are surrounded by communities of Native Americans.

Seventy-seven other waste-disposal sites and contaminated areas at Los Alamos are located on potential floodplains.

Following only a modest postfire rainfall in September 2000, the concentration of cesium 137 in suspended run-off mixed with clay and soil in the water was 5 to 20 times higher than prefire levels, plutonium was 5 to 10 times, and strontium 90 was 2 to 5 times higher.

Flash floods inundate the region almost every year.[45, 46, 47]

HANFORD NUCLEAR RESERVATION. On July 28, 2000, a wildfire near Richland, Washington, sparked by a fatal car collision, burned 190,000 acres, including parts of the Hanford Nuclear Reservation.

An eight-foot wall of fire came to within 400 yards of 330 50-gallon barrels of waste containing uranium powder and chips, and other toxic and hazardous waste material. A single drum, if ignited, could send flames 20 to 30 feet into the air, releasing all the radioactive and toxic contents.[48]

The fires also passed through an area of known radioactive dump sites. The firefighting operation was hampered by lack of adequate maps detailing radioactively contaminated nuclear sites.[49] The fires burned through highly contaminated B/C cribs (storage sites) in the 200 West area, which probably contain more radioactivity than the entire Los Alamos inventory.

Plutonium was detected in air monitors around the area, but the monitoring was inadequate. Because federal officials misjudged the seriousness of the fire, the plutonium measurements were incomplete; the most reliable testing by the EPA was performed after the fires ended. Levels measured at that time were still 100 times the normal amount. It is unknown what the measurements were during the height of the blaze.

Plutonium could potentially enter the lungs of people hundreds of miles away depending on wind direction. One millionth of a gram of inhaled plutonium is a carcinogenic dose.[50]

IDAHO NATIONAL ENGINEERING & ENVIRONMENTAL LABORATORY. In July 2000, a fire burned 49,000 acres in and around the Idaho National Lab, producing higher-than-normal levels of radioactivity in the air. The fire entered a test reactor area. Evacuation from the facility was ordered.

Another fire in September at the same labs consumed 8000 acres

and resulted in an accident that officials admitted was very dangerous. One chamber of an incinerator that was used to "burn" mixed
radioactive and toxic waste containing plutonium continued to burn
overnight without supervision after worker evacuation. Lab officials
claim that workers shut down the incinerator before they left, but
one chamber reignited because of the fire. Safety procedures required that the incinerator be attended at all times, but they were not
followed. Operated by Bechtel—a DOE contractor—the incinerator
has since been closed.[51]

It is evident that radioactive material should never be subjected to
incineration, as it is transferred unchanged into the air to be dispersed by the wind.

OTHER NUCLEAR FACILITIES. Several major nuclear weapons facilities
were closed over the past ten years, leaving behind large quantities of
unguarded, unstable nuclear materials, including 189 tons of com-
bustible, highly enriched uranium at the Oak Ridge Y-12 weapons
plant in Tennessee, stored in old wooden buildings. If a wildfire ignited the uranium metal, water used to fight the fire would generate
hydrogen, converting the blaze to a small holocaust.[52]

The department of energy recently admitted for the first time that
four tons of plutonium had been injected into the Nevada Test Site
over a period of four decades. Vast quantities of deadly fission products accompany the plutonium. This material is moving rapidly
through underground water systems toward communities that reside
nearby.[53]

Government Compensation

Thousands of people who once worked in nuclear weapons production plants are, for the first time, to receive compensation from the
federal government. These people mined, milled, and enriched uranium, operated nuclear reactors, reprocessed deadly radioactive materials, machined plutonium, uranium, and thorium, and handled
radioactive waste. Many have already died, others are now dying of
cancers and diseases related to their radioactive and toxic chemical
exposure. Yet for sixty years the government stubbornly denied a link

between work exposure in the nuclear weapons complex and subsequent disease processes. Very few nuclear workers, if any, were informed of the medical dangers implicit in their work. Rather, the emphasis was on the cold war–related emergency production of nuclear weapons. This was a national security imperative, and the health of the workers was a secondary consideration.

Finally, Congress has offered a one-time 150,000-dollar payment plus free health care to those who have suffered. The total cost to the government is estimated at 1 billion dollars over the next five years, compared with the billions doled out by Congress to the military corporations, the Pentagon, and the nuclear labs.

Another, possibly larger group of people exposed during the forties and fifties were employed by more than 200 private companies across the nation. Ranging from mom-and-pop machine shops to large chemical firms, these facilities were quietly converted to the production of nuclear weapons components. In total ignorance, workers handled tons of dangerous uranium, thorium, polonium, beryllium, and other toxic and radioactive substances.

Most of the factories were located in the industrial belts of New England, New York, Pennsylvania, New Jersey, around the Great Lakes, and through the Ohio and Mississippi River Valleys, as well as in the cities of Detroit, Chicago, St. Louis, and Cleveland. In all these facilities, many thousands were exposed to levels of radiation hundreds of times higher than the arbitrary limits imposed at the time, limits that have since been shown to be many times too high. Workers in the most dangerous jobs were exposed to lung doses of 130 rems or higher—ten times that accepted today. (A *rem* is a biological measurement of radiation.)

No dose of radiation is safe, and radiation is biologically cumulative—each dose adds to the risk of cancer development years later. Some of these workers were so contaminated they were 200 percent more likely than unexposed people to die of radiation-induced cancer. Government reports documenting the medical risks were classified and hidden.

The new Congressional compensation bill applies specifically to government employees, excluding those who were privately employed. Many of the private nuclear companies have shut down, and records have been displaced or lost. The surrounding communities are largely unaware of the permanent radioactive and toxic contamination of their environments—a medically tragic legacy of this secret weapons work. As a single example—one of many—the Harshaw Chemical Company in Cleveland pumped 350 to 500 pounds of radioactive uranium dust from its stacks.

In light of this ongoing danger, the SS & M program will perpetuate and make worse an already catastrophic environmental and health problem. There is no cold war. There are no enemies except terrorists, and they will not be stopped by the use of nuclear weapons. We the people must demand that the labs cease to function: They are killing us all to make the bombs to kill us all better.

Chapter Six

STAR WARS:
THE STORY OF NATIONAL MISSILE
DEFENSE SYSTEMS

If the U.S. proceeds to destroy the ABM treaty.... We can and will withdraw not only from the START II treaty ... but from the whole system of treaty relations having to do with the limitation and control of strategic and conventional arms.

—Russian President Vladimir Putin, 2001

Any amendment, or abolishing of the treaty, will lead to disastrous consequences. This will bring a halt to nuclear disarmament now between the Russians and Americans, and in the future will halt multilateral disarmament as well.

—Chinese Arms Control Ambassador Sha Zukang, 2001

A T ROUGHLY THE SAME TIME that nuclear scientists conceived the idea of a "stockpile management program" to prolong their careers after the end of the cold war—and as a cover for development of new nuclear weapons—Bill Clinton and George W. Bush, in response to pressure from weapons manufacturers, worked on a parallel effort to craft a missile defense system. Shaped, as always, by the politics of the day, the plan evolved from Lyndon Johnson's Sentinel to George W. Bush's national missile defense program (NMD), via Ronald Reagan's memorably named Star Wars plan. Each successive incarnation has added new approaches to creating a comprehensive missile shield for the U.S., and it is important to understand both the evolution of missile defense and the various components of the latest plan being put forth by George W. Bush—including his proposal to put nuclear reactors and possibly nuclear weapons in space as well as on earth and in the immediate atmosphere—in order to evaluate the viability and implications of our current policy. This chapter looks at the history of missile defense and its current components. Chapter Seven looks at plans to militarize space.

FROM SENTINEL TO NATIONAL MISSILE DEFENSE

Every military weapon ever built has instigated another weapon to counter it. Ever since scientists designed missiles capable of delivering nuclear weapons through space, the next imperative became an antimissile system. To this end, in 1967 President Lyndon Johnson proposed a system called Sentinel. President Richard Nixon called his hypothetical version Safeguard, and Ronald Reagan's version became known as Star Wars. Eventually, all these plans were abandoned because none of them worked. Building thousands of hydrogen bombs proved far easier than building a system to foil them.[1] Nevertheless, Reagan's charisma and powers of persuasion swayed public opinion in favor of Star Wars—a "shield" to be constructed over the continental U.S. to protect against incoming Soviet ballistic missiles. His Star Wars speech in 1983 gave the imprimatur to a plan recognized by every reputable scientist to be unworkable. Reagan's speech also gave the whole concept of missile defense an indelibly memorable name and many people—myself included—now use the term "Star Wars" for all comprehensive missile defense plans, despite each successive administration's renaming efforts.

Seventy billion dollars later, after enormous amounts of work and research in many of the universities, colleges, and corporations around the nation, none of the evolving technologies has been shown to be effective against incoming ballistic missiles. Following his election in 1992, Clinton directed his defense secretary, Les Aspin, to end the Star Wars program, or the strategic defense initiative (SDI) as it was then called. In May 1993 Aspin created as an alternative a new organization called the ballistic missile defense organization (BMDO). Moving away from the concept of space-based weapons, the new plan was to acquire and develop ground-based systems designed to defend American forces overseas from battlefield missiles. Eighty percent of the BMDO budget was appropriated to "theater" or short-range missile defense; 20 percent for research into national or long-range missile defense.[2] But since the same technology is used to design both short- and long-range systems, the Republican Right was actually quite pleased with Aspin's plan,[3] and Frank Gaffney, former assistant to Reagan's undersecretary of defense, said that Aspin was really just "rearranging the deck chairs."

As early as 1991, the navy, army, and air force had quietly begun to develop their own theater missile defenses. The navy and army worked on two similar systems—a lower-tier defense designed to intercept short-range missiles in the lower atmosphere, and an upper-tier defense designed to intercept missiles in the upper atmosphere.[4] The air force, meanwhile, had been developing several theater missile defense (TMD) programs, including a boost-phase laser system intercept that would be deployed in a piloted plane. Aspin's BMDO specifically endorsed three of these systems—the army's Patriot (PAC-3) lower-tier system, the navy's Aegis program to be based aboard Aegis ships, and the army's theater high altitude area defense (THAAD).[5] (It is a generally accepted notion that theater or short-range missile defense does not violate the Antiballistic Missile—ABM—treaty. However, THAAD operates at altitudes of 40 kilometers, almost outside the atmosphere, so in effect it does violate the ABM.)

But the shock of the political loss of the House and Senate to the Republicans in 1994 had a dramatic effect upon Clinton's opposition to Star Wars. Among the dictates of Speaker Newt Gingrich's "Contract with America" was a provision calling for a "highly effective defense" of the continental United States at the earliest practical date.[6] In order to placate the now-powerful Republican Congress, Clinton specifically embraced the Star Wars issue, retitling it once again, this time as the seemingly more benign national missile defense (NMD).

The American Right remained adamantly wedded to the Star Wars idea, despite the fact that a 1995 U.S. national intelligence estimate found that "no country, other than the major declared nuclear powers, will develop or otherwise acquire a ballistic missile in the next fifteen years that could threaten the contiguous 48 states and Canada."[7] Upset by this report, the Republican-controlled Congress appointed Donald Rumsfeld, secretary of defense in the Ford administration (and now secretary of defense for George W. Bush) to head an "independent" commission to counter the assertions. According to Bob Aldridge's background paper on national missile defense titled "Son of Star Wars," the commission was directed to consider the worst-case possibilities, but to exclude the most likely scenarios in its deliberations.

They were told to assess real or potential threats from ballistic missiles carrying nuclear, biological, or chemical weapons, but were not to decide their probability or feasibility. Nor were they to consider that there could be other easier ways to deliver these weapons. In other words, the commission was directed to find specific threats for Congressional promotion of its NMD ambitions.[8] General Henry Shelton, chairman of the Joint Chiefs of Staff, gave some perspective on the Rumsfeld report in a letter he wrote to Senator James Inhofe on August 24, 1998: "The [Rumsfeld] commission points out that through unconventional, high-risk development programs and foreign assistance, terrorist nations could acquire an ICBM capability in a short time, and that the intelligence community may not detect it. We view this as an unlikely development."[9]

Unfortunately, Shelton's letter arrived just as North Korea launched a Taepo-Dong missile containing a satellite over the Japanese mainland in August 1998, an event that gave new momentum to national missile defense. This missile was based upon primitive scaled-up Scud missile technology, built by a country that has a gross domestic product smaller than Delaware's.[10] (The prestigious journal *Jane's Defense Weekly* said of the North Korean long-range missile site that it looks "more like an abandoned oil derrick than the nerve center for annihilating the 'running dogs of capitalism.' ") Inherently incapable of reaching the U.S. mainland, the primitive Korean medium-range missile crashed into the sea off the coast of Japan. Nevertheless, it provided the American Right an enormous boost of moral ammunition. It also prompted Japan, which had previously been reluctant to become involved with the U.S. on plans for missile defense, to sign a cooperative agreement in August 1999 to develop a theater missile defense.

The Rumsfeld report was now followed by another assessment from the National Intelligence Council, published on September 9, 1999. This new report warned that proliferation of medium-range ballistic missiles, driven primarily by missile sales from North Korea, presented an "immediate, serious and growing threat . . ." (This was not even an allegation that North Korea presented a threat, but that it was selling missile components to *other* countries that *might* be threats.) Among other allegations, the report said that Iran, with the help of Russia, *could* test a missile before 2010 that *could* deliver a several-hundred-kiloton warhead against the U.S.[11] And that over the next fifteen years the U.S. "most likely will face ICBM threats from Russia, China, and North Korea, probably from Iran, and possibly from Iraq."

While these reports were designed to sound comprehensive and authoritative, in their zeal to justify a multibillion-dollar defense program they failed to acknowledge the fact that any country or person in the world could smuggle a nuclear, chemical, or biological weapon into the United States aboard a ship, in a suitcase, or in a small private plane. A truck could be driven in from Mexico or Canada loaded with weapons. A cruise missile flying beneath radar, undetectable by any NMD system, could also be used as a suitable delivery mechanism. Or, as we witnessed on September 11, 2001, American aircraft loaded with civilians and thousands of gallons of jet fuel could be used as ballistic missiles, the primary weapons—simple, inexpensive box cutters. As the *Mercury News* argued on September 10, 1999, attack through these means was much more likely than attack through space.

Joseph Cirincione, the director of the Carnegie Endowment for International Peace, incisively stated that the new report "reflects a lowering of previously established intelligence standards for judging threats." The report arbitrarily shifted the missile threat to incorporate all fifty states instead of forty-eight (as allowed under the antiballistic missile treaty, which excluded Hawaii and Alaska), and it advanced by at least five years the possible date of a "rogue state" long-range-missile deployment. The report itself acknowledged that "some analysts believe the prominence given to missiles countries 'could' develop gives more credence than is warranted to developments that may prove implausible." [12]

Meanwhile, in Washington, an independent review team headed by former air force chief of staff and retired four-star general Larry Welch, and comprised of twelve experts on missile defense, issued another report. This team was touted as "the most experienced collection of civilian and retired military officers to have studied the antimissile effort." They found that the missile-defense program was plagued by inadequate testing, spare parts shortages, and management lapses. The report criticized the government and contractors for exhibiting over-optimism about their ability to develop a reliable missile interceptor. It found failures based in poor design and fabrication, lax management, and lack of rigorous government oversight. The report said that the test schedules had been so compressed that the program was essentially "a rush to failure." [13, 14] The panel also pointed out that an *actual* kill vehicle had not been tested on an *actual* booster (as opposed to prototype warheads and surrogate boosters) and there was major concern that the kill vehicle would not be able to withstand the actual shock loads, because the actual booster is much faster and the loads are "more than an order of magnitude greater than those of the surrogate booster now being used." The panel recommended that Clinton delay his decision to build the national missile defense. [15]

Clinton, however, was under impeachment proceedings in January 1999, and in an exceedingly vulnerable political position. By the end of the month, Defense Secretary William Cohen, acting for Clinton but also agreeing in principle himself, increased the missile defense budget by 6.6 billion dollars over four years and announced a timetable that included a deployment decision before Clinton left office. [16] While the Clinton administration had initially endorsed a modest missile defense system in response to a theoretical small ICBM attack from a "rogue" state, the defense budget increase announced by Cohen allowed the Star Wars lobby to get their proverbial foot in the door, and an animated debate on the efficacy, technical validity, and viability of the proposed NMD ensued. As scientists from both sides of the fence attacked each other, three tests for the missile system failed, North and South Korea made peace overtures to each other, and the rationale for NMD disappeared.

Clinton had originally enumerated four criteria for making the decision about deploying national missile defense: the threat, the cost, the technology, and overall American security. The threat was now gone, the cost was incomparable, the technology did not seem to work, and many felt that American security would be endangered rather than enhanced by deployment of NMD, a view confirmed by a classified intelligence report issued at the time on "Foreign Responses to U.S. National Missile Defense Deployment." The report warned that NMD would prompt China to expand its nuclear weapons arsenal tenfold and cause Russia to place multiple hydrogen bombs on missiles that currently carry only one bomb. The report also stated that if China were prompted to deploy 200 warheads by 2015 (as noted, they currently have only twenty hydrogen bombs capable of hitting America) this would prompt India and Pakistan to respond with their own nuclear buildup.[17]

In response to the report (and with obvious relief), Clinton passed the Star Wars problem on to the next president and thus avoided being labeled the president who destroyed the ABM treaty. (Even as he failed definitively to decide the future of NMD, in typical Clinton fashion he directed his secretary of defense to pursue a "robust program of technological development." So, unofficially, the program proceeded unabated.)

In contrast, George W. Bush now enthusiastically endorses a full-scale, no-holds-barred, multilevel NMD system.[18] The Heritage Foundation has been busy setting the stage and leading the charge, including circulating the following petition during the presidential election year 2000, some months before Bush was declared president:

Citizen's Petition to Protect America Now

Whereas China and Russia have threatened the U.S. with nuclear attack, and rogue nations such as Iraq, North Korea and Iran have acquired or are acquiring missiles equipped with weapons of mass destruction;

Whereas the United States currently cannot stop even one missile after it is launched;

Whereas the Administration has declared that it must have the permission of the Russian government before deciding to deploy any missile defense for the United States;

Whereas the limited, land-based missile defense system the Administration says it may decide later this year to deploy will not be able to protect our families until 2005 at the earliest;

Whereas the United States Navy could be ordered to immediately begin the process of deploying a sea-based defense that would provide some missile protection several years before 2005;

Whereas senior Pentagon officials have judged that a comprehensive missile defense with a combination of land-, sea-, air-, and space-based components would offer the American people the most effective protection against missile attack; and

Whereas the Administration is currently engaged in treaty negotiations with Russia that would prohibit the United States from deploying sea-, air- or space-based defenses;

Therefore I, [fill in name] of [fill in state], call upon my elected representatives and candidates for public office to pledge to my family and all of the families of the United States to support immediately beginning the process of deploying a sea-based missile defense as the first layer of protection for America's families; and further to pledge to reject the notion that any other nation may exercise a veto of the U.S. military's ability to offer the American people the most effective protection available.

Jack Spenser and Michael Scardaville, Heritage Fellows, fashioned an op-ed piece for the *Miami Herald* on October 17, 2000, justifying such a commitment to NMD. They reminded readers that Iran tested a Shahab missile with an 800-mile range on September 21, 2000, and announced that Iran is "dangerously close to developing nuclear weapons." They also noted that on September 23, Syria acquired a new model of Scud missile from North Korea, allowing it to attack Israel from bases deep within its own territory. Libya, they said, began receiving North Korean Nodong missiles on September 24, giving Libya the ability to attack Israel and southern Europe. They wrote that Pakistan and India were also planning new missile tests for intermediate-range ballistic missiles, and they ended by stressing that the threat to "our troops and friends abroad is growing," that the U.S. needs an antiballistic missile system, and that reliance upon the ABM treaty is folly.[19]

In response, Steve LaMontagne, a research analyst at the Council for a Livable World, wrote that Spenser and Scardaville omitted the fact that the missile developments of Libya, Iran, and Syria *occurred within a week of and in response to Israel's successful test of its new Arrow 2 anti-tactical ballistic missile system,* and that none of the above-mentioned missiles could reach the U.S. His article pointed out that if—as the Heritage Foundation claimed—antiballistic missile systems deter proliferation, "why do Iran, Syria, and Libya seem unfazed—and even provoked—by Israel's missile defenses?" And "why is Russia determined to preserve its retaliatory strike capability against possible U.S. defenses? . . . The lesson from the Middle East and Russia is that missile defenses encourage proliferation." [20]

Nevertheless, any ongoing debate about the need for or feasibility of national missile defense takes place even as the corporations and the Pentagon quietly go about designing, contracting, and constructing most of the elements. There is no public discussion, no informed debate within or by the media, and the American public is being asked to foot the multibillion-dollar bill and take the catastrophic risks such developments entail. William Cohen, Clinton's secretary of defense, had enthusiastically endorsed NMD when he increased the missile defense budget in January 1999, referring to North Korea by saying, "We affirm that there is a threat and the threat is growing." Congress added to the pressure two months later by endorsing legislation introduced by Republican Senator Thad Cochran mandating national missile-defense deployment "as soon as is technically possible," [21] and stating, "It is the policy of the United States to deploy a national missile defense."

Star Wars had been revived.

On October 2, 2001—21 days after September 11—the Senate unanimously passed a massive 345 billion dollar Defense Appropriations bill, which included George W. Bush's demands for flexibility on missile defense (which itself cost 8.3 billion dollars). [22]

COMPONENTS OF MISSILE DEFENSE

The categorization of Star Wars or missile defense systems is complex and intertwined, and the nomenclature is continually changing. During the nineties' revival of Reagan's Star Wars concept, less belligerent terminology was devised to make the whole concept seem more acceptable. *Missile defense* was the chosen lexicon, and, as noted previously, it had two components: theater missile defense (TMD) and national missile defense (NMD). TMD was to be used to hit in midair, low-flying short-range missiles—sometimes known as "tactical missiles"—like Scuds, which were used by Iraq in the Gulf confrontation. (The flight time of these missiles is minutes only.) NMD was conjured up to describe the interception of intercontinental ballistic missiles, usually nuclear armed. (The flight time of sea-launched ballistic missiles—sometimes known as "intermediate-range missiles"—is fifteen minutes; the flight time of land-based ballistic missiles—sometimes known as "strategic missiles"—is thirty minutes.)

Star Wars and each of the options that have succeeded it encompass plans to protect against the whole spectrum of weapons, from the most primitive to the most dangerous and sophisticated. Individual politicians, lobbyists, and others endorse more or less extensive versions of missile defense, ostensibly related to the level of threat they perceive (but clearly often driven by more mercenary factors):

LIMITED MISSILE DEFENSE

Some believe that America need only protect itself against "rogue" states or "states of concern" like North Korea, Iraq, Iran, Libya, etc. These countries possess conventional weapons but none possess missiles capable of hitting the U.S., and none currently possess nuclear weapons. Advocates of this approach favor antimissile missiles, based on land, on sea, and in the air.

EXTENSIVE MISSILE DEFENSE

Others argue that China must now be considered the new global threat, although it maintains only twenty primitive nuclear-armed ICBMs that are liquid-fueled and take days to prepare before they can be launched against the U.S. But the Pentagon is projecting that China will shortly be arming itself with ever more nuclear-armed ICBMs, and therefore argues for a more extensive missile defense than that currently planned for rogue states. Russia, on the other hand, retains a nuclear arsenal capable of destroying the U.S. and inducing nuclear winter. It is obvious that no antimissile system could ever protect the U.S. against some 5000 Russian nuclear weapons descending upon it from space. But the missile defense system makes sense in conjunction with the other components of the overall U.S. official policy to "fight and win" a nuclear war against Russia. In a surprise attack the U.S. will initiate a first strike, which means it will go first and win the nuclear war by taking out most of the Russian missiles before they are launched from their silos. Star Wars will then "mop up" the few missiles that have escaped destruction and have actually been launched into space, so there will be no more Russian missiles to hit the U.S. This scenario will create nuclear winter, of course.

SPACE-BASED DEFENSE

An even more aggressive contingent within the official U.S. establishment is pushing for a still more extensive, space-based system, both to provide a greater degree of missile defense and to protect America's *economic* interest in space. Beyond protecting America's current borders from missile attack, this contingent plans to exploit natural resources by "mining" the moon, the asteroids, and the planets for rare minerals. Naturally, if the U.S. invests billions of dollars in space research and development, it must be prepared to "protect" its investment. This logic led to the establishment of a new military entity—the U.S. space command, created by the Joint Chiefs of Staff in 1985 to help "institutionalize the use of space in U.S. deterrence." [23]

The U.S. space command explicitly states that the U.S. must "[dominate] the space dimension of military operations to protect U.S. interest and investment," domination that will be attained by the militarization of space with antisatellite weapons, antiballistic missile weapons, laser beam weapons, nuclear missiles, nuclear reactors, and possibly orbiting nuclear weapons. (So concerned is the rest of the world that on November 1, 1999, 138 nations voted at the United Nations for a resolution titled "Prevention of an Arms Race

in Outer Space," which recognized "the common interest of all
mankind in the exploration and uses of outer space for peaceful purposes" and "reaffirmed the will of all states that the exploration and
uses of space shall be for peaceful purposes and shall be carried out
for the benefit and in the interests of all countries. . . . Prevention of
an arms race in outer space would avert a grave danger for international peace and security." Only the United States and Israel refused
to support this resolution.[24]

THREE WAYS TO DESTROY AN
INTERCONTINENTAL BALLISTIC MISSILE

A ballistic missile is like a bullet shot from a gun. It leaves its launch-
pad or silo on a predetermined trajectory, cannot be recalled, and will
land where it is targeted. Missile defense systems are categorized
based on the point in flight at which they intercept enemy missiles:

- *Boost-phase systems* hit "enemy" missiles immediately after they
  are launched, in their "boost" phase—the five minutes available
  after launch and before the missile leaves the atmosphere
- *Midcourse systems* hit missiles in space during their "transit"
  phases, as the bombs, or "passengers," separate from their missiles
  and coast through space at tremendous speeds
- *Terminal systems* hit missiles as they reenter the earth's atmosphere to land on and "kill" their target

Destruction of a ballistic missile at any stage—boost, transit, or terminal—carries grave medical implications.

BOOST PHASE

The boost phase is possibly the best time to destroy the missile, particularly if it is MIRV'ed (multiple independent reentry vehicles), for
it carries numerous hydrogen bombs that are much harder to target
once they have separated. If the missile is loaded with numerous sub-
munitions of chemical or biological weapons, the only efficient time
to destroy them is during the boost phase. During the boost phase, the

missile itself is large and slow compared to tiny warheads barreling through space at many times the speed of sound. During its rapid ascent the missile pours forth great jets of fire, which are readily identifiable by infrared-tracking early-warning satellite, thus making them "easy" targets.

There are three disadvantages to boost-phase destruction. First, the missile must be detected within two minutes of launch, leaving no time for human decision or intervention either to detect or to attack the missile. This means that World War III could be computer initiated by error or by design, with software determining our future.

Second is a medical problem of grave import. If ten hydrogen bombs on one missile were destroyed in the atmosphere, approximately 100 pounds of carcinogenic plutonium would rain down upon the population, causing long-term havoc and mayhem. Prevailing winds would scatter the deadly, long-lived carcinogenic pollution hundreds to thousands of miles. The contaminated earth would be polluted forever. Likewise, if the missile were carrying biological or chemical weapons, lethal genetically modified viruses and bacteria, or highly toxic chemicals, would descend upon the underlying population.

The third disadvantage is that the intercepted nuclear weapons could accidentally explode when intercepted.

TRANSIT PHASE

As a MIRV'ed missile zooms through space, the launch rocket separates from the front end, or "bus," which contains its "passengers"— the ten hydrogen bombs.

This transit phase lasts about 25 minutes. It is very difficult to detect hydrogen bombs hurtling through space at very cold temperatures. But because the metal bombs originate in the earth's atmosphere, they retain their warmth relative to the subfreezing temperatures of space. Heat-sensing mechanisms on an antiballistic missile or "kill" vehicle are designed to detect the temperature differential and allow the missile to seek out its target.

However, it has long been recognized that it is relatively easy to fool an antiballistic missile system. Numerous decoys could accom-

pany the bombs—such as mylar balloons inflated to bomb size and
coated with the appropriate radar reflecting material to simulate the
bomb, or pieces of aluminum to confuse the radar systems of the kill
vehicle. Balloons can be made to be the same shape as the warhead,
and if they contain a lightbulb and a battery, they maintain the same
temperature as the warhead, thus confusing the interceptor sensors.
Or the real bomb can be surrounded by a cooled balloon to make it resemble a decoy. The truth is that the Pentagon has never tested an interceptor system against a large array of decoys. Burton Richter,
winner of the 1976 Nobel Prize in physics, compares the task to hitting a gnat with a gun that fires pins, with only one pin in each gun.
Not surprisingly, most of the tests performed thus far by the Pentagon using a hit-to-kill missile have failed.

Richter and other eminent scientists suggest that the only way to
effectively halt or intercept missiles and bombs in space is to deploy
nuclear weapons in space. Decoys would then be irrelevant, because
the nuclear explosion would destroy bombs and decoys over a wide
area.[25] But even an effective space-based missile defense would create
what are known as "exotic" effects, including electromagnetic pulse
(EMP). In 1962, for example, the United States exploded a hydrogen
bomb 248 miles high in space. In an unexpected turn of events, it was
thus discovered that destructive electromagnetic radiation emitted
from a nuclear blast in space travels vast distances.

It has since been calculated that a single bomb exploded 200 miles
above the continental U.S. could paralyze North America, destroying
most electronic systems, including long runs of cable, piping, or con-
duit; large antennae and their feed cables; guy wires and their support lines; overland power and telephone lines; long runs of electrical
wiring; railroad tracks; aluminum aircraft bodies; computers; power
supplies; alarm systems; intercoms; life-support control systems;
transistorized receivers and transmitters; base radio stations; satellites; and some telephone equipment. Fewer than five explosions
could blanket the U.S. with as much as 100,000 volts per square
meter.[26]

Ted Taylor, one of the inventors of the miniaturized hydrogen
bomb, estimates that there are approximately fifty exotic effects from
a nuclear explosion, including many types of EMP, gamma radiation,
X rays, and electron effects from bomb debris.

TERMINAL PHASE

As the hydrogen bombs reenter the earth's atmosphere, at 20 times the speed of sound, it is very difficult to destroy them. Even if some of them could be successfully hit, they would spread plutonium across the targeted country.

•   •   •

Despite all these drawbacks, missile defense systems seem destined for manufacture unless the American people, realizing that their lives are in great jeopardy, rise up to save themselves, their children, and all future generations.

While I have tried to give a neat overview of missile defense systems, as recently as August 2001 the Pentagon changed the terminology again, which will keep the public—conveniently for the Pentagon—confused. TMD and NMD are now intertwined, the differences between them unclear. This terminology shell game means that those who previously supported TMD only, including many Democratic politicians, may be forced to support the whole system, unless they have the courage to challenge the Pentagon.[27]

WEAPON SYSTEMS INVOLVED IN MISSILE DEFENSE [28]

I invite you to absorb the following with a skeptical eye, being ever aware of the innate dangers technology brings to the world. You need to understand how the U.S. government is spending your tax dollars, and how this spending spree is contributing to the destabilization of an armed world seething with ancient animosities between nations. Bear in mind that in determining numbers of weapons systems needed, the Pentagon's overall strategy has been to prepare the equipment to fight two conventional wars simultaneously (although before September 11, Defense Secretary Rumsfeld had planned to downscale to a single major war).

In each case, I have described the particular weapon system, given the cost to taxpayers, indicated who will benefit from the contract to build it, and evaluated the weapon's usefulness, track record, feasibility, etc., drawing on reports of the General Accounting Office and others who have analyzed each system in detail. I have also tried to indicate which systems are in violation of existing treaties, but because the Antiballistic Missile (ABM) treaty is not absolutely specific and does not cover theater missile defense, it is unclear whether some of the systems under development constitute violations or not. Some Americans would contend that theater defense does not violate the ABM, for example, but Russia is not so sure. Several of the systems with bilateral functions definitely do violate the ABM treaty, as they cross the line between the theater defense arena and NMD. It is deeply worrying that the U.S. military-industrial complex is already constructing many of these systems regardless of treaty violations.

Many Americans are under the impression that weapons developed under the rubric of "missile defense" do not count as new weapons or are permitted by current arms control treaties. This was the case with a man from the national guard in Alaska, who told me that he is involved in installing the foundations for the first 100 missiles near Fairbanks, the initial part of the exoatmospheric missile defense system initiated by Clinton. The man was very surprised by an anti–Star Wars speech I gave, saying that he had been under the impression that NMD was specifically for defense. The fact is that missiles used in missile defense violate all arms control treaties and will likely initiate a massive new nuclear arms race involving China, Russia, India, Pakistan, and others, despite the express purpose of the ABM and other international agreements.

LOWER-TIER DEFENSE (ENDOATMOSPHERIC)

The army and navy are in charge of these particular systems, designed to intercept missiles or bombs at low levels in the atmosphere. Components of the systems include the antimissile missiles themselves, and detection and tracking systems to locate and target enemy missiles for destruction.

Patriot PAC-3 Army System

This is a hit-to-kill warhead on a missile guided by aerodynamic fins. The current version is an upgraded model of the Patriot PAC-2 defense used against Iraqi Scud missiles during the Gulf War. The Pentagon, despite the dazzling TV propaganda at the time, has been forced to admit that not one of the Patriot missiles intercepted a single Scud,[29] a fact that does not bode well for the future development and upgrading of the Patriot. Although the missiles certainly seemed to be hitting the Scuds, these images that played and replayed clearly did not represent what was actually happening in "real time" during the Gulf conflict.

The new, upgraded version of the Patriot missile, PAC-3, will be 17 feet long and weigh 640 pounds with a 22-mile or 33-kilometer range. The warheads will be equipped with sensors to locate and home in on the target, with small rocket thrusters to maneuver the bomb onto a collision course. Destruction of the enemy missile will be accomplished by energy of the impact. Sixteen of these interceptor missiles are to be loaded onto a Patriot launcher.

COST: Original estimates for the upgraded Patriot came in at 5 million dollars for each interceptor, based on building 2200 PAC-3s to meet the two-war criteria. This figure is now reduced to 1200 PAC-3s at 2 million dollars each.

The total estimated cost of the PAC-3 system is 7.4 billion dollars. But according to the Government Accounting Office, this figure may be an underestimate because contractor costs could exceed current estimates, and twelve to fifteen additional flight tests may be conducted as well, meaning twelve to fifteen replacements.

BENEFICIARIES: Principle contractors are Lockheed Martin Missiles and Fire Control for the interceptors, and Raytheon Company for the launchers and the fire control vehicle with its small phase-array radar and the engagement control vehicle with computers and displays.

There are five subcontractors.

EVALUATION: There is no guarantee that these weapons will work if the performance of their predecessors is any indication. Note that the destruction of one missile will cost 2 million dollars just for one antimissile, and this amount does not include the infrastructure, plus the R and D necessary for its construction.

Navy Area Defense

The missiles in this system—called Block-4A—have a range of 62 to 124 miles, longer than that of the army's PAC-3, and are to be placed within vertical launch tubes on Aegis destroyer ships. These are an updated version of the Standard-2 anti-air missile, which is already deployed. They will be equipped with a hit-to-kill warhead for endo-atmospheric intercepts, an infrared seeker to supplement their radar seeker, and a radio-frequency adjunct sensor.

Development and operational testing are already complete; the system is in low-rate initial production.

COST: The total cost to American taxpayers is estimated at 8.98 billion dollars.

BENEFICIARIES: Raytheon is the main contractor with five subcontractors.

EVALUATION: The General Accounting Office warns: "The Navy plans to contract for the low-rate initial production of 185 Block-4A missiles, at an estimated cost of $568.2 million, prior to the completion of any realistic operational testing. . . . We are concerned that the Navy will make a premature commitment to production of unproven missiles."

However, the navy is convinced that their system is superior to the army's Patriot system because the army requires more than 126 C-5A airplane flights to Korea, for example, to rapidly deploy a single Patriot battalion (194 missiles) just to "protect" U.S. troops. The navy would need only three to four Aegis ships to "protect" most U.S. troops in Korea and Japan. (Nevertheless, the navy intends to build 1500 missiles to put on fifty-seven Aegis destroyers and twenty-two Aegis cruisers by the year 2011.)

Medium Extended Air Defense System (MEADS)

MEADS is designed to be a rapidly deployable, highly mobile theater missile defense system to be used in the battlefield to protect soldiers.

Traversing rough terrain and maneuvering with troops, it will provide a protection of 360 degrees.

There will be sixteen missiles per launcher and 100 launchers in a battery.

COST: Under pressure by the U.S. government, Germany and Italy have been persuaded to cofinance this particular antimissile system—the U.S. will fund 55 percent, Germany 28 percent, and Italy 17 percent. In 1996 MEADS was estimated to cost a total of 40 billion dollars, but new estimates are now predicted to be many times this amount.

BENEFICIARIES: Prime contractors are Lockheed Martin Missiles and Fire Control; Alenia Marconi Systems in Rome, Italy; and Daimler Chrysler Aerospace AG in Munich, Germany.

EVALUATION: The 1996 estimate for developing and producing 100 complete MEADS systems—sixty for the U.S. and forty for Europe, was estimated at 40 billion dollars over fifteen years, based on the PAC-3 missile costing 2 million dollars each. The subsequent increase to 3 million dollars per missile caused an uproar in the MEADS program.

Airborne Warming and Control System (AWACS)

The air force already has a fleet of thirty-four AWACS—a strange Boeing 707 aircraft with a saucer-shaped radar dish on the top of the plane—as do Britain and Saudi Arabia. NATO operates eighteen AWACS. South Korea, Turkey, and Italy are interested in buying. The AWAC planes are to be upgraded by Boeing to track missiles and provide target information specifically for Star Wars operations.

COST: Upgrades will cost 60 million dollars, and the infrared tracking system for each plane is to cost 8 to 15 million dollars.

BENEFICIARY: Boeing Defense and Space Group.

EVALUATION: This radar will be very useful for missile tracking and it has been modified to track elusive cruise missiles.

Joint Surveillance and Target Attack Radar System (J-STARS)

The J-STARS surveillance plane is designed to detect, track, classify, and support the attack on moving and stationary targets from a distance of 120 miles. A joint army and air force project, it will either pinpoint mobile missile batteries, destroying them before their missiles are launched, or it will provide early detection of missiles after launching.

COST: 11 billion dollars.

BENEFICIARY: Northrop Grumman Corp.

EVALUATION: These new planes were tested during the Bosnian war in 1995–96, and they were found to be unsuitable for their task. Despite this problem an undersecretary of defense approved full-scale production. The GAO blasted this move as being premature and raising the program's level of risk.

UPPER-TIER DEFENSE (EXOATMOSPHERIC)

In this area, once again, the army and navy are competing with each other. Upper-tier defense systems are designed to attack incoming missiles and bombs at high levels in the earth's atmosphere or just above the atmosphere in space.

Theater High Altitude Area Defense (THAAD)

THAAD is a ground-based launcher of upper-tier interceptors—i.e., missiles launched from the ground to intercept other missiles high in the atmosphere. Defending an area of 120 miles at heights of more than 90 miles, it is more extensive than the lower-tier systems.

Its missiles will have a range of 650 miles and will deploy a hit-to-kill interceptor destroying its target with collision energy, not explosive forces. However, THAAD cannot sit alone in the field because it is vulnerable to attack from cruise missiles or weapons launched from planes. So it must be protected with a Patriot or some other lower-tier defense system—protecting a missile with a missile so it can destroy a missile.

Each THAAD launcher is designed to hold ten interceptors. A total of nine to thirteen launchers compose a battery. A tactical operations center and an X-band TMD-GBR (theater missile defense ground-based radar) are needed.

COST: The current estimate for the acquisition of THAAD and its twenty years of operational life is 23 billion dollars.

BENEFICIARIES: Lockheed Martin Missiles and Space is the prime contractor. They are constructing a plant forty miles west of Huntsville, Alabama, specifically for THAAD work. On June 28, 2000, Lockheed Martin signed a 4-billion-dollar eight-year contract with the army for full-scale engineering, manufacturing, and development for configuration 1—the first stage of THAAD. This will include twenty-seven flight tests. The company hopes that sales to other countries could be in the range of several billion dollars, exceeding national Pentagon purchases. THAAD has twelve subcontractors, including Raytheon, Boeing, United Technologies, Northrop Grumman, Honeywell, and Westinghouse.

EVALUATION: The first two trial flights of the THAAD interceptors at White Sands Missile Range in New Mexico in April and July 1995, tested only the ability of THAAD to fly, maneuver, and separate from the warhead. One test worked, the other test failed. A third test in October was reported as successful. Subsequent flight tests for the missiles' infrared sensors had dismal results, six attempts and six failures spanning four years. During the parade of failures, the army kept justifying more tests in order to compete with the navy for the upper-tier interceptor that will eventually prevail.

The General Accounting Office is critical of THAAD. "A suitable target for testing the THAAD system against longer-range missiles does not exist, and funds have not been requested for target development and production. Without a longer-range test target to represent the more formidable higher-velocity missiles that THAAD could face, the system's operational effectiveness will remain in doubt, and DOD will not have reasonable assurance that it could rely on THAAD in an actual conflict."

When THAAD finally intercepted a target missile in 1999, the army optimistically decided that the program was so successful that final flight tests would be unnecessary. Phillip E. Coyle III, the director of operational test and evaluation for the Pentagon, was scathing in his criticism. He said the THAAD missiles used at the White Sands range were prototypes and not the correct configuration that will be used. He called the tests "highly scripted" and nowhere near the situation that would be encountered with actual hostile missiles.

Retired Air Force Lieutenant General Larry Welch called the extraordinary push to deploy THAAD and other hit-to-kill vehicles as a "rush to failure." An aid to a senior Democratic senator said, "The taxpayers have paid for something we still don't have." Bob Aldridge, (writer of "Son of Star Wars") who compiled much of this material, described the system as a corporate golden goose.

Naval Theater Wide (NTW) Missile Defense

An upper-tier system to be deployed on Aegis ships, NTW will use a Standard-3 missile to carry a twenty-pound hit-to-kill lightweight exoatmospheric projectile (LEAP) as a warhead. With a range of 370 to 620 miles, it is designed to intercept missiles above the atmosphere, and as such is classified as exoatmospheric. NTW will require space-based and/or airborne early-warning sensors to detect and to help it hit the ballistic missiles. It is to be developed in two segments, Block-1 and Block-2.

Block-1 will have eighty interceptors carried on four ships. To be deployed by 2010, it will protect against rudimentary missiles like the North Korean Nodong-1 with ranges of 1000 kilometers. Block-2 is to be used against missiles with ranges of up to 3000 kilometers—missiles from China, and Russian ballistic missiles—and as such constitutes a clear violation of the ABM treaty.

Block-3 or Standard-3 is a four-stage missile. The first two stages launch the interceptor into space, the third stage boosts the interceptor farther, and the fourth stage is the LEAP kill vehicle which, using infrared sensors, is designed to detect and hit the target. The third stage of the rocket will take readings from NAVSTAR global positioning system (GPS) satellites for course correction.

COST: 1.9 billion dollars is earmarked to be spent on the naval theater wide missile defense system between 2000 and 2005.

BENEFICIARIES: Principle contractors are Lockheed Martin, Raytheon, and Boeing. The navy has established its own specific missile defense office to implement NTW. The Aegis-guided missile cruiser USS *Lake Erie,* home ported at Pearl Harbor, is to be dedicated to navy missile defense tests over the next two years.

Obviously the navy will need more Aegis ships (and crew) to compensate for those being used for NMD. New ships would cost 1 billion dollars to build and 20 million dollars a year to operate.[30]

EVALUATION: A report from the Council for a Livable World said that sea-based and boost-phase alternatives to NMD could cost between 30 and 36 billion dollars, would be detrimental to other naval operations, and would not be deployed until 2014. This estimate precludes hidden costs to the navy and does not include costs of space-based tracking sensors. The addition of seven more ships to cope with simultaneous geographical threats could raise the cost to 43 billion dollars, the report says.[31] The report also points out that it would be impossible to incorporate boost-phase interceptors with very high acceleration and high burnout velocity on Aegis ships in the present vertical-launch system modules, so new ones would have to be built. Despite the navy's enthusiasm, the General Accounting Office warned that the NTW has significant technical and schedule problems. It also questions the navy's ability to design a kill vehicle capable of discriminating between an actual bomb and decoys in the time allocated to testing.

On an even more frightening note, it is important to understand that if the missiles were to be used for boost-phase interception, the ships that carry them would need to be located near the enemy coun-

try, making them an easy target. Furthermore, the theater commander would have virtually no time to assess the threat of enemy
missile launches, so the launch of antimissile missiles would be initiated by a computer, a process aptly described as the tyranny of reaction time.

Operational testing will not occur until 2010. Despite this time
frame, more than 50 percent of the interceptors are to be deployed by
2008.

HIGH ENERGY LASER WEAPONS

A whole other category of laser-based weapons, appropriately called
"killer lasers," is also planned as part of overall missile defense.
These weapons directly violate the ABM treaty because they are to be
used against intercontinental ballistic missiles. Under development
since Reagan's Star Wars program began, they are now divided into
three types.

Air Force Airborne Laser (ABL)

Carried aboard a Boeing 747 plane, this laser is designed to destroy
an intercontinental missile in its boost phase. The 747s will be
equipped with passive infrared sensors and megawatt-class chemical oxygen-iodine lasers (COILs), which will focus intense laser
energy on "hostile" missiles at altitudes between 39,000 to 70,000
feet. The intensity of the focused laser beam will burst the motor
casing of the missile. Each plane will carry chemicals for twenty to
forty shots, and each shot will cost 1000 dollars. It is planned that two
planes will circle constantly at 40,000 feet, ever-ready for
an attack.

COST: 11 billion dollars.

BENEFICIARIES: Lockheed Martin, Boeing, and TRW.

EVALUATION: Serious technical obstacles face chemical laser weapons,
including diffusion of the beam through the atmosphere, accurate

target tracking during air turbulence, and miniaturization and packing of the equipment so that it will fit into a plane. David Collier, chief scientist for the army space and strategic defense command, said, "Laser geeks tend to overestimate their effectiveness. . . . There's a major disagreement on the effectiveness of almost any laser system." Finally, depending upon whether the missile is carrying hydrogen bombs or chemical or biological weapons, the country that launches the missiles and/or its neighbors will be contaminated either by plutonium, highly toxic chemicals, or genetically modified lethal bacteria or viruses.

Space-Based Laser (SBL)

A Reagan concept, conceived in 1977, the SBL has been resurrected to become the Pentagon's first space-based weapon for use in both the ballistic missile defense and theater missile defense programs, both overt violations of ABM. Jointly funded by the ballistic missile defense organization and the air force, and operated by the air force, SBL will employ twenty to twenty-five satellites, each equipped with a cylindrical hydrogen-fluoride chemical laser capable of destroying 100 missiles from a range of 2672 miles. The first SBL launch is scheduled for 2012.

COST: The total cost is estimated to be in the billions of dollars.

BENEFICIARIES: Lockheed Martin, Boeing, and TRW were awarded an initial contract of 125 million dollars in February 1999 to begin a space-based laser integrated flight experiment.

EVALUATION: A technology demonstration phase scheduled in autumn 2001 will culminate in a systems definition review. Each review and modification tends to increase the cost of the system.

Tactical High Energy Laser (THEL)

THEL is a ground-based laser incorporating command, control, communications, and intelligence systems, as well as a fire-control and target-acquisition radar, and a laser pointer/tracker. The laser can fire sixty shots without reloading, each shot costing 3000 dollars. THEL is to be used to defend Israel's northern border against the small Katyusha rockets fired by Hezbollah guerrillas from Lebanon. (Katyusha rockets are much cheaper, and the THEL system can readily be overwhelmed by more rockets). THEL is jointly funded by Israel and the U.S. and managed by the U.S. army, but it is not designed for American use.

COST: 201.8 million dollars has been spent on the program since 1996, with Israel's contribution at 67.5 million dollars.

BENEFICIARY: TRW Space and Electronics.

EVALUATION: Yiftah Shapir, from the Jaffee Center for Strategic Studies in Tel Aviv, said on May 26, 2000, that THEL is not cost-effective or practical. Each truck-mounted system can launch only forty of these 120-mm diameter rockets without reloading, but a Katyusha battery has six trucks that can ripple-fire 240 rockets. Major General Gaby Ashkenazi, commander of the Israel Defense Force's northern command, said, "It's like trying to protect the entire northern part of Israel from rain with a single umbrella."

BATTLE MANAGEMENT/COMMAND, CONTROL, AND COMMUNICATIONS (BM/C3)

This intricate computerized system will be the nerve center of all missile defense. It will receive information from myriad sensors and sources the U.S. has deployed on land, on sea, and in space around the world. The information will be instantaneously processed by a battle-management computer, designed to produce a detailed picture of the missile attack. Because missiles move so fast, there will be no time for human input; the computer will therefore be programmed to initiate its own antimissile attack (obviously the computer can never be tested under the realistic conditions of an attack).

The elements that must be in place for BM/C3 to function include rockets, radars, satellites, transmitters, and command centers as follows:

Ground-Based Interceptor (GBI)

The GBI is the NMD system which is ground-launched. It consists of a "booster stack" missile with an exoatmospheric kill vehicle (EKV) deployed atop this three-stage rocket. The GBI will travel at speeds of 25,000 miles per hour, firing the EKV into space to shatter the enemy missile by impact.

BOOSTER STACK
In July 1998, the department of defense selected a booster stack design deploying commercial off-the-shelf motor stages.

COST: Each booster stack is estimated to cost 3 million dollars.

BENEFICIARIES: Boeing is the main contractor; Alliant Tech Systems and United Technologies are subcontractors.

EVALUATION: The first test of a booster stack will not take place until August or September 2001 at the earliest. This means Clinton was pressured to make a decision to proceed with NMD before the rockets. had been constructed, let alone tested.

EXOATMOSPHERIC KILL VEHICLE (EKV)
The following description of the EKV was provided by Raytheon, the prime contractor. The EKV "has its own [long wavelength infrared] seeker, [liquid bipropellant] propulsion, communications, guidance, and computers to support intercept targeting decisions and maneuvers." Cold gas thrusters are used to control the altitude (position) of the 55-inch long, 130-pound EKV and aim its seeker as it approaches the target at 4500 miles per hour.

The EKV will have six to eight minutes to home in on the target and destroy it with a combined impact velocity of 12,000 to 20,000 miles per hour, taking place at an altitude of 140 miles.

COST: A total of twenty-four integrated test flights are planned (six have already occurred). Each test costs about 100 million dollars, so the testing alone will cost about 2.6 billion dollars before actual deployment occurs.

BENEFICIARIES: Raytheon, and subcontractor Axsys Technologies.

EVALUATION: It was announced by the Clinton administration that two out of three flight tests of a prototype GBI-EKV must be successful before presidential approval would be given to develop NMD. The first qualifying test took place on October 2, 1999. The test was rigged to score a hit, as were some of its earlier predecessors. The hostile missile launched from Vandenberg Air Force Base in California carried a large balloon that traveled alongside the target bomb. Because there is no friction in space, the balloon traveled as fast as the bomb, but it was designed so that its infrared signal was constant and did not flicker like a normal signal from a tumbling bomb. Although the Pentagon claimed that the balloon was a decoy, it actually served as a marker buoy to lure the EKV close enough to site the target, because the EKV had failed to orient itself correctly with the stars and had drifted off course.[32]

Eventually it "saw" the balloon from the corner of its visual field, and, after homing in on the balloon, it was able to see the bomb's flickering signal and make a "kill." This strange sequence was described by Undersecretary of Defense Dr. Jacques Gansler:

> In this early test what we were trying to do was to pull it off and so used something that was even larger and much more obvious, and we figured that might pull the interceptor off to the target, and in fact, it did, in the flight. It found this decoy first because it was larger, did have more radiation, and it found it first, and it said, "Oh, there's the target," and started to go for it. . . . And its software said "That's the wrong target," and then it shifted to the target that had the characteristics it was supposed to have had . . .[33]

As reported by the *Washington Post*, both the interceptor and the target missile used the NAVSTAR global positioning system (GPS) to maneuver onto a collision course. Obviously a "hostile" missile would not be so obliging as to broadcast its position and trajectory, to signal its position and to send up a marker balloon for its bomb.

The next test was conducted on January 19, 2000. The EKV failed to intercept the target bomb because of a leak of liquid nitrogen utilized to cryogenically cool its infrared sensors. As in the previous test, a large balloon was also deployed, and the NAVSTAR GPS accurately positioned the missile and interceptor. Space-based sensors and the battle management/command, control, and communications system were also deployed and the field of view for the EKV was increased by 210 percent. Still it failed.

The last test before Clinton was to make his decision took place on July 8, 2000. It failed for three reasons: the balloon did not inflate, the interceptor missile veered off course, and the EKV did not separate from the surrogate booster rocket.

Apart from these problems, the tests in no way resemble the conditions that would exist in battle. Russian, North Korean, or Chinese missiles would fly from west to east, but the NMB test "offensive" missiles are launched from California, to be intercepted by "kill vehicles" launched from an atoll in the mid-Pacific. As of this writing, fourteen more test flights are scheduled, with all the artificial Band-Aids that the previous tests deployed. As one senior official was heard to say during a briefing, "I am trying to avoid defining, 'What means success?' " However, Secretary of Defense Cohen, after the last failed test, said, with what journalist Mary McGrory of the *Washington Post* called "striking sophistry" that "the test itself was a disappointment but it was one of those failures that was least expected. . . . That happens from time to time—that you have a failure of something that's fairly routine." [34]

Ted Postol, a professor at MIT who was a scientific advisor to the chief of naval operations in the eighties and helped develop the Trident-2 missile, said that the Pentagon had rigged missile tests to ensure success. After a 1997 test of the antimissile revealed that it couldn't effectively distinguish decoys from warheads, the Pentagon stopped using decoys that would seriously challenge the defensive weapon. [35] Nina Schwartz, a senior physicist who worked at TRW in 1995 and 1996, charged that the TRW corporation had falsified work in an effort to portray a "kill vehicle" as more capable than it actually was. She said that TRW certified to the government that interceptors using its computer programs would succeed more than 95 percent of the time in the identification of enemy warheads, but in fact they could do so only 5 to 15 percent of the time. Dr. Schwartz said that at some level the Pentagon and its contractors were in collusion. "It's not a defense of the United States, it's a conspiracy to allow them to milk the government. They are creating for themselves a job for life."[36] Schwartz said that TRW fired her when she protested about alleged efforts to fudge test data to hide flaws in the system's ability to distinguish warheads from decoys.

Postol alleges that the Pentagon colluded with TRW to collate fraudulent test documents. (The FBI is investigating these charges of fraud.)[37] Postol also accused the Pentagon of significantly reducing the difficulty of the next sixteen tests planned.[38] Postol and David Wright conducted a study of the efficacy of NMD and found that the defense would not work because it can be overwhelmed with simpler, cheaper technology—decoys.[39] Three major scientific groups supported Postol in his stand. The American Physical Society with 42,000 physicists, the Federation of American Scientists and the Union of Concerned Scientists, and fifty Nobel laureates called the planned system "premature, wasteful, and dangerous."

Theater Missile Defense Ground-Based Radar (TMD-GBR)

This particular radar is a small, ground-based portable sensor that can be transported by plane. It can search, track, and discriminate for specific missiles. Designed to receive and instantaneously process data from all relevant sensors (satellites, other radars) it can form a detailed picture of the attack. A commander will then theoretically be equipped with the necessary data to direct the TMD weapons to intercept a hostile missile attack—if he has the time.

COST: An estimated 5.4 billion dollars.

BENEFICIARY: Raytheon is the primary contractor.

EVALUATION: No evaluation available.

Ballistic Missile Early Warning System (BMEWS)

This is one of two early-warning radar systems that feed into the ground-based radar system. The radar at Fylingdale in Yorkshire,

England, has three faces and therefore operates over a 360-degree circle. (Other installations at Clear, Alaska, and Thule, Greenland, consist of two-faced phased-array radars that monitor 240 degrees of azimuth; each face monitors 120 degrees of azimuth—the arc of the heavens from horizon to zenith.)

COST: Not available.

BENEFICIARY: BMEWS radars are made by Raytheon.

EVALUATION: The Pentagon wishes to upgrade these facilities to become X-band radars, but neither Denmark nor Britain is willing to approve any new installations that do not comply with the ABM treaty. The U.S. is assessing alternative plans, including placing X-band radars on commercial ships in international waters.

Perimeter Acquisition of Vehicle Entry Phased-Array Warning System (PAVE PAWS)

ANOTHER RADAR REQUIRED FOR BM/C3
There are two of these two-faced phased-array radars in the United States, one at the Cape Cod Air Force Station in Massachusetts and one at Beale Air Force Base in California.

COST: Not available.

BENEFICIARY: Manufactured by Raytheon.

EVALUATION: PAVE PAWS has been in place for many years as an integral part of the early-warning system, but it is to be upgraded to a more sophisticated system for NMD.

SPACE-BASED INFRARED SYSTEM (SBIRS)

Radar systems must be supported and complemented by infrared tracking satellites that detect heat and flames emanating from the tail ends of missiles. The current system of infrared satellites is called the defense support program (DSP) and consists of three satellites deployed in geosynchronous orbit—they move at the same speed as the earth's rotation, and continuously overlook one area of the earth, namely the Indian, Pacific, and Atlantic Oceans. There may be more DSP satellites, but the exact number is classified. Three upgraded replacement satellites of the DSP system are about to be launched, the last scheduled for 2003.

Apart from DSP, the Pentagon is about to deploy another set of satellites specifically for Star Wars:

High Orbit Space-Based Infrared System (SBIRS-High)

Approved by the Pentagon since 1994, this system will consist of four satellites in geosynchronous orbit around the equator, plus another two satellites in highly elliptical polar orbits, providing effective coverage of the northern regions of the globe.

SBIRS-High will monitor the hot exhaust plumes of missile launches, and is due to replace the DSP system in 2004. This system will be better able to determine the exact launch and impact points of a missile, and its trajectory.

COST: 2 billion dollars for six geosynchronous-orbit satellites and infrared sensors that will ride piggyback on other satellites.

BENEFICIARIES: The main contractor is Lockheed Martin; there are six subcontractors.

EVALUATION: The comptroller's office has instructed the air force to delay the launches of the satellites 2 through 4 by one year so that money can go to other programs.

Low Orbit Space-Based Infrared System (SBIRS-Low)

Low orbit satellites will complement the high orbit satellites by tracking hostile missiles and hydrogen bombs through space (the midcourse phase) after their booster motors have died, thus providing better targeting and engagements for the kill-vehicles. SBIRS-

Low will consist of between eighteen and thirty-two small satellites in low orbit—about 250 miles high. They will have the ability to look through clouds and darkness; some will use electronic cameras. Data is to be relayed from one low orbit satellite to another by laser beam, reaching the relevant command center with the speed of light. The information will be rapidly relayed to the ground-based radars. In turn, they will send the trajectory information about the missiles to the kill interceptors.

COST: The air force plans to spend a total of 11.8 billion dollars on SBIRS-Low.

BENEFICIARIES: Eleven contractors are already working on this project. The prime contractor is to be Spectrum Astro, with Northrop Grumman Corp. as its main partner.

EVALUATION: In February 2001 the GAO warned, "the air force's current SBIRS-Low acquisition schedule is at high risk of not delivering the system on time or at a cost with expected performance." It identified three problem areas:

1. The current acquisition schedule does not provide for flight-test results or crucial satellite functions and capabilities until five years after production has started.
2. Five of the six critical technologies have been judged immature for the current state of the program.
3. Alternative terrestrial systems to the SBIRS-Low have not been investigated.

Single Integrated Air Picture (SIAP)

SIAP will provide a sophisticated common battlefield picture for aircraft, cruise missile, and ballistic missile defense. It will be designed to integrate huge quantities of information from sensors and intelligence information from the three services, and the results will be instantaneously available to every commander.

The navy already has such a system, called cooperative engage-

ment capability (CEC), in place. Computers combine all the fleet's
radar, sensor, and targeting systems into a single picture displayed on
computer screens in ships and aircraft that determine which ship or
aircraft should track the targets and which should engage them. By
2007 the navy hopes to have CEC equipment on all cruisers and destroyers with Aegis radars. The army wants CEC for its Patriot PAC-
3 batteries, and the air force will also develop their own form of CEC
for its AWACS.

COST: Tens of billions of dollars.

BENEFICIARIES: Lockheed Martin and Raytheon.

NMD INFRASTRUCTURE

Even a relatively simple missile defense system requires a mas-
sively complex interconnecting system of ground-based radars,
sensors, detectors, satellites, command centers, computers, radio
transmitters, and personnel. Let us now examine this infrastructure,
remembering that it could be modified for a full-scale first-strike
system.

Radar stations already exist in strategic locations around the
world, as part of the U.S. early-warning system. These can also be
used for the Star Wars systems. Coordinating their data collection
with space-based infrared sensors on satellites, they will be able to
detect launches of "hostile" missiles and to give an imprecise idea of
the missile's location. Once the imprecise location is determined,
newly constructed X-band radars, which would violate the ABM
treaty, will take over and give the precise location and condition of
the missile by tracking the target. The X-band radar will then provide the "kill assessment."

The construction of the first X-band radar is planned for Shemya
Island, part of the Aleutian chain of islands in Alaska, the most western point of the United States—in direct line with any attack on the
U.S. from North Korea, but also conveniently in direct line with Russia and China. Three other X-band radars are to be constructed in
other strategic locations of the globe, including Fylingdale in York-

shire, England, and in Vardo, Norway. There are also rumors that America is planning a total of nine X-band radars in places such as Pine Gap, Australia, and possibly in Japan and South Korea.

A multiweek exercise called integrated ground test (IGT-6) was conducted in February 2001 at the Integrated System Test Capability-2 facility, a new site located at the Army Space and Missile Defense Command's Advanced Research Center in Huntsville, Alabama. This IGT-6 operation involved the test of the next NMD intercept. The previous three have failed.

Officials assessed the operability of the NMD integration efforts by deploying "nodal" computers representing each element of the complex system, using the most advanced software and processors. The exercises were conducted in "real time"—meaning no delay— and, according to Pentagonese language, were designed to validate "the functionality" of element-to-element interface and to mitigate the risk to NMD intercept tests. These ground tests are crucial to the NMD program because they will provide, as the military says, the vast majority of information needed for "milestone" decisions along the way to a fully integrated and operational Star Wars system. IGT-6 was used to test engagement scenarios involving limited attacks from three geographical regions: North Korea, the Middle East, Libya, and from accidental unauthorized launches from Russia and China.

The Ballistic Missile Defense Organization (BMDO) already has operational IGT nodes for the antiballistic missile's battle management/command, control, and communication system, for the ground-based X-band, the upgraded early-warning radar, the in-flight interceptor communications system, the defense support program satellites, the space-based infrared system satellites, and the ground-based interceptor.[40]

This infrastructure will all feed into a battle management computer.

OVERALL EVALUATION OF BATTLE MANAGEMENT/ COMMAND, CONTROL, AND COMMUNICATIONS (BM/C3)

The crux of the Star Wars system—a battle-management computer designed to plan, coordinate, direct, and control the Star Wars weapons and its sensors—is essentially a computer system with millions or billions of lines of programming. No computer is perfect, even the simplest desktop computers fail because of software problems. According to software experts, the increase in difficulty of writing software is not linear but exponential. Moving from ten to twenty lines is not twice but 100 times as difficult. The difficulties inherent in a program of millions upon millions of lines of computer code are impossible to imagine. A bug in a desktop computer is a nuisance, but in a missile-defense computer it could mean nuclear winter.[41]

Under conditions of attack, there will be virtually no human input, except perhaps a split-second decision by a military operator. Certainly there will be no time for civilian or political input. John Pike, a space and military policy analyst, formerly of the Federation of American Scientists, says that by the time the missile-defense system is operational, the computer software that assesses the attack and analyzes response options "will be the culmination of many thousands of work-years of modeling and calculation and simulation and refinement and testing. The software is going to be in an infinitely better position to make a considered judgment about what should be done than the few human beings sitting in the room. There will be too much stuff going on too fast for any human operators to figure it all out. There just won't be any time for mere human meddling."[42]

In other words, the decision to go to war or to annihilation will be removed from the president in the oval office and given instead to a computer manned by a military officer sequestered in an underground command post. Computerized or fully automated war would definitely be necessary in a boost-phase counterattack, favored by George W. Bush, where there would be only a few tens of seconds to detect a launch and another few seconds to fire. Unfortunately, the battle-management computer can never be tested under operating conditions; the first actual test will occur when the U.S. is under attack.

Here is one scenario: North Korea fires a missile containing five chemical warheads. In response, the U.S. launches a dozen interceptor missiles, which appear on China's primitive early-warning radar screen. Believing it is under attack, China launches its nuclear missiles at the U.S. before they can be destroyed in their silos from a U.S. first strike. America, detecting this unexpected Chinese attack, immediately launches its hair-trigger missiles, initiating a full-scale nuclear war.[43]

Another scenario, postulated by former missileer Bruce Blair: "What if a country is just going to test a missile? Are we going to knock it out just because it has the range to reach our country? It could be a peaceful launch."

THE INNATE CHAOS OF COMPLEX COMPUTER SYSTEMS

Other insuperable problems plague the Star Wars systems. The most fundamental is an inherent aspect of rocket science. Called the "brittle" problem by students of complexity theory, it is simply this: Should one tiny part of a hugely complex interconnected system fail, the whole thing fails. Compounding the brittle factor is the "flub" factor. The more complex a system, the more likely it is that something unanticipated will fail.

With thirty minutes or less from the time a missile is launched until it reaches its target, there is no time to fix anything. As Gottfried J. Mayer, adjunct professor of kinesiology at Pennsylvania State University, memorably noted some years ago, "the booster fails to separate from the payload—and New York is history,"[44] a particularly chilling speculation in light of the September 11 attacks.

IS NMD JUST A FRONT FOR FIRST-STRIKE WINNABLE NUCLEAR WAR?

In 1977 and 1980 Jimmy Carter's Presidential Directives 18 and 59 clearly described the four components of first-strike capability:

1. *Antisatellite (ASAT):* Weapons to knock out the Soviet early-warning system
2. *Decapitation:* Destruction of the Soviet leadership with extremely accurate Pershing 11 missiles before they pressed their button

3. *Counterforce:* Destruction of most Soviet missiles in hardened silos, submarines, mobile launchers, and the strategic bomber fleet by MX and D5 missiles
4. *Strategic Defense Initiative (SDI):* A ballistic missile defense system to mop up any Soviet missiles that survived counterforce and had been launched[45]

No presidents have signed any significant treaties agreeing to back away from a stance that was adopted at the height of the cold war, and I would submit that first-strike winnable nuclear war is the real (secret?) agenda of Star Wars revitalization.

DOES NMD VIOLATE INTERNATIONAL TREATIES?

Almost all the plans for NMD and most involving TMD will violate the ABM treaty, the cornerstone of all other nuclear arms control treaties. The ABM treaty, for example, directs that America and the former Soviet Union—now specifically Russia—can operate only one regional interceptor defense system each. (The current systems are in North Dakota and Moscow, respectively, making the new Alaska-based system a clear violation.)

The treaty would also be violated by upgrading the present U.S. radar systems, by implementing a defense system covering all fifty states instead of the agreed-upon forty-eight, by installing a new satellite network, or by shifting the interceptor system to a new location—all of which are currently proposed as a part of George W. Bush's national missile-defense plan.

The ABM treaty states that because no country can protect itself against a nuclear attack, each side must therefore live in fear of mutually assured destruction. Logically, under these circumstances, no country would be foolish enough to launch a nuclear war. Thus, the ABM treaty has always been intended as a brake on unrestrained nuclear arms buildup, and has proven effective since its signing in 1972. Its violation by either party would be an unconscionable and extraordinarily destabilizing act in a world bristling with nuclear weapons.

Yet the U.S. openly plans to violate the ABM treaty. In justifying his plans, George W. Bush told an audience in Iowa in 1999, "When I was coming up, it was a dangerous world, and you knew exactly who they were. . . . It was us versus them, and it was clear who them was. Today, we are not so sure who they are, but we know they're there." [46]

Violation of the ABM would in turn jeopardize other international treaties. Currently, for example, the Russian Duma has ratified a new nuclear arms treaty, START II, calling for the bilateral reduction of strategic nuclear weapons to 3500. Should the ABM be violated, Russia has indicated that it may well cancel plans to reduce its nuclear arsenal and refuse to consider additional reductions under START III. Surprisingly, START II actually allows the U.S. to maintain 3500 deployed strategic weapons, as well as 950 operational tactical nuclear weapons, 2500 "hedge" strategic weapons, and 2500 in the "inactive reserve." [47] Furthermore, the START II treaty does not actively call for the elimination of the hydrogen bombs, only for destruction of the launch platforms, so that in the future the bombs could be hauled out of storage and redeployed.

START III, however, if agreed upon, would reduce Russia's and America's strategic arsenals to fewer than 2500 nuclear bombs each, and would, for the first time, include requirements for the actual destruction of nuclear bombs, with the plutonium and uranium disposed of in such a way that they will never be available for the future construction of nuclear weapons. (It is relatively easy to monitor these procedures technically, given the goodwill that currently exists between the countries concerned, but this may not continue to be the case under the Bush administration.) [48]

Furthermore, President Putin, wishing to discourage America's NMD developments and wanting to move rapidly toward nuclear disarmament, recently offered unilaterally to reduce Russia's nuclear arsenal to between 1500 and 1000 weapons, or even less—at least 1000 to 1500 fewer than the number demanded by START III. This offer comes with the proviso that America not proceed with national missile defense, abide by the ABM treaty, and that the Senate ratify the Comprehensive Test Ban Treaty.

However, at the Crawford ranch meeting in Texas between President George Bush and President Vladimir Putin during the second week of November 2001, Bush proposed a unilateral reduction of U.S. strategic weapons to between 2200 and 1700 to take place over a period of ten years, from the current level of more than 6000. This would obviate the START II treaty ban on Russian land-based missiles with multiple nuclear warheads, and would leave most of the U.S. deterrent on submarines invulnerable to surprise attacks. Putin left the meeting without a response, although he is expected to reciprocate in kind. The Bush move is intended to "soften up" the Russians for the U.S. intended violation of the ABM treaty.[49, 50]

But the U.S.'s attachment to NMD is so bizarre that the state department actively encouraged Russia to maintain "large, diversified, viable arsenals of strategic offensive weapons capable of delivering an annihilating counterattack," as long as Russia allows the U.S. to violate the ABM treaty and to proceed with national missile defense.[51, 52]

China, with its twenty intercontinental nuclear weapons, has already confirmed that it might well speed up deployment of a new generation of weapons systems if America goes ahead with NMD. Indeed, China will be encouraged to do so. In a speech in early November 2000, foreign minister spokesman Zhu Bangzoa said:

> The United States is a country with the largest and most sophisticated arsenals of both nuclear and conventional weapons in the world and now it is engaging itself to develop NMD and TMD (theater missile defense). Such an act is contrary to the trend of the times because it is not conducive to the international efforts of disarmament and arms control. It will also exert a lasting negative impact on world peace. The Chinese side expresses serious concern, and in particular if the U.S. is to develop TMD and to include Taiwan, this is something that will be by no means accepted by the Chinese side.[53]

(Ironically, the small NMD system for "rogue" states that Clinton advocated would actually be an adequate "defense" against China's twenty nuclear-armed intercontinental missiles that could reach the U.S.—as opposed to the multilayered missile defense planned by George W. Bush.)

Likewise, European allies are increasingly worried that violation of the ABM will initiate a new nuclear arms race and separate European security from that of the U.S. French President Jacques Chirac said in the *New York Times* on December 17, 1999, "If you look at world history, ever since men began waging war, you will see that there's a permanent race between sword and shield. The sword always wins. The more improvements that are made to the shield, the more improvements are made to the sword." [54]

WHAT THE WORLD THINKS OF NMD

Star Wars is designed to protect only the United States, but obviously should other countries be persuaded to host Star Wars facilities, they are not necessarily protected but become targets of a nuclear attack.

Citizens of certain countries due to participate in Star Wars are not happy about the prospect. England, for instance, has been deeply involved in the U.S. early-warning system for many years, hosting two American bases at Menwith Hill and at Fylingdale. And the level of British participation is increasing. Over the past year, almost 500 British military-scientific representatives visited the U.S. under the auspices of a 1958 mutual defense agreement, a twofold increase in visits from 1995. And the U.S. military establishment visited the British scientific military facility at AWE Aldermaston 110 times during the same period. Two Aldermaston staff were seconded to Los Alamos and one to Lawrence Livermore "to assist with the technical development of facilities of mutual interest." [55] Washington plans to upgrade the U.S. base at Menwith Hill in North Yorkshire, giving it a crucial role in America's plans for a space-based infrared missile-launch-detection system. Tony Blair has already granted approval for Fylingdale Moor to be upgraded, but the Parliament has not concurred. The U.S. also plans to construct a fifteen-story–sized radar building at some unknown location in the U.K. [56]

But strong opposition is mounting in England as U.S. plans expand. Aware that Bush is in favor of the full Star Wars system, a committee of twelve members of Parliament concluded after deliberation: "The government should articulate the very strong concerns that have been expressed about NMD within the U.K. We are not convinced that the U.S. plan to deploy NMD represents an appropriate response to the proliferation problems faced by the international community. We recommend that the government encourages the U.S. to seek other ways of reducing the threats it perceives." [57]

And Hugo Young, writing in the *Guardian*, says NMD is "born of an arrogance that Russia could not be expected to watch in silence, nor China, with its relatively small missile armory, to countenance without increasing its own nuclear force," adding that "for Europe, the project is all downside risk," because Iran and Iraq are closer to Europe than to North America.[58]

Similar opposition exists in Denmark about the upgrading of early-warning radars in Thule, Greenland, a Danish province. Strategically significant early-warning radars that require upgrading to X-band status include the facilities in Thule, Greenland; Grand Forks, North Dakota; and Clear, Alaska. According to Ted Postol, these upgrades are exactly what the U.S. will need for a national missile defense program aimed specifically at Russia and China.[59]

Thus, incredibly, the U.S. seems to have allowed the perceived threat by North Korea, Iran, and Iraq to justify a system actually aimed at China and Russia.

The most obvious clue about these intentions is the current deployment of the world's most sophisticated advanced tracking and imaging intelligence-gathering radar on the northern tip of Norway, forty miles from the Russian border. This new X-band radar, along with the one to be deployed at Eareckson Air Station at Shemya Island, 1500 miles southwest of Anchorage, will be used to collect data on Russia's long-range missiles tests, rendering Norway a prime Russian target.

Called Vardo, code-named HAVE STARE, this U.S.-owned, Norwegian-based radar could well present a formal violation of the ABM treaty. With a potential resolution of about 10 to 15 centimeters, it will provide extremely detailed images of Russian warheads and their missiles. (To date, the most sophisticated radars have resolutions of at best 5 to 10 meters.) The two radars in Norway and Shemya will be capable of monitoring the entire trajectory of Russian missile tests, including their powered flight, the "bus" maneuvers, deployment, and separation of warheads and decoys. Precise data will be collected on every phase of the missile and its bombs from launch to splashdown. The radars will be linked directly to the nerve center of the proposed NMD, buried deep inside Cheyenne Mountain in Colorado. This data will be entered into the NMD database, increasing enormously the discrimination capabilities of the NMD system against Russian intercontinental ballistic missiles.

As Ted Postol says, "If the purpose of a national missile defense system is to protect the United States from North Korean missiles, why is the world's most advanced tracking and imaging radar about to go online at the northern tip of Norway instead of northern Japan?" According to Postol, Russia and China will be constantly concerned "that the U.S. will eventually expand and modify their missile defense with nuclear armed interceptors instead of the pitiful hit-to-kill interceptors now planned for the system." [60] Postol points out that the U.S. should at least be honest about its intentions. Both Russia and China are under no illusions about the U.S. agenda, he argues, but America is lying to the rest of the world—including its own population—using North Korea as a camouflage to disguise its true intentions.

As noted, Shemya Island is to receive the next X-band radar. Part of the Aleutian Islands chain, Shemya is a remote, windswept place. The closest inhabited point is an Eskimo village 100 miles away. Shemya is therefore not the most convenient place for this facility. Because of its isolation, it is also an easy target for destruction, either from a missile or a small artillery piece mounted on a fishing trawler.

The U.S. claims that this particular site has been chosen because it is in line with a missile attack from North Korea.[61] But there is a political reason that Shemya was chosen as a site. Senator Ted Stevens, the powerful ex-head of the Senate appropriations committee, is from Alaska. And because Clinton needed his support, an attempt had to be made to protect Alaska from Russian attack, even though this radar was precluded under the ABM treaty.

The Rumsfeld report stated that "a number of countries with regional ambitions do not welcome the U.S. role as a stabilizing power in their regions and have not accepted it passively. Because of their ambitions they want to place restraints on the U.S. ability to project power or influence into their regions."

But perhaps the U.S. should begin by questioning its right to project its power into other regions of the world: 6.5 billion people inhabit this planet, not just 280 million Americans. Given the reality of past and present U.S. interference in the politics of numerous foreign, sovereign states, the U.S. missile shield signals to the world that America maintains a significantly hostile intent. A working nuclear shield above the United States would be the equivalent of giving a sniper a bulletproof bodysuit. Would he be more or less likely to shoot others if he himself were immune?[62]

Chapter Seven

SPACE: THE NEXT AMERICAN EMPIRE

It's politically sensitive, but it's going to happen. Some people don't want to hear this, and it sure isn't in vogue, but—absolutely—we're going to fight in space. We're going to fight from space and we're going to fight into space. That's why the U.S. has developed programs in directed energy and hit-to-kill mechanisms. We will engage terrestrial targets someday—ships, airplanes, land targets—from space. We will engage targets in space, from space.

—General Joseph Ashy, former commander in chief
of the U.S. space command, 1996 [1]

The threat, ladies and gentlemen, I believe is real. It's a threat to our economic well-being. This is why we must work together to find common ground between commercial imperatives and the president's tasking me for space control and protection.

—General Richard B. Meyers, former commander in chief of the
U.S. space command, 1999, now the new chairman of the
Joint Chiefs of Staff for President George W. Bush [2]

With regard to space dominance, we have it, we like it, and we're going to keep it.

—Keith Hall, the air force assistant secretary for space
and director of the National Reconnaissance Office [3]

COMMISSIONED BY Congress, John Collins's 1989 book *Military Space Forces: The Next 50 Years,* was one of the earliest studies to explore in depth the notion of fighting a war from space and in space. Collins, a senior specialist in national de-

fense at the Library of Congress, was funded by the air force association and the association of the U.S. army, which meant that his
book had a particular point of view. Endorsed by prominent members of Congress, including John Glenn and John Kasich, the book
described the possibilities and problems associated with space warfare. Other endorsees included Senator Sam Nunn, chairman of the
Senate armed services committee, who said, "Space, a distinctive
military medium, deserves a new school of thought. This book will
be an indispensable starting point," and former Representative Les
Aspin, later secretary of defense for President Bill Clinton, who
said, "No other military space study puts all the pieces of the puzzle
together."

Collins begins the book by paraphrasing Halford J. Mackinder's
"Heartland statement":[4]

Who rules circumterrestrial space commands Planet Earth;
Who rules the moon commands circumterrestial space;
Who rules L 4 and L 5* commands the Earth-Moon System.

Military Space Forces is a recipe for space-based warfare. It is simultaneously belligerent, nationalistic, provocative, well researched, and
extremely scary. And it forms the basis for much official U.S. policy
regarding the militarization of space.

Among other topics, Collins discusses the fact that the moon in
particular is rich in many natural resources that could be mined and
brought back to earth for economic returns. He says that parties "that
hope to satisfy economic interests in space must maintain ready access to resources on the moon and beyond, despite opposition if necessary, and perhaps deny access to competitors who seek monopolies."
He warns, however, that rival forces may lie in wait to hijack shipments on return from the moon. Obviously, if America invests huge
capital in mining the moon, it must then defend its investments.
Antisatellite warfare is analyzed.

Collins's thinking is dangerous, advocating "soft kill" weapons
that penetrate target surfaces without impairing them, and that can
selectively disorient, damage, or destroy human beings as well as

* areas in space where the respective gravitational forces of the moon and earth are in
balance

damage sensitive equipment within satellites or space stations. He also suggests jamming communication systems, spray-painting satellite camera lenses, focusing blinding light onto laser reflectors, or the surreptitious introduction of foreign objects into booster fuel of enemy rockets, and he discusses the merits of laser-beam weapons, and of particle beam weapons consisting of highly energetic protons, neutrons, electrons, or hydrogen atoms.

He talks of the use of nuclear weapons in space and of the efficacy of various forms of nuclear radiation, which, he says, is unimpeded because there is no atmosphere in space, and could therefore cover much more space volume than if used in the atmosphere near the earth's surface. It would work especially well against targets in low space orbit. However, he concedes that nuclear radiation cannot distinguish friend from foe. Electromagnetic pulse from nuclear explosions could "wound" users as well as the intended victims.

Collins explores war on the moon, saying that strike forces there could use the full range of offensive maneuvers that are now used on earth. Space mines could be easily positioned. He describes how space-based "civilian" vehicles could be used surreptitiously for military activities. He says that lasers, sensors, and telecommunications devices can be concealed within satellites that appear perfectly harmless. Weapons could "piggyback" on satellites that are ostensibly for reconnaissance and surveillance.

He is particularly keen on biological and chemical warfare in space, saying that self-contained biospheres like a space station offer a "superlative" environment for these sort of attacks because they rely on a closed-circuit life-support system that continually recirculates air and water. Clandestine agents could dispense into space stations lethal or incapacitating chemical or biological agents, which—because they are colorless and odorless—are impossible to spot before symptoms appear.

He introduces the notion of fighting from space, targeting particular installations on earth, and quotes former astronaut Michael Collins, who said that space is an ideal place from which to attack surface combatants and aircraft carriers, because ships "stand out as clearly as billiard balls on green felt" when seen from space.

Collins advocates the use of psychological operations (psyops). These techniques of psychological warfare would be used to control

elitist and popular opinion as nonlethal weapons systems, or to convince rivals that it would be useless to start or to continue military
space operations. Collins says that these psyop maneuvers would
"deprive opponents of freedom of action, while preserving it for one-
self," and advocates using psyop propaganda to spread subversive
ideas, including the futility of space for the achievement of military
superiority, the perils to world peace by militarizing space, and the
waste of global resources better spent on people than on a fruitless
arms race. He says that U.S. superiority in space "could culminate in
bloodless total victory, if lagging powers could neither cope nor catch
up technologically."

This is not a pleasant scenario for 95 percent of the earth's population who do not happen to be American, and who rightly feel that the
moon and the heavens belong to them, too.

U.S. PLANS FOR WAR IN SPACE[5]

During the sixties and seventies, the army, navy, and air force came to
rely upon advanced and expanded space technologies in communications, meteorology, geodesy, navigation, and reconnaissance. The
military use of space supported strategic deterrence by providing
treaty verification, arms control, and early-warning systems of impending nuclear attack. In 1985 the Joint Chiefs of Staff officially in-
stitutionalized the military use of space by establishing a new unified
command called the U.S. space command, whose motto is *Master of
Space*. During Operation Desert Storm in the Persian Gulf in 1991,
military space operations were used to produce what is called a "multiplier" effect, which considerably enhanced communications, navigation, and targeting.

The U.S. space command then took on more responsibilities. Composed of three active elements—the United States army space command, the fourteenth air force, and the naval space command—the
U.S. command's mission statement calls for it to "integrate space
forces into war-fighting capabilities across the full spectrum of conflict," in addition to "dominating the space dimension of military
operations to protect U.S. interests and investment," as previously
noted.

In 1996 the space command published a pamphlet called "Vision for 2020" in which it overtly enunciated its goals of war in space.[6] In 1998 the space command expanded the original 1996 plans in a comprehensive 100-page document, "The Long Range Plan" (LRP), written with the cooperation of seventy-five military corporations, including Boeing, Aerojet, Hughes Space, Lockheed Martin, Raytheon, Sparta Corp, TRW, and Vista Technologies. During the year 2000, a coalition of aerospace corporations engaged in a campaign called "declaration of space leadership," meant to persuade their congressional allies to introduce the idea of the militarization of space in the form of a House resolution. The declaration calls for funding of "defensive" systems and NASA at levels that "guarantee American leadership in the exploration of space."

The aerospace corporations produced rafts of propaganda designed specifically to convince American children that everything that happens in space is exciting and must be supported, while NASA—working closely with the U.S. space command—has designed a program to reach every science teacher in the U.S. with the efficacy of their space message. The aim is to program children to believe that a large portion of the U.S. national treasure should be spent on Mars exploration, and that war in space is inevitable.[7]

The long range plan opens by stating that the military must guard against allowing its dependency on space to become a vulnerability and thus must develop an ability to "deny" others (the enemy) the use of space. The way a nation makes wealth, it proclaims, is the way it makes war. According to the plan, the time has come for national policy-makers to understand that space is now the center of gravity for both the department of defense and for the nation—exactly the tack that the Bush administration is adopting.

The plan sets out five basic goals:

1. To assure the means to get to space and to operate once there
2. To surveil the region to achieve and to maintain situational understanding
3. To protect America's critical space systems from hostile action
4. To prevent unauthorized access to, and exploitation of U.S. and allied space systems
5. To negate hostile space systems that place U.S. and allied systems at risk

The LRP then discusses global engagement, which it says is "the combination of worldwide situational awareness and precise application of force from space." There must be "a seamlessly integrated force of theater land, sea, air, and space capabilities through a worldwide global defense information network."

U.S. space command will observe "high interest areas" on the earth from space so the military will have "complete awareness in peace, crisis, or war." The plan is to defend America against ballistic and cruise missile attacks from an enemy—aka, Star Wars. The space command will also "hold at risk" a finite number of "high value" earth targets with near-instantaneous force application—i.e., the ability to kill from space. The long term plan continues:

> One of the long acknowledged and commonly understood advantages of space-based platforms is no restriction or country clearances to overfly a nation from space. We expect this advantage to endure. . . . Achieving space superiority during conflicts will be critical to the U.S. success on the battlefield.

The LRP, however, does acknowledge that there could be problems: "At present, the notion of weapons in space is not consistent with U.S. national policy. Planning for this possibility is the purpose of this long range plan should our civilian leadership later decide that the application of force from space is in our national interest." (Is the Bush administration this civilian leadership?)

The long range plan envisions an end state: "By 2020, a robust and fully integrated suite of space and terrestrial capabilities will provide dominant battlespace awareness enabling on-demand targeting and engagement of all ballistic and cruise missiles; and if directed by the National Command Authority [the President] the ability to identify, track and hold at risk designated high value terrestrial targets." One of the space command members, retired General Ronald R. Fogleman, former chief of staff of the air force and a member of the Joint Chiefs of Staff, said, "I think that space, in and of itself, is going to be very quickly recognized as a fourth dimension of warfare."

The long range plan gives an indication of how the military elite in U.S. society view the world and their place in it:

- The United States will remain a global power and exert global leadership.
- It is unlikely that the United States will face a global military peer competitor through 2020.
- The United States won't always be able to forward base its forces (fight wars in other people's territory).
- Widespread communications will highlight disparities in resources and quality of life—contributing to unrest in developing countries.
- The global economy will continue to become more interdependent. Economic alliances, as well as the growth and influence of multinational corporations, will blur security agreements.
- The gap between the "have" and "have-not" nations will widen—creating regional unrest.
- The United States will remain the only nation able to project power globally.[8]

This last statement means that as the world becomes more and more divided economically, the U.S. can use its military and space superiority to maintain the imbalance between the rich and the poor. In this context, it is well to remember that the U.S. contains 5 percent of the world's population and uses 40 percent of the world's natural resources.

U.S. SPACE FORCE

At the start of the twenty-first century, for the first time since the air force was created in 1947, there is talk of creating a specific new service within the Pentagon (even though the established Pentagon services ruthlessly guard their domains and are fiercely resistant to change). First proposed by General Ronald Fogleman when he and his staff concluded that the air force should evolve into a space and air force, the service would be quite different from the space command, which is not an official arm of the Pentagon.

The idea gained ground after the Gulf conflict and the Kosovo war, in which use of space was critical. The Pentagon's GPS satellite constellation guided precision bombs to their targets in bad weather.

Spy satellites monitored Serbian troop movements and intercepted conversations among top officials. And satellites tracked the impact point of thousands of NATO bombs (though they did not count the number of people killed or injured). This kind of space-controlled war is easier for U.S. soldiers to handle psychologically because it means long-distance killing, eliminating the trauma of close-up death. In a statement issued on June 17, 1999, the space command proclaimed that "any questions about the role or effectiveness of the use of space for military operations have been answered by NATO's Operation Allied Force in Kosovo." [9]

Republican Senator Bob Smith of New Hampshire enthusiastically supports the concept of a space and air force service, contending that the air force, which controls most of the military's space assets under the space command, spends too much time on aircraft and not enough time on spacecraft. A thirteen-member congressional panel has been established to examine all aspects of how a space force would operate. [10]

The air force organization magazine reported on an air force association conference in February 2000, at which General Michael Ryan pronounced that the military implications of the increased use of space systems are immense. He supported the concepts of the space command, noting that the U.S. must be able to control space when need be, as it controls the atmosphere. Space and air are not separate domains for the air force; they are two parts of the same whole, as closely related as the oceans and seas, he said. "We should think of the aerospace domain as a seamless volume from which we provide military capabilities in support of national security," he continued. For instance, the Kosovo "effort" connected forty different locations in fifteen countries using a variety of military and civilian lines and satellites, and many new ones were established. We worked over 44,000 spectrum requests, some terrestrial, some atmospheric, some for space systems, and, as you may know, these are very gnarly issues with our host countries," he told his audience. He added that partnerships with industry were very important. "We are on a journey, combining and evolving aerospace competencies into a full-spectrum aerospace force." [11] This cyberspace technology is being used just as effectively in the Afghanistan war, and here again the equipment fails to monitor the number and variety of civilian casualties, but was used only to locate "targets" and to guide the missiles, planes, and bombs.

CIVILIAN USES OF CYBERSPACE

The military is muscling into cyberspace territory that has become an essential ingredient for the daily lives of millions of people—cell phones, the internet, weather predictions, traffic control and monitoring, and accurate locating mechanisms for ships and terrestrial events via the GPS satellite systems. International currency and stability are dependent upon space. Trillions of dollars are transferred with a flick of the finger through cyberspace. Business and international globalization could not function without space.

What will happen, then, if America proceeds with its plans to militarize space? How will antisatellite warfare, space-based killer lasers, or nuclear explosions in space affect our daily lives? Does any country have the right to invade space for its own nationalistic purposes?

MERGING OF CIVILIAN AND MILITARY ACTIVITIES

Without a distinct separation between the military and civilian life, agendas become blurred, as was demonstrated recently by a project designed to use the space shuttle for a mission to map the earth's topology. On January 31, 2000, the space shuttle *Endeavor* took off from Cape Canaveral on a secret military mission: an eleven-day journey to obtain high resolution, three-dimensional maps for 80 percent of the earth's surface. The Pentagon gave NASA 200 million dollars for the shuttle flight, and most of these high-resolution maps will be classified, under military control, but the American people were not told that this was a military expedition. Instead, it was billed simply as a NASA earth topology mapping mission in the Pentagon-funded Global 3-D Mapping Mission.

While the maps may indeed provide better global mapping, they will also increase the ability of the Pentagon to identify and hit targets virtually anywhere on the planet using space technology. These pictures are designed to provide the military not only with the location, but the precise height of every tree, hill, and mountaintop, the depth of every ditch, valley, and canyon in the mapped area. As John Pike, former space policy chief at the Federation of American Scientists in Washington said, "Smart weapons need smart maps, and right now the military does not have smart maps." [12] Thus, under the guise of NASA exploration, the Pentagon has developed new technology that will enhance its ability to kill people or destroy property with extraordinary precision.

This detailed mapping by NASA has been enhanced by an experimental satellite launched in September 2000 from Kirtland Air Force Base in New Mexico. The satellite carries a hyperspectral imaging instrument that uses hundreds of very narrow wavelength bands to "see" reflected energy from objects on the ground. Military questions such as, *Is this field too muddy for a tank assault? Are breaking waves too high for an amphibious landing? What is the natural foliage? Am I looking at a distant parking lot or a grassy playground? Is this an armored personnel carrier or a school bus?* may now be satisfactorily answered.[13] Thus, although it was initially established in 1958 for "peaceful" space exploration, NASA is becoming progressively militarized.[14]

In another example of the militarization of the civilian sector, the air force decided to expand its space-lift partnership between commercial industry and the federal government. Because space launches are almost prohibitively expensive, a White House interagency working group initiated a report titled "Future Management and Use of U.S. Space Launch Bases and Ranges," to explore the cooperation of the department of defense and the civilian sector in space. Encouraging this partnership, Dr. Neal Lane, assistant to President Clinton for science and technology, said that "U.S. commercial launch rates have more than tripled since the early 1990s and now make up about 40 percent of the launch manifest at Vandenberg Air Force Base, California, and Cape Canaveral Air Force Station, Florida." Proceeding apace, the air force is putting mechanisms in place to benefit both the government and the private sector, in order to maximize the effectiveness of everyone's investment.[15] So once again, the lines are becoming blurred.

RECENT DEVELOPMENTS

The space command has recently conducted a range of exercises to demonstrate the supposed need to expand the scope of their program. On July 10, 2000, for example, an annual joint warrior interoperability demonstration (JWID) took place at Peterson Air Force Base in Colorado, during which industry and government joined forces to demonstrate that earth-bound war-fighters could be supported by integrating space forces and space-derived information with land, air, and sea forces. During this exercise, demonstrations were conducted at many locations around the world, including Cheyenne Mountain Operations Center near Colorado Springs; the U.S. Pacific Command at Camp Smith, Hawaii; and the U.S. Joint Forces Command in Norfolk, Virginia. Facilities in many NATO nations were included as well as U.S. bases in Australia and New Zealand.

As Air Force General Ralph E. Eberhart, commander in chief of the space command said, "It's clear this reliance on space will continue to grow. Traditionally we've talked about space as a combat multiplier in a combat support role. . . . However, now space has become much more basic and intrinsic than just a force multiplier. Space is a prerequisite. It's not a luxury any more; it's a requirement for conducting military operations. Space has proven itself vital to our national interests." [16]

Meanwhile, the air force announced on September 8, 2000, that their aerospace operations center (AOC) at Hurlburt Field in Florida had become an official weapons system. The AOC is essentially a forward-deployed war room described as "light, lean, and lethal." During an exercise on September 15, 2000, which assessed air force expeditionary forces using new technologies and capabilities in a simulated war-fighting environment, the AOC was the hub for all the information coming in from combined live-fly forces, models, simulations, and technology insertions at eleven different sites across the U.S. Information from space played a major role in this exercise. [17] According to Air Force Chief of Staff General Michael E. Ryan, the AOC will be the eyes, ears, hands, and legs of the commander during a real war operation.

And at Fort Bliss, Texas, a simulated military exercise called Roving Sands 2000 took place, again utilizing cyberspace for coordination. Using sophisticated computerized systems, military teams from different locations in the U.S. engaged in separate missions supporting an overall military objective. Not only was the battlefield a simulated target area, all the missile systems and other tools of engagement were also simulated so that smaller numbers of troops could command a greater range of territory.[18]

This was one of the first virtual cyberspace war exercises.

Space-Based Star Wars Weapons Under Development

Space-based weapons are exotic imaginary systems that have never been tried or tested, but many are already under construction. These include space-based lasers, hypersonic military space planes, various forms of antisatellite weapons, electronic jamming satellites, and space-based nuclear weapons.

Swords into Lasers

At least two specific, space-based laser weapons are already under development, both of which involve a concept the magazine *Space Daily* calls "turning swords into lasers."

- *The Space-Based Laser Demonstrator*, the first step in space-based weaponry, is currently being developed by Lockheed Martin, TRW, Boeing, the U.S. Air Force, and the Ballistic Missile Defense Organization.
- *The Alpha High-Energy Laser* is the second space-based laser under development. Also constructed by TRW, it underwent its twenty-second successful test firing in April 2000. The success of this test was trumpeted by *Space Daily* as "a significant step forward in the nation's disciplined maturation of the technology required to deploy the Space-Based Laser Integrated Flight Experiment."[19, 20]

The military excitement over and the moral implications of these weapons are reflected in a quote from a 1996 air force board report:

In the next two decades, new technologies will allow the fielding of space-based weapons of devastating effectiveness to be used to deliver energy and mass as force projection [read killing] in tactical and strategic conflict. These advances will enable lasers with reasonable mass and cost to affect very many kills. This can be done rapidly, continuously and with surgical precision, minimizing exposure of friendly forces. The technologies exist or can be developed in this time period.

The report continues, "Force application by kinetic kill weapons will enable pinpoint strikes on targets anywhere in the world. The equivalent of the Desert Storm strategic air campaign against Iraqi infrastructure would be possible to complete in minutes to hours essentially on immediate notice." [21]

(There is dissent. Mike Moore, the former editor of the *Bulletin of Atomic Scientists,* wrote in 1999: "The notion that the United States—or any country—might actually place weapons in space, as envisioned by the U.S. Space Command, is so repugnant that the United States ought to clearly repudiate it. Better yet, it should push to amend the Outer Space Treaty so as to definitively prohibit all weapons in space, not just weapons of mass destruction." [22] This attitude is reflected by the international community who repeatedly vote at the UN to endorse the Outer Space Treaty prohibiting the militarization of space. The U.S. consistently abstains.)

HYPERSONIC MILITARY SPACE PLANES

The air force is also in the process of developing a plane designed to perform reconnaissance, space control, and strike missions from orbit. Called an aerospace operations vehicle (AOV), it is a two-stage-to-orbit vehicle with a reusable booster. It has a "mission specific" upper stage, which is based upon Lockheed Martin's X-33 reusable launch vehicle technology demonstrator. Boeing is also involved in the development of the plane, and full-scale development is projected within three years.

The most contentious part of the plane is the upper stage, or common aero vehicle (CAV), a lifting-body-boost-glide vehicle that is designed for immediate attack on earth targets. So although the space plane is not technically an "in-orbit" weapon, and thus avoids Clinton's ban on these, it is a "strike" system that violates the belief—and indeed the UN Outer Space Convention—that space should be weapons-free.[23]

While the Clinton administration was reluctant to militarize space, the Bush team will probably endorse this new space-plane. This will allow the air force to maneuver outside the atmosphere and to place systems in orbit that can be recovered and reused.

ANTISATELLITE WARFARE

A whole other area of space-based weapons development involves building and protecting satellites, as well as potentially destroying those of other nations. (The Pentagon's term for satellite destruction is "Navigation Warfare" or "NavWar".) Because satellites have become essential to commercial, scientific, and national security services, the United States believes that it must control all satellite use. Satellites have no built-in protective mechanisms and are extremely vulnerable to attack, but until recently, no one thought to protect them. As Allen Thomson, a retired CIA analyst, said, attack on a satellite would be like an act of war.

Yet lasers can readily destroy satellites. So can something as simple as buckshot introduced into low-earth orbit where the satellites function. Computer hackers can interrupt signals sent between satellites and their ground operators. And commandos can attack ground stations that serve as control centers or relay points for data. NASA and the air force are also building a space maneuverable vehicle (SMV). Billed as giving the air force a new flexibility in space operations, the SMV has antisatellite applications as well. Other methods of satellite destruction—many of which rely on cyber technology—are in development. An order from the National Security Command Authority in 1999, backed by President Clinton and his secretary of defense, William Cohen, recently instructed the military to gear up to wage cyberwar. Cyberwar involves attacking satellites and infecting them with virus-like systems rendering them inoperable. To this end, Lieutenant General Edward Anderson, deputy commander in chief at the U.S. space command, was assigned the task of creating cyberwar strategies, including massive "denial-of-service" assaults that can be unleashed by launching crippling viruses called *trojan horses,* and jamming the enemy's computer systems with electronic radio-frequency interference.[24]

Threat to U.S. Satellite Systems

Because the Pentagon has been planning antisatellite warfare, it is intensely aware that its own satellites are at risk. Indeed, so vulnerable is America's satellite program that her present critical advantage in warfare could be destroyed if her GPS system was damaged. Private satellites now used for military communications are also vulnerable. For instance, the Iridium satellite constellation could be irreparably damaged if just one receiving building on the ground were destroyed. Signals from GPS satellites travel like radio waves and are available to anyone with a receiver. It is thought that China could develop antisatellite techniques within ten years, while a private Russian company has already developed a handheld GPS jammer with a range of 150 miles. In fact, "enemy" countries already use the American GPS system to enhance the accuracy of their weapons, including Scud missiles in North Korea, Iran, and Iraq.

Meanwhile, American satellites continue to become more and more sophisticated. The next generation of spy satellites was launched in 2000—smaller and more numerous than those in orbit—and is able to distinguish ground objects as small as 6 inches from a height of 500 miles. Canada is about to launch a satellite with these capabilities, with more to follow.

The Philosophy of Antisatellite Warfare

Antisatellite warfare is a tenuous proposition. How do you destroy other countries' satellites without endangering your own? How can you separate yourself from other countries when the communication systems are so interdependent? For instance, the army conducted a war game in 1998. The enemy was a fictitious country in the Middle East. During the exercise, China provided the "enemy" with satellite imagery of U.S. troop movements using the same satellites the U.S. uses to monitor its own troops. Should the U.S. destroy the satellites under these circumstances?

And how can we distinguish between peaceful and legitimate uses of satellite technology and those that are aspects of an overtly militarized "defense?" For example, it is now commonplace for the Pentagon to intersperse radomes for intelligence gathering with Star Wars radomes. Buckley Air Force Base, located east of Denver in Aurora, Colorado, the largest consolidated intelligence center in the western hemisphere—is jointly used by the National Reconnaissance Office (NRO) and the National Security Agency (NSA). Buckley boasts thirteen radomes—big white domes that envelope downloading stations for satellite data. Used for space-based intelligence gathering, they are also an integral component of the Star Wars system and will download information from the new high orbit space-based infrared system (SBIRS-High). A similar comingling of uses is happening at Pine Gap in Australia and at Menwith Hill in England. Because intelligence gathering is top secret, this technique of combined intelligence gathering and Star Wars planning can also be used to prevent local politicians from inspecting American Star Wars bases, vehemently opposed by the general public in those two countries.

Because the military is so dependent upon them, the space command stopped publishing information on the whereabouts of their twenty-seven GPS satellites, previously posted on the NASA web site. Most satellites, military or commercial, have no defenses against attack by laser beams or other objects targeted to destroy them. It is very expensive to add protective mechanisms to satellites because they add extra weight and launch costs become prohibitive. (It costs 10,000 dollars a pound to launch a payload into low earth orbit, and shielding mechanisms are heavy.)

Former Virginia Democratic Senator Charles Robb, a member of the Senate arms committee, said that the development of space weapons, including antisatellite capabilities, would be "a mistake of historic proportions" that would trigger an arms race in space. He noted that other nations would necessarily follow the U.S.'s example, and frantic generals, unable to know exactly who has put what in orbit—would plead for extravagant countermeasures.[25]

The increasing interdependency of the global economy and all military systems on satellite technology means that all destructive military thinking must cease and be replaced by an international resolution to preserve space for peaceful purposes only. In other words, the civilian lawmakers must exert control over their aberrant military.

MARS AND THE ASTEROIDS

While John Collins said that the moon contains valuable minerals and resources, he did not mention that the asteroids and other planets are also being examined for possible economic exploitation. The U.S. has plans to send manned and unmanned missions to Mars in the near future to explore and extract valuable minerals for earthly use.

Enthusiasm for the project was somewhat tempered in 1999, when NASA experienced two manmade catastrophes: the Mars Climate Orbiter and the Mars Polar Lander both mysteriously disappeared. The Climate Orbiter was lost after a navigational error sent it skimming too deeply into the Martian atmosphere, because engineers failed to convert English to metric units. The Polar Lander, which incorporated innovative lightweight materials, extraordinarily small microchips, and a low-cost laser-based navigational system, was scheduled to make a soft landing on September 23, 1999, at the Martian south pole. It would drop two probes, which, falling at high speed would penetrate a few feet into the Martian crust to explore for evidence of groundwater. NASA realized just prior to Lander's arrival that the mission was doomed because of a fatal design flaw. Lander probably blew up.[26]

But NASA scientists, undeterred, are planning future expeditions, including missions to recover rock samples from Mars and to do deep drilling to search for water, microbes, and minerals. Shell Oil and Los Alamos National Lab are among the outside groups assisting NASA in these investigations. The orbits of Earth and Mars offer favorable flight opportunities once every twenty-five months, when they are in such a position that the trip takes less than a year.[27] The current Mars schedule is as follows:

• In the spring of 2001, the Mars Odyssey Orbiter was launched, equipped with remote sensors to study surface minerals.
• In 2003, two small roving vehicles will be launched to land on

Mars in January 2004. These are 300-pound wheeled robots capable of traveling 300 feet a day while taking pictures, analyzing rocks, and investigating surface geology and possible subsurface water deposits.

- In 2005, NASA plans to send a Mars reconnaissance orbiter, which will be modeled on the now-successful Mars Global Surveyor still in orbit mapping Mars, for further mapping.

- In 2007, a "smart" landing craft will be launched, equipped with precision guidance and navigation, and hazard avoidance systems so that future missions will be able to land in the prescribed place all in one piece.

- Also in 2007 the first scout mission, deploying instrument-bearing balloons or a small airplane, will be launched.

- Again in 2007, NASA and the Italian space agency may team to place an orbiting satellite around Mars to help relay the increasingly heavy communications load from the Martian spacecraft. France may also participate.

- In 2009, NASA may team with the Italian space agency to deploy ground-penetrating radar to prospect for water while in orbit. These flights are being planned to search for water and traces of life, past or present.

- NASA's long-term plan is to launch a sample-return mission sometime during 2011 to 2014.[28]

Manned trips to Mars are on the drawing board. There is a possibility that some very primitive forms of life exist on the planet. The atmosphere probably contains traces of hydrogen peroxide, a strong oxidizing agent, and the planet is bathed in searingly high levels of ultraviolet light. Hence any trace of life would be found only at some depth from the surface.

Human habitation of Mars, a dream of many at NASA and other influential scientific organizations, will present huge physiological problems. An article written by Jerome Groopman, professor of medicine at Harvard Medical School, in the *New Yorker* in January 2000 summarizes this medical dilemma. Groopman questions whether human beings can survive weightlessness and deep-space radiation for prolonged periods. He worries about the possible psychological ramifications of isolation, stress, and confinement, and the problem of medical emergencies that could arise during the trip. Among other problems, it is virtually impossible for the human body, which evolved under the influence of gravity, to survive intact without it. Blood, which under the influence of gravity normally pools in the legs and lower body, rushes to the head, triggering severe pounding headaches. The fluid-controlling mechanisms are fooled by this redistribution, and dehydration rapidly develops as the kidneys excrete the "excess" fluid. The thickened blood then sends signals to the bone marrow to cease making red blood cells, inducing a mild anemia.

Muscles and bones almost melt in a weightless environment. Tendons and ligaments deteriorate, and minor stresses cause both ligaments and muscles to tear like tissue paper. Bone mass dissolves at a rate of 1.5 percent per month. Then there is the danger from radiation emanating from cosmic rays. These are essentially iron particles traveling at the speed of light that go right through the body, causing breakage of chromosomes and destruction of genes. Chromosomal and genetic damage increases the risk of developing cancer, and a recent review by the National Research Council found a 40 percent increased cancer risk from a trip to Mars, more than 10 times higher than the level deemed acceptable.

Surgery under any circumstances would be highly dangerous; if someone seriously injured a leg, the most appropriate treatment might well be amputation rather than an arduous repair. And a head injury would be almost impossible to treat. Neurosurgery at zero G could not be imagined.

Sleep deprivation, monotony, claustrophobia, anxiety, and depression will produce mental instability. It has been noted during missions in harsh, lonely environments that more than 10 percent of subjects develop serious problems of psychological adaptation and up to 3 percent develop psychiatric disorders, such as major depression. It has been recommended that older astronauts be chosen for a Mars trip because they would not live long enough to develop cancer from the cosmic radiation, or have fewer years to lose if they did. Also, younger men would be unable to have children because of radiation damage to their sperm.[29]

There are also grave concerns that the introduction of Martian material into the earth's biosphere may inject microorganisms that could unleash serious hazards. (Until the recent NASA Mars failures, plans to return Martian samples to earth were scheduled for 2008, but that date has been delayed until 2011.) Barry DiGregorio, who founded the International Committee Against Mars Sample Return, pointed out some pertinent lessons from history:

- In the early- to mid-1300s, one quarter of Europeans died when a flea from China carrying an unfamiliar microbe was introduced into a susceptible population.
- When the Spaniards explored the Americas, they introduced the smallpox virus that decimated tens of thousand of native inhabitants.
- European explorers infected the susceptible native inhabitants of the Polynesian and Hawaiian Islands with many different infectious diseases. Nearly half of these populations died.

At present NASA plans to return the Martian samples to earth in a passive Earth-entry capsule that will enter the atmosphere without a parachute and slam into the Utah desert, where it will sustain a 300–400 G force impact. Engineers say that the capsule will remain intact, but the potential ramifications of a mistake are difficult even to contemplate.[30] A report issued by the space studies board of the national research council (NRC), a research arm of the National Academy of Sciences, concluded that space samples will require very careful handling, and NASA must create a special facility to contain any material that might be contaminated with dangerous organisms. While they point out that the risk of bringing back something very dangerous is extremely low, it is not zero. NASA must err on the side of being prudent.[31]

John Rummel, NASA planetary protection officer, said that NASA will quarantine the Martian samples in a high-level containment facility similar to those used to harbor the world's deadliest viruses.[32] But DiGregorio said, "If we make one mistake it could mean the extinction—maybe for our species—or maybe another; for instance, bumblebees or photoplankton, which are a huge part of our ecology."

NASA's interest is not limited to Mars. A NASA mission scheduled for November 2003 will orbit Europa, a moon of Jupiter, which may have a deep, watery ocean. The next Europa mission may launch a "submarine" into this ocean to explore it, which exposes the probes to massive concentrations of damaging extraterrestrial radiation, similar to that experienced in post–nuclear war.[33]

The Colorado School of Mines, long involved in the concepts of space mining and minerals extraction, and in space-based market development and minerals economics, is the motivating force behind these extraordinarily ambitious mining plans. Engineering students and faculty are currently establishing an ongoing space utilization roundtable to calculate methods to retrieve useful products and services from space. Everything from tourism, to mining, solar power, water extraction, and manufacturing on the moon is under consideration. Space mining may be ten to twenty years away, but someone has to start thinking about these possibilities now, they say.[34]

INTERNATIONAL SPACE STATION

On October 31, 2000, a three-member Expedition One crew was launched from the Baikonur Cosmodrome on a Russian Soyuz rocket to dock at the International Space Station (ISS) two days later. This eighth mission marked the start of a permanent human presence in space, initiating a planned permanent occupancy of ten years. It is intended that the ISS will eventually be the launching pad for missions to other planets.[35] A total of sixteen countries are involved in this project: Russia, Germany, Belgium, Canada, Italy, Japan, the Netherlands, Denmark, Norway, France, Spain, Sweden, Switzerland, the U.S., the U.K., and Brazil. More than 900 researchers from these and other countries are developing experiments to be conducted in zero-gravity conditions in fields such as biotechnology, combustion science, fluid physics, materials science, life sciences, engineering and technology, and earth sciences.

The stated goals of the International Space Station are as follows (most are worthy, but some are troublesome):

- To find solutions to crucial problems in medicine, ecology, and other areas of science

- To lay the foundation for developing space-based commerce and enterprise
- To create great worldwide demand for space-related education at all levels by cultivating the excitement, wonder, and discovery that the ISS symbolizes
- To foster world peace through high-profile, long-term international cooperation in space[36]

It would appear that the internationalism of the ISS would mitigate against unilateral exploitation and control of space by a single nation. However, I do not trust the present Bush administration, and Congress has rarely acted in the best interests of the international community. The military and space corporations, along with other multinationals, paid billions of dollars for the last U.S. election, and have control over upcoming legislation. Furthermore, the Republican right-wing openly supports U.S. militarization and domination of space.

Is the function of the ISS just window-dressing for a more ominous future?

NUCLEAR DEVICES IN SPACE

The surface of Mars is bone-dry and covered with a fine dust of an average particle size of about two microns—the same dimensions as cigarette smoke. The dust is so fine and pervasive that it would gum up space suits, scratch helmet visors, induce electrical shorts, sandblast instruments, and clog motors. The corrosive hydrogen peroxide in the Martian atmosphere could also slowly wear away rubber seals.

Astronauts would need to maintain a dust-free environment because tiny particles of inhaled silicon dust induce a severe lung disease called *silicosis*. The particles will be electrically charged so the dust will cling to everything. But the dust means something else. Solar power necessary to fuel a mission would become almost impossible to generate, because Martian powder would accumulate on the solar panels. On the Mars Pathfinder mission, for instance, the electrical output from the solar panels fell 1 percent every three days as powder covered them.

Therefore, the preferred choice for power generation becomes nuclear, in the form of a 100-kilowatt nuclear reactor.[37] And this brings us to some of the worst of the Star Wars hazards that will threaten planet Earth: nuclear-powered rockets; orbiting nuclear reactors; nuclear reactors destined for asteroids, the moon, or Mars; and plutonium-fueled space probes to investigate other planets—all of which pose potentially severe risks to the earth's biological systems.

NASA consistently plays down these nuclear threats, which are an integral part of its space program, while emphasizing the glory of space research, and of extraterrestrial adventure. But the threats are very serious.

THE HISTORY OF NUCLEAR DEVICES IN SPACE

Over a period of decades, while Russia launched more than thirty nuclear space reactors, America has launched only one. Some of these Russian reactors have crashed to Earth, permanently polluting swathes of hundreds of miles with potent, long-lived, radioactive material. The most serious Russian nuclear space accident occurred in 1978 when a Cosmos 954 satellite carrying a nuclear reactor smashed into the Northwest Territories of Canada. Sizable amounts of radioactive debris were distributed over a 600-kilometer path from Slave Lake to Baker Lake. Fifty large radioactive fragments were recovered, along with other chunks, flakes, and slivers. But a wide area stretching southward from the Great Slave Lake was also affected by smaller, scattered particles from the reactor core. The total search covered 124,000 square kilometers of the Northwest Territories. These carcinogenic, radioactive particles posed a serious risk to the population, because they could be either inhaled or ingested through the food chain.

The most recent Russian accident happened in 1996 when its Mars space probe, carrying half a pound of plutonium 238 (not a nuclear reactor), fell from space. President Clinton urgently contacted the prime minister of Australia, offering help when it was thought that the probe would hit Australia. Instead, it fell into the less politically important countries of Bolivia and Chile, and international concern ceased. (Not a word was uttered again about the risk to biological systems or to human life.)

Russia is not alone in its nuclear space accidents. The most significant U.S. accident occurred in 1964 when a Transit 5BN-3 satellite with a SNAP plutonium power system crashed. Some 2.1 pounds of plutonium 238 were dispersed around the world. A report prepared in 1989 by the health and radiation agencies in Europe stated that, "a worldwide sampling program carried out in 1970 showed SNAP debris to be present at all continents and at all latitudes." (Small quantities of plutonium 238 are used to provide electricity to space probes, which is generated by the decay heat of the radioactive element. Plutonium 238 is used because it has a shorter half-life than plutonium 239 and therefore produces more heat.) Dr. John Gofman, professor emeritus of medical physics at the University of California–Berkeley, relates that accident to a subsequent worldwide increase in lung cancer.[38]

Between the U.S. and Russia, there has been a 15 percent accident rate in both countries' space programs.

NUCLEAR POWERED SPACE PROBES

Despite these disasters, NASA has continued for thirty years to use plutonium 238 for its space exploration power systems and has launched a total of twenty-five missions with radioactive power packs. Plutonium 238 is 280 times more carcinogenic than the more prevalent isotope, plutonium 239. Glenn Seaborg, plutonium 239's discoverer, called plutonium 238 the most dangerous material on Earth. And plutonium 239 is almost the most carcinogenic substance known to the human race—as previously stated, one pound, if adequately distributed, could induce lung cancer in every human being on the planet.

NASA is playing with the most deadly of materials with seeming impunity, evidently not caring if one of its rockets malfunctions and sprays plutonium 238 onto countries that happen to be located beneath. Previous plutonium 238–fueled NASA missions included the Apollo lunar scientific packages, and the Pioneer, Viking, Voyager, and Ulysses deep-space probes. More recent missions include the Mars Pathfinder mission, launched in 1996, and the Cassini mission, launched in 1997.

Future NASA plans include plutonium 238-power systems for the

Pluto-Kuiper Express mission scheduled for launch in 2004, the Europa Orbiter mission scheduled for 2006, and the solar probe mission for 2007. The Pluto-Kuiper Express mission will require about 16.3 pounds of plutonium 238, and the Europa Orbiter and solar probe missions each will require about 6.6 pounds.

Eight plutonium 238–fueled RHUs will also be required for each Mars Surveyor mission over the next decade. Approximately thirty will be launched. Each plutonium 238 capsule will weigh 0.7 pounds. Small amounts of curium 242, curium 244, and cobalt 57 will also be required for scientific instruments. Each of these radioactive elements is almost as toxic as plutonium. According to the General Accounting Office report, *Space Exploration: Power Sources for Deep Space Probes,* NASA is contemplating eight more nuclear-fueled electric generator space missions by 2015.

HEALTH CONSEQUENCES OF PLUTONIUM 238 PRODUCTION

By law, the department of energy is responsible for the supply of plutonium 238 for the space program. Historically, the military reactors and reprocessing plants at Savannah River, South Carolina, were used to manufacture this plutonium. However, these dangerously polluted facilities were closed down in 1996 when the end of the cold war determined that plutonium 239 for bombs was not needed (plutonium 238 and 239 were manufactured in parallel).[39]

Because the plutonium 238 supply of the U.S. was limited, in 1992 the DOE signed a five-year contract with Russia to supply it. In 1997 this contract was renewed for another five years. But because the long-term viability of Russian plutonium could be in jeopardy, and the inventory of plutonium 238 for space missions might be depleted by 2005, the DOE is considering restarting old military nuclear reactors or using civilian light-water reactors for its plutonium 238 production.[40]

Episodes of worker contamination are frequent. The plutonium 238 for the Cassini mission was manufactured at Los Alamos Lab. The total amount of radiation exposure increased during this production period at Los Alamos and the number of people contaminated with plutonium 238 rose from 139 to 244 (between 1993 and

1995). More recently, eight more Los Alamos workers were exposed to plutonium 238 at potentially dangerous levels in March 2000. These people received medical treatment, but in truth, there is no effective way to decontaminate workers once plutonium 238 has entered their bodies.[41]

Significantly, the European Space Agency has developed high-efficiency solar space cells to replace nuclear generators. In 2003 this agency will launch its Rosetta probe to travel beyond the orbit of Jupiter and to rendezvous with a comet named Wirtanen—the first such probe. Wirtanen is 675 million kilometers from the sun, where the sunlight is twenty times weaker than on earth.[42] If solar power is capable of supplying the very small amount of electricity needed for these missions, why does NASA persist in using plutonium 238? To ascertain the source of pressure for nuclear space probes, follow the money.

For many years, General Electric made the nuclear space systems. Now this lucrative business has been subsumed by Lockheed Martin. Over the years, both companies have lobbied long and hard for nuclear space systems. Los Alamos National Laboratory and Oak Ridge National Laboratory are also heavily invested in the development of nuclear space systems.

The militarization of the space program has had a significant effect upon NASA's nuclear commitment. One reason that NASA insists on using nuclear power instead of solar power is because the military is enthusiastic about nuclear weapons in space. One recent NASA plutonium 238 space launch was the Cassini Saturn probe, which flew atop a Lockheed Martin Titan-4 military rocket. Cassini carried 72.3 pounds of plutonium 238—more plutonium than had ever been launched into space. The Titan-4 rocket is an unreliable, dangerous old rocket with a one-in-ten record—one catastrophic accident in every ten launches. Not long after the Cassini launch, three Titan rockets blew up, either on the space pad or shortly after launching. NASA designed Cassini to circle Venus and then to return toward earth via a "gravity assist" slingshot in order to increase its momentum to Saturn. Cassini circled the earth above the atmosphere at 42,300 miles per hour, at an altitude of 700 miles on August 1999. Luckily, unlike Apollo 13, the vectors were accurate, and Cassini with its plutonium load did not enter the atmosphere to disintegrate and spread its deadly cargo across the planet.

In its final environmental-impact statement, NASA said that if the flyby did not go as planned, and Cassini made an inadvertent reentry into the atmosphere, the plutonium 238 would have been released and "approximately five billion of the . . . world population at the time . . . could receive 99 percent or more of the radiation exposure." NASA also acknowledged that if plutonium rained down on areas of natural vegetation, it might have to "relocate animals"; if it fell on agricultural land, it might need to "ban future agricultural land uses"; and if it rained down upon urban areas it would have to "demolish all or some structures" and "relocate affected population permanently." Dr. Gofman of the University of California–Berkeley, who is also the codiscoverer of uranium 235, predicted a death toll of 950,000 as a result of a Cassini accident.

The Outer Space Treaty specifically states that "states shall be liable for damage caused by their space objects." However, in 1991 NASA and the department of energy drew up a "space power agreement" to cover American nuclear space flights using the government-sponsored Price-Anderson Act as its basis. Price-Anderson allocates a domestic liability of 8.9 billion dollars in the event of a nuclear accident, but just 100 million dollars for damage incurred in all foreign nations.

NUCLEAR POWERED ROCKETS

At the thirty-sixth Joint Propulsion Conference in Huntsville, Alabama, in July 2000, at least a dozen papers were presented devoted to space propulsion using nuclear thermal rockets (NTR). (This particular project had been terminated in 1973 because of growing antinuclear feelings among the U.S. population, but it is now back on the drawing board.) Stanley Borowski, a nuclear engineer who manages the NTR studies at NASA's Glenn Research Center, enthusiastically sees NTR as a "three-fer," offering three mission types for the price of a single engine: "We could use it to fly missions to the moon, to Mars, and to near-Earth asteroids—all with the same vehicle," he said. (As one of NASA's spokemen, Borowski speaks to audiences ranging from kindergartens to retirees and receives a nearly uniform response. He must be a very persuasive speaker because the audiences are enthusiastic: "Why hasn't this country developed this option yet?" they ask.)[43]

Some add that the NTR could be used for defending space systems, for rebooting the international space station, and for the eventual colonization of Mars. Russia will participate in the NTR program because they developed robust fuel nuclear rods that could be used in the nuclear engine. It has been suggested that the air force invest a small part of its budget in development of the nuclear thermal rocket, which could be used to assist the North American Aerospace Defense Command in the tracking and defense of U.S. space systems. Borowski predicts that the rocket could be ready to fly in ten years. NASA and the department of energy have recently undertaken a major public relations campaign to sell the nuclear rocket to the public. A conventional rocket would take a year to get to Mars, they explain, but the nuclear option would cut travel time in half.

NASA's Marshall Space Flight Center in Huntsville, Alabama, will be coordinating work on the nuclear rocket with Los Alamos National Lab, NASA in Cleveland, and the University of Florida's nuclear engineering department. In January 2000, at the seventeenth annual Symposium on Space Power and Propulsion, 600 conferees from NASA, DOE, aerospace corporations, nuclear academia, and the air force met to discuss the expansion of nuclear power in space. NASA scientist Roger Lenard, who works at the Marshall Space Flight Center, said, "Want to go to Mars quickly? Detonate some nuclear warheads and months later you're there." He had another proposal: How about a nuclear-powered "space tug" capable of deflecting a comet or asteroid heading for impact with earth? Less exotic proposals focused on using nuclear power to fuel human exploration and colonization on the Moon, Mars, Jupiter, and Saturn.

NUCLEAR POWERED WEAPONS

Some of the weapons that are currently proposed in the Star Wars plans, including laser-beam weapons, particle-beam weapons, and others, will require orbiting nuclear reactors for their power sources.

The 1996 air force board report points out that because "power limitations impose restrictions" on space-based weapons systems, making them "relatively unfeasible . . . a natural technology to enable high power is nuclear power in space." The report's authors seem amazingly confident that their ideas will be viable. "Setting the emotional issues of nuclear power aside," they say, "this technology offers a viable alternative for large amounts of power in space."

OZONE DEPLETION AND THE SPACE PROGRAM

Quite apart from the obvious dangers of nuclear war, nuclear accidents, and the like, many of the efforts that make up America's space-based defense program presuppose ongoing and continuous launching of rockets into space, posing the imminent danger that the ozone layer will be seriously damaged.

Solid fuel used in U.S. rockets and in the space shuttle releases chlorine atoms into the stratosphere. The space shuttle, for example, releases 240 tons of concentrated hydrochloric acid (HCl) at each launch. Chlorine, which splits off from the HCl molecule, is the substance that combines with and destroys ozone molecules. Scientists in 1989 predicted that if NASA continued to launch solid-fuel rocket boosters at a rate of ten per year, this would induce a 10 percent depletion in the ozone by 2005.[44, 45, 46] Yet the number of civilian and military launches have increased alarmingly since that prediction was made. (For each 1 percent decrease in stratospheric ozone there will be a 4 to 6 percent increase in skin cancer. We are experiencing these effects in Australia, where we see a proliferation of skin-cancer clinics within our cities, and where the hole in the ozone layer of the southern hemisphere was larger in the year 2000 than ever before.)

INTERNATIONAL CONCERN

At the opening of the conference for disarmament in Geneva in January 2000, UN Secretary General Kofi Annan called for nations to join together to maintain space "as a weapons-free environment." China received wide support for a proposal to create "an international legal instrument banning the testing, deployment and use of any weapons, weapons systems and their components in outer space, with a view to preventing the weaponization of outer space." Nevertheless, the U.S. is attempting to block the proposal.

International concern about American plans is so great that in November 2000, 138 nations voted in the UN to reaffirm the Outer Space Treaty, stating specifically that space be set aside "for peaceful purposes." The motion was titled "Prevention of an Arms Race in Outer Space." As noted, only the United States and Israel abstained.[47] The Clinton administration quietly acquiesced to the pressure exerted by the military-industrial complex to militarize space.

With George W. Bush in the White House, and an administration staffed by major hawks enthusiastic about a full-blown Star Wars system, many of the proposals discussed above will become reality unless we rise up and use our democracy in an efficient and passionate way.

Chapter Eight

NUCLEAR WAR
IN THE GULF AND KOSOVO

I N 1990, SHORTLY before he invaded Kuwait—which had
been drilling oil beneath Iraq's border and selling it at a steep
discount—President Saddam Hussein of Iraq approached the
U.S. ambassador, April Glaspie, about his plan, and she indicated that
the U.S. had no defense treaties or security commitments to Kuwait.
In a subsequent face-to-face meeting with Glaspie, Hussein told her
that Iraq was in dire economic straits, and the low oil price induced
by Kuwait's and the United Arab Emirates' overproduction was hurt-
ing them badly. She told Hussein that Iraq had "a right to prosper";
and Glaspie continued, "I know you need funds. We understand that,
and our opinion is that you should have the opportunity to rebuild
your country. But we have no opinion on the Arab-Arab conflicts, like
your border disagreement with Kuwait." ¹ (Subsequently Glaspie lied
about this conversation when she testified before the Senate Foreign
Relations Committee: "I told him orally we would defend our vital
interests, we would support our friends in the Gulf, we would defend
their sovereignty and integrity.")

The U.S. response when Iraq invaded Kuwait belied Glaspie's reas-
surances. Contrary to Glaspie's "no opinion on the Arab-Arab conflicts," the U.S. staged a military operation on Kuwait's behalf that
had been planned for months and amounted to a veritable arms
bazaar for U.S. weapons manufacturers. Eighty-eight thousand, five
hundred tons of bombs (the equivalent of more than seven Hiro-
shimas) were dropped on Iraq and Kuwait (fewer than 7 percent of
the weapons used were "smart"; most were old fashioned "dumb"

bombs), and 70 percent of these did not hit military targets, but fell on civilian areas. (Smart bombs have computer guidance systems and maps of the terrain to guide them accurately to their targets. This technology, however, often fails. Dumb bombs are dropped from planes and may or may not land where they are intended.)

Contrary to accepted norms of wartime behavior, the U.S. attacked columns of retreating Iraqi soldiers and civilians with carrier-based planes, using cluster bombs and napalm—the petroleum compound that adheres to the skin while burning. (Returning pilots spoke of partaking in a "duck or turkey shoot" and of "shooting fish in a barrel.") And, in an equally controversial move, U.S. forces failed to support Iraqi dissidents or the Kurdish or Shi'a uprising at the end of the war, preventing the Iraqi troops who were rebelling against Hussein in the south of the country from reaching captured arms depots, and circling in planes overhead as Hussein's helicopters slaughtered his own dissenting troops.[2] (Not one American or allied soldier was killed by Iraqi troops, though some died through "friendly fire.")

The U.S. response to Iraq's invasion of Kuwait also made history for another horrific reason: Operation Desert Storm was the first conflict in history to create a radioactive battlefield. America's deployment of radioactive-uranium weapons in the Gulf countries—used as a basic tool of combat for the first time—have permanently contaminated the area and will continue to affect citizens of the region for thousands of years after the war ended.

HISTORY OF URANIUM WEAPONS

During the fifties, the department of defense became interested in using uranium 238 to manufacture weapons for several reasons. Over 700,000 tons of the element were dispersed in various locations around the United States, a by-product of nuclear weapons and nuclear power production. It had no specific use, it was free, and it was dangerous. Several uses for the element were conceived:

- Uranium is 1.7 times more dense than lead and is therefore extremely effective as ammunition for penetrating metal armor. A 120-mm tank round, for example, contains about ten pounds of solid uranium, which at high speed can slice through tank armor like a hot knife through butter. (The Pentagon refers to uranium shells and bullets as "nuclear tipped." They are not: the shells are composed of solid uranium. The uranium is alloyed with other elements that may also be medically dangerous, but these materials are classified.)

- Uranium 238 can also be used as armor plating in tanks because its density prevents penetration by conventional weapons.
- Uranium is heavy, and thus works as ballast in cruise missiles and aircraft.

The U.S. began testing uranium weapons in 1954 at a secret place near the Los Alamos Lab. They continued researching and testing at various locations around the U.S. during the sixties and seventies, and the first usable ammunition was produced in 1978, though it was not used in battle until Operation Desert Storm in 1991.

COMPONENTS OF URANIUM WEAPONS

Natural uranium, found in the earth's crust, is composed primarily of two isotopes: Uranium 235, the most valuable, which is present in concentrations of only 0.7 percent, and uranium 238, which is virtually worthless and constitutes the remaining 99.3 percent.

Uranium 235 is the fissionable material, and is used as fuel for nuclear weapons and nuclear reactors. It must be enriched to concentrations of 3 percent for reactors and over 50 percent for nuclear weapons. Enrichment is a process that involves converting the uranium ore to a gas, which is then forced through minute pores in a large nickel shield, separating the two isotopes. Also called *gaseous diffusion*, this process is extraordinarily energy consuming. (The process was first used during the Manhattan Project in the early forties, and the Hiroshima bomb was a uranium-fueled weapon.) Uranium 238, the unfissionable isotope remaining after enrichment, is dubbed *depleted uranium*, or DU.

Over sixty years of uranium enrichment saw very few safeguards put in place, and regulations controlling the enrichment process were virtually nonexistent. Most of the enrichment was conducted at the

Paducah Gaseous Diffusion Plant in Kentucky. It involved not just the pure uranium that had been extracted from the ground, but reclamation of uranium from nuclear reactors dedicated to the manufacture of plutonium—at Savannah River, South Carolina; at Hanford, Washington; and at Oak Ridge, Tennessee.

Enrichment of reclaimed uranium poses special problems because a variety of other radioactive elements come into play during the process, "polluting" the uranium and posing additional health hazards. When uranium 235 is fissioned in a nuclear reactor, over 200 new radioactive elements are created, and the uranium, when mixed with its fission products, becomes 1 million times more radioactive than in its natural state. One of the most valuable by-products of the fission process is plutonium, which is created when a uranium 238 atom captures a neutron. Plutonium is not a fission product, but a transuranic element with an atomic weight greater than uranium. Plutonium is the most efficient fuel for nuclear weapons—ten pounds, a chunk the size of a grapefruit, is fuel for a hydrogen bomb. An enormous quantity of plutonium was created during the cold war, when the U.S. manufactured 70,203 nuclear weapons. Pure bomb-grade plutonium was obtained from the mess of fission products in the fuel rods by dissolving the rods in concentrated nitric acid, and removing the plutonium from the thermally hot, highly radioactively corrosive solution.

Along with plutonium, unfissioned uranium remaining in the fuel rods was also extracted for further use. This reclaimed uranium is a mixture of uranium 238 and uranium 235. The uranium 235 must then be reenriched to 3 percent for use again in nuclear reactors.

Consequently, uranium 238 again accumulates. But because it came from spent fuel rods, it is contaminated with plutonium and other dangerous elements such as neptunium (also a transuranic element), and possibly with fission products such as technetium, strontium, and cesium. Shipments of this polluted reclaimed uranium were sent to Paducah for more than twenty years. (Although Paducah was a department of energy plant, the private contractors responsible for its well-being were Lockheed Martin and Union Carbide. Recently, the department of energy admitted that the Paducah plant is surrounded by high concentrations of plutonium contamination. Pollution has been detected over a mile from the plant; the Ohio River, two miles from the plant, contains elevated levels of plutonium; and the element has contaminated streams, ponds, and groundwater.[3])

Uranium purified after extraction from the soil contains three isotopes: 234, 235, and 238. (*Purification* means the removal of soil together with daughter products such as radium, radon, polonium, and many other long-lived radioactive decay products.) Uranium 238 has a half-life of 4.5 billion years. In the depleted form after the enrichment process, it still contains small amounts of uranium 235 and uranium 234. All three uranium isotopes are alpha emitters and as such are potentially highly carcinogenic. In 1 gram of uranium 238, 12,400 atomic transformations occur each second, and each throws off an alpha particle consisting of two protons and two neutrons.

The depleted uranium 238 used for weapons has half the radioactivity of the original natural uranium (uranium 235 is 0.7 percent, and uranium 238 is 0.93 percent), because uranium 235 itself is very energetic. Nevertheless, the radiation emanating from 238 can be dangerous if it enters and resides within human or animal bodies. Uranium 238 weapons are made even more dangerous by the contaminant isotopes from Paducah plutonium 239, alpha emitter—half-life 24,400 years; and neptunium 237, alpha and gamma emitter—half-life 2 million years. (The U.S. military is fond of saying that depleted uranium is less radioactive than naturally occurring uranium. However, uranium 238 is 100 percent uranium, unlike the uranium ore in the ground, which is considerably diluted with soil. Thus, comparing DU with natural uranium ore is like comparing apples and oranges. It is simply not relevant.)

MEDICAL RISKS OF URANIUM PROCESSING

Uranium processing exposes hundreds of thousands of people to inhaled and ingested radiation throughout the nuclear-fuel cycle—which includes mining, milling, enriching, fuel fabrication, nuclear fission, reprocessing, and storage of radioactive waste.[4] Uranium miners are at significant risk for developing lung and other forms of cancers, as demonstrated in workers in Canada, Germany, Namibia, Czech Republic, France, Russia, and the United States.[5]

Workers at and neighbors of uranium milling and processing plants are also at risk for cancers. For example, the Feed Materials Production Center at Fernald, Ohio, which commenced operation in 1953, manufactured uranium pellets for plutonium production reactors at Hanford and Rocky Flats, and parts for nuclear weapons made at Rocky Flats and the Y12 plant at Oak Ridge, Tennessee. During its decades of operation it released 298,000 pounds of uranium dust into the air—167,000 pounds into the Great Miami River and 12.7 million pounds into unlined earthern pits. Large silos on the reservation contain 9700 tons or 1600 to 4600 curies, which continually emit high concentrations of carcinogenic gas. Local people have developed highly malignant bone sarcomas and other cancers secondary to uranium deposits in their bodies.[6]

There are radioactive facilities such as this all over the United States as well as in other countries—all integral components of the nuclear fuel cycle, producing uranium ammunition, uranium fuel rods for nuclear power plants, and plutonium for nuclear weapons. Up to eighty sites in America have been involved in the production, manufacture, development, testing, and storage of uranium 238.

Firing ranges for uranium 238 weapons in Madison, Indiana; Yuma, Arizona; and Aberdeen, Maryland may never be decontaminated. Uranium-polluted soil was discovered almost a mile away from a munitions production plant in Concord, Massachusetts, where 400,000 ponds of uranium wastes lie in an unlined pit. Groundwater and a nearby cranberry bog are contaminated.[7] (For a comprehensive list of uranium weapons–related sites, I refer you to the excellent book, *Metal of Dishonor*, pages 212 to 216.)[8]

As far back as 1943, scientists in the Manhattan Project postulated that uranium could be viewed as an air and terrain contaminant, saying that inhalation would cause "bronchial irritation coming on in a few hours to a few days." They also noted that the acute radiation effects could induce ulcers and perforations of the gut, followed by death.[9] On January 29, 2000, the U.S. department of energy finally acknowledged—after many years of denial—that employees of uranium-processing facilities experience significantly high rates of leukemia, Hodgkin's disease, and cancers of the prostate, kidney, liver, salivary glands, and lungs. In England, a study commissioned by British Nuclear Fuels and released in July 2000, found a link between radiation and lung cancer at the Springfield uranium-fuel fabrication plant near Preston in Lancashire.[10] And the highest incidence of childhood leukemia in the United Kingdom has been reported around a uranium firing range at Duindrennan, Scotland.[11] The National Academy of Sciences recently reported that of 144 highly contaminated nuclear sites around the U.S., 109 would remain radioactive in perpetuity, because it was virtually impossible to clean them up.[12]

MEDICAL IMPLICATIONS OF URANIUM WEAPON USE IN THE GULF WAR

During Operation Desert Storm, American M1A1, M1, and M60 tanks fired 14,000 depleted uranium (DU) anti-tank shells. Seven thousand rounds were used during training before Desert Storm, fired into sand berms in Saudi Arabia; 4000 were fired during combat; and 3000 more were lost in fires and other accidents. The air force A-10 "tank-killer" planes also fired approximately 940,000 30-mm DU rounds in combat, totaling 564,000 pounds of DU that either hit their targets or were scattered over the desert floor. (For those that hit their targets, it is important to note that uranium 238 is pyrophoric: when it hits a tank at high speed it burst into flame. Up to 70 percent of the shell is vaporized and converted to tiny particles of oxidized uranium 238. Sixty percent of the particles are tiny—less than 5 microns in diameter. Because these particles are light, they can be transported many miles on wind currents, and they are small enough to be inhaled into the terminal bronchi—the tiniest air passages of the lungs. They can reside in these terminal bronchi for many years, irradiating a small volume of surrounding cells with high doses of radiation. The larger particles can be wafted up to the throat carried by the mucous and cilial action of the airways and then swallowed.)

One third, or 654 of the 2054 American tanks used during Desert Storm, were equipped with uranium armor plating, providing them with a tactical advantage, because the conventional Iraqi weapons would have no chance of penetrating them. But by their use, the American tank crews were exposed to whole-body gamma radiation, similar to X rays emanating from the uranium armor.

At the end of the operation, between 300 and 800 tons of uranium 238 with a half-life of 4.5 billion years lay across the battlefield of Iraq, Kuwait, and Saudi Arabia, never to be retrieved, in spent rounds, in solid and powdered form, in various states of decay and dispersal.

External Dose

External gamma radiation emitted from uranium shells can be as high as 200 millirads per hour, more than the yearly dose received from natural background radiation. One DU penetrator found at the port of Dammam in Saudi Arabia measured 260 to 270 millirads per hour. If, for example, a person picked up a shell and kept it in her pocket for ten hours, she would absorb 2.7 rads of gamma radiation, a relatively high dose. Children have been found playing with the empty shells and people collect shell fragments to display in their houses. Soldiers took home the radioactive ammunition as souvenirs, unaware that it was dangerous.

Internal Dose

The water supplies in the affected areas are at risk. The dissolved uranium will concentrate in the food chain, thousands of times at each step, particularly in milk—including human breast milk. (As noted, it is not possible to taste, smell, or see radiation.) Children and babies are ten to twenty times more sensitive to the carcinogenic effects of radiation than adults.

The geographical areas in the Gulf that are now contaminated with uranium will remain radioactive for the rest of time, the inhabitants being at risk for cancers and congenital deformities forever more. Insoluble, tiny ceramic particles of uranium dioxide aerosol will be inhaled into the lungs of the surrounding population, be they soldiers, adult civilians, or children. And the radioactive water will cause pollution of the food supply.

Because the uranium, its daughter isotopes, and the contaminants named above emit both alpha and beta particles, the lung cells with which they are in contact will absorb high doses of radiation. It takes a single alpha or beta particle or gamma ray to damage a single regulatory gene in a single cell to kill the patient. Like a parasite, cancer uses up the nutrients of the body, and the patient wastes away and then dies.

Insoluble uranium is also transported from the lungs by macrophages (white blood cells that ingest insoluble or foreign bodies), to the lymph glands in the center of the thorax. The cells in the glands receive a radiation dose ten times that of the lung cells. The complications of irradiated lymph tissue are leukemia and lymphoma. Indeed, some of the NATO troops who were exposed to uranium weapons in Bosnia and Kosovo are now reporting an increase in leukemia, as are the civilians in Iraq. Uranium is solubilized in the lymph glands and transported to the liver, where it can cause liver cancer, and to the bone, where it can induce bone cancer or leukemia.

The biological half-life of uranium 238 in bone is 300 days.[13] This element can also be deposited in brain, kidney, muscle, spleen, and— most important—in the reproductive organs.[14] In 1997 uranium 238 was found in the semen of five out of twenty-two American veterans who had been carrying uranium fragments in their bodies since 1991.[15] This finding is significant because there have been reports of an increased incidence of congenital abnormalities in the offspring of veterans and also in the newborn babies in Iraq; the uranium is finding its way into testicles where it is mutating genes in the sperm cells. Uranium can also induce testicular cancer.

Uranium crosses the placenta, where, like the drug thalidomide, it can induce severe fetal abnormalities by killing cells that are imperative to normal fetal development. This is called *teratogenesis*.[16]

Uranium is also a heavy metal. As such, it can cause a particular form of nephritis or kidney disease. It is excreted through the kidney, so this organ is at particular risk. It is known that many Gulf War veterans are suffering from kidney disease. The kidney is also at risk because the heavy-metal uranium is also radioactive. As the kidney is the main organ of excretion for the uranium that is stored in the body, there is the risk of renal carcinoma. No epidemiological studies have been done by the Pentagon to determine the true incidence of renal disease amongst the veterans. Nor have there been any studies to determine whether malignancies have increased.

The Pentagon is also steadfastly refusing to conduct studies of the civilians living in the contaminated areas. What is their prognosis or life expectancy? What will happen to future generations? Instead, the Pentagon and the British ministry of defense are blocking efforts to study their troops for relevant diseases, disclaiming any association of the so-called Gulf War syndrome with uranium ammunition, even though a secret report issued by the United Kingdom atomic energy authority in April 1991—a month after the conclusion of Desert Storm—warned that only 40 tons of uranium debris left from the DU weapons could cause over 500,000 deaths.[17] (Actual debris amounts to not 40 tons but 300,000 to 800,000 tons.)

Aware of the radioactive dangers, Saudi Arabia demanded that the U.S. army collect all the tanks, vehicles, and instruments of war destroyed by uranium munitions on their territory. Because Saudi Arabia is a close American ally, the request was honored and the contaminated equipment taken back to the U.S. to be stored with extreme care.[18] To this end, the Pentagon has constructed a high-priced, high-security, high-tech cocoon at the Savannah River Nuclear Facility in Georgia to process radioactive materials from the contaminated equipment. This building, Building 101, has special walls and flooring to prevent air or dust from escaping to the outside world.

Kuwait and Iraq have not been so lucky. There is no U.S. commitment to decontaminate their radioactive land.

PRIOR KNOWLEDGE

It is clear that the Pentagon understood the medical hazards of uranium munitions well before Desert Storm. Numerous reports from the military acknowledged that uranium 238 can cause kidney damage, cancers of the lung and bone, nonmalignant lung disease, skin disorders, neurocognitive disorders, chromosomal damage, and birth defects.[19] In July 1990, an army contractor warned, "Aerosol DU exposures to soldiers on the battlefield could be significant with potential radiological and toxicological effects. Under combat conditions, the MEIs [most exposed individuals] are probably the ground troops that reenter a battlefield following the exchange of armor-piercing munitions, either on foot or motorized transport." However, no warnings about the dangers of uranium were given to the American or coalition forces deployed during Desert Storm, let alone to the surrounding civilian population.[20]

Finally, in their only statement of responsibility, the department of defense admitted in January 1998, "Our investigations into potential health hazards of depleted uranium point to serious deficiencies in what our troops understand about the health effects DU posed on the battlefield. . . . Combat troops or those carrying out support functions generally did not know that DU contaminated equipment, such as enemy vehicles struck by DU rounds, required special handling. . . . The failure to properly disseminate information to troops at all levels may have resulted in thousands of unnecessary exposures."

The military cover-up was partially explained in a statement made by Lieutenant Colonel M. V. Ziehmn of Los Alamos Lab in 1991: "There has been and continues to be a concern regarding the impact of DU on the environment. Therefore, if no one makes a case for the effectiveness of DU on the battlefield, DU rounds may become politically unacceptable and thus, be deleted from the arsenal. . . . I believe we should keep this sensitive issue at mind when after-action reports are written."[21] Because of the cover-up, support personnel were not told to check soldiers for uranium-contaminated shrapnel wounds, nor were they told to wear protective suits during their own contact with contaminated soldiers, equipment, or soil. In direct violation of the operative army and Nuclear Regulatory Commission regulations, there was no medical testing or follow-up of the soldiers who were either wounded by uranium or who may have inhaled or ingested uranium dust.

The symptoms of Gulf War syndrome are difficult to collate within a specific disease entity. Nevertheless, the complaints of the veterans are surprisingly similar in pattern to the various pathologies induced by uranium exposure as described by the U.S. military. Without definitive medical and epidemiological studies, it is at this stage impossible to know exactly what the future holds for the people exposed to uranium from the weapons used in the Gulf and the Balkans. Estimates must suffice. The president of the American Gulf

War Veterans estimates that 50,000 to 80,000 veterans are afflicted with Gulf War syndrome, 39,000 have already been dismissed from active service, and 2400 to 5000 have died. In Britain about 4000 returned servicemen have Gulf War syndrome and 160 have died.

What were the causes of death? Why the cover-up? Collation of the diagnoses would make plain the link between pathology and uranium.[22] If there is nothing to hide, why not publish the data?

And the intrigue continues.

The World Health Organization (WHO) has steadfastly resisted conducting studies on the health effects of exposure to uranium 238 following Desert Storm, Bosnia, and Kosovo. The reason for this refusal is an agreement forged in 1959 between the International Atomic Energy Agency (IAEA), which actively promotes nuclear power worldwide, and the WHO, stating that if one agency wishes to carry out a study that affects the work of the other, mutual agreement is required. The IAEA has never agreed to such studies.[23]

However, even Dr. Mike Repacholi, WHO's coordinator for occupational and environmental health, acknowledged that young children face a particular risk from depleted uranium: "Young children could receive greater depleted uranium exposure when playing within a conflict zone because of hand-to-mouth activity that could result in high depleted uranium ingestion from contaminated soil."[24] Medical reports from Iraq indicate that childhood malignancies have increased to seven times what they were and the incidence of congenital malformations has doubled in the areas where the bombing was the most intense.[25] International sanctions have worsened the medical situation. Pediatric physicians are unable to treat these patients because they have no access to chemotherapeutic agents, no antibiotics, and no radiotherapy.

CLEAN-UP

Back in the U.S. the concern about uranium has been so great that large, contaminated areas of soil were dredged, containerized, and removed during the clean-up of uranium 238 contamination at the Starmet plant in Concord, Massachusetts; at Sandia National Labs; and at Kirtland Air Force Base in New Mexico (where DU penetrators had been test fired). The army knows that it should have cleaned up its radioactive battlefield. In a report in July 1990, it warned, "Assuming U.S. regulatory standards and health physics practices are followed, it is likely that some form of remediable action will be required in a DU post-combat environment."[26] However, once the scale and cost of the clean-up were realized, the U.S. army Environmental Policy Institute informed U.S. policy makers that "no international law, treaty, regulation, or custom requires the United States to remediate the Persian Gulf War battlefields."[27] As Dan Fahey of the Military Toxics Project said, "The United States established a precedent during the Gulf War which permits an armed force to use depleted uranium weapons without warning civilian populations about contamination of the land."

PROLIFERATION OF URANIUM WEAPONS

The U.S. has either encouraged the construction of uranium weapons in, or exported uranium munitions to, sixteen other countries, including Australia, Britain, France, Greece, Turkey, Russia, Israel, Saudi Arabia, Kuwait, Bahrain, Egypt, Thailand, Taiwan, Pakistan, Japan, and New Zealand.[28] Other sources say that Iraq itself, Oman, Jordan, Abu Dhabi, and the United Arab Emirates may also have these weapons in their arsenals.

The UN subcommission on human rights has condemned uranium munitions as weapons of indiscriminate destruction. As such they fail:

- *The temporal test:* their effects continue after the war ends
- *The environmental test:* they pollute food, water, and soil
- *The humanness test:* they have effects beyond those necessary to achieve military objectives
- *The geographical test:* the particles can potentially travel to non-combatant countries

And the manufacture and testing of uranium weapons affects civilians, even if the weapons are not used.[29]

The navy has been testing their uranium munitions on a training range at Vieques, Puerto Rico. They admitted to firing 263 uranium bullets, of which they recovered only fifty-seven. (You may be sure these figures are underestimates.) The people in Vieques blame the navy for higher-than-normal cancer rates in that area. The navy denies that their activities have damaged anyone's health.[30]

Britain has been test firing uranium munitions in various locations, including Eskmeals Cumbria, Solway Firth, and Leelworth in Dorset. They were also test fired in Germany at Lower Saxony in the early seventies and at the upper Bavarian town of Schrobenhausen, where they were tested for seventeen years until 1996. And they were used by the U.S. in combat in Mogadishu in the early nineties, when a warning was issued to medics that they might encounter soldiers "who had unusually high levels of contact with depleted uranium."[31] Israel has almost certainly been using uranium armor plated tanks and uranium weapons against the Palestinians on the West Bank and in Gaza.[32]

BOSNIA AND KOSOVO

Two other "radioactive" wars have been fought in recent times, primarily by the United States and its NATO allies, in Bosnia and Kosovo.

As of this writing, an international furor is erupting, as soldiers and peacekeepers deployed in Kosovo are developing malignancies, including leukemia. Approximately 31,000 rounds of uranium ammunition were fired in Operation Allied Force—the seventy-eight day war in Kosovo in 1999—and over 10,800 uranium shells were fired in Bosnia in 1994–95, mainly around the city of Sarajevo,[33] where American A-10 Warthog planes fired uranium ammunition from its 30-mm Gatling guns at a rate of 3900 rounds per minute.

Initially, NATO officials were reluctant to give their member countries specific information about the use of uranium ammunitions in Kosovo or Bosnia, although in July 1999 NATO had warned those countries with armies and aid workers in the Balkans that there could be a "possible toxic threat" arising from the use of uranium weapons, and advised them to take preventive measures. (The head of the UN environment program criticized NATO for not being more forthcoming about where it had used the ammunition.)

Concern about uranium weapons began percolating among the NATO countries in December 2000, when Italy announced an investigation into thirty sick soldiers who had served in Bosnia in 1994–95 and Kosovo in 1999. Twelve have cancer and five to seven have died of leukemia. About 30,000 to 40,000 Italian soldiers served in the Balkans, and the Italian defense minister, Sergio Mattarella, said, "I must express my bitterness that the competent international organizations have waited until now to answer our request for information that is important to the Bosnian community and members of the military."

Spain will test all 32,000 of its soldiers stationed in the Balkans since 1992. Two confirmed cases of leukemia have been reported amongst the Spanish contingent. Apart from the leukemia deaths, an unknown number of soldiers who served as peacekeepers in the Balkans have an array of symptoms similar to the Gulf War syndrome, including hair loss and chronic fatigue.

Other countries concerned about the future health of their men include Kosovo, Denmark, France, Belgium, Portugal, and Holland. Ireland, Latvia, and Romania will also test their troops. Five Belgian soldiers have malignancies, as have two Portugese, two Finnish, and two Dutch soldiers. Portugal will send scientists to measure radiation levels in the affected areas. Russia is sending a team to check the zones where its people are deployed as international peacekeepers, and plans to test all military personnel before January 20, 2002.[34] Portugal and Italy have accused NATO of a cover-up.[35]

A former environment minister from Finland, Pekka Haavisto, who headed the UN inquiry into Kosovo, said after an inspection of the Kosovo battlefields, "We found some radiation in the middle of villages where children were playing. We were surprised to find this a year-and-a-half later [after the war]. People had collected ammunition shards as souvenirs and there were cows grazing in contaminated areas, which means the contaminated dust can get into the milk." Haavisto and his team discovered low-level beta radiation at eight of the eleven sites they sampled. They recommended that the contaminated areas be marked and fenced off, because, he said, the local people do not understand the material.

The eleven sites examined were chosen from 112 areas that NATO admitted it had targeted with radioactive munitions, although to

Haavisto's anger, NATO procrastinated, taking almost a year and a half before providing the necessary geographical data to the UN team. Haavisto also expressed concern that the use of controlled explosions to clear mines, unexploded munitions, and cluster bombs would scatter the radiation and toxic materials yet again.[36] After several weeks of European consternation and banner headlines in December 2000 and January 2001, NATO (which to a large degree is controlled by the U.S.) was finally forced to order a full investigation into the possible effects of depleted uranium. Apart from NATO, the fifteen-member European Union ordered its own inquiry.

After months of steadfast denial about the dangers, the British ministry of defense has asked for an independent study on the possible effects of uranium weapons. The House of Commons met on January 10, 2001, to decide whether to summon ministers to explain the government's policy.[37] Britain finally agreed that—along with the other NATO countries—it would conduct tests on its troops, 1400 of whom are said to be suffering from the Gulf War syndrome (469 of these have died; causes of death have yet to be made public).[38]

No doubt medical tests will benefit families and soldiers, but the doctors will be unable to ascertain whether or not these people have actually inhaled or ingested uranium particles. Blood tests will reveal only whether or not the patient has leukemia at the time of testing. X-ray scans of the body will determine whether there is an advanced cancer. Urine tests will reveal if the person is excreting uranium. If positive, the patient is at risk for developing a malignancy years later. Even if the urine shows no trace of uranium, it does not mean that uranium is not deposited in bone or in other organs. There is no way to determine whether or not there is uranium in the body, apart from placing the patient in a whole-body scanner, where a tiny specific spectrum of radiation can be detected, indicating the presence of uranium or its decay products. If the whole body scanner fails to detect traces of radioactivity, this still does not exclude damage. Uranium could have been in the body previously, mutated some regulatory genes, and then excreted. The patient could still go on to develop cancer.

Medically, one would not expect the symptoms of leukemia to arise for two to ten years following exposure. So the troops who were present at Operation Desert Storm and in the 1994–95 operation in Bosnia may well be developing leukemia, but it is early for soldiers exposed in 1999 to be manifesting malignancies. The incubation period for cancer may be shorter than we have been led to believe when exposed to internal uranium deposits. We have much yet to learn. Dr. Eric Wright, a British radiobiologist, said "I am not aware of any real radiobiology research in depleted uranium." [39]

That the soldiers and peacekeepers will be followed medically is appropriate. But there are tens of thousands—or indeed millions— of innocent civilians at risk in Saudi Arabia, Kuwait, Iraq, Bosnia, and Kosovo, as well as the other places around the globe where radioactive weapons have been aerosolized by testing.[40] These people must also be followed up and cared for. On January 17, 2001, the Swiss Federal Institute of Technology in Spiez also discovered traces of uranium 236 in the weapons used in Kosovo.[41] As Uranium 236 is made only in a nuclear reactor, these weapons are definitely contaminated with fission and transuranic products from nuclear fission. The U.S. military and department of energy must have known about this contamination. If there is uranium 236, almost certainly there will be plutonium, together with americium, neptunium, strontium 90, and cesium 137. This situation has extremely serious medical implications for the public health of the people who have been and will be contaminated.

Chapter Nine

THE LOCKHEED MARTIN PRESIDENCY AND THE STAR WARS ADMINISTRATION

We enter the twenty-first century locked in a mortal arms race with ourselves. Though the needs for more advanced weaponry are at best unclear, we proceed on the premise that "if we build it, they will come."

—M. W. Gruzy [1]

It's not right to have all those people in one building without a single watchdog. We're all in trouble . . . when the generals get that much power.

—Harry Truman on the Pentagon

EORGE W. BUSH ASCENDED to the presidency propelled by a Republican-dominated Supreme Court. His cabinet is composed mostly of corporate executives. Among them are Dick Cheney, former CEO of Halliburton Oil; Andrew Card, chief of staff—General Motors vice president; Paul O'Neill, treasury secretary—chair of Alcoa; Don Evans, secretary of commerce—former CEO of Tom Brown Inc. Oil Company; Donald Rumsfeld, secretary of defense—former CEO of G. W. Searle and General Instrument; Condoleezza Rice, national security advisor—Chevron board of directors. [2]

Forty million dollars, the largest amount ever donated, paid for the festivities at the inauguration, including 100,000 dollars each by 168 corporations and individuals. More than forty-five corporations wrote five-digit checks for events that honored Texans. A news release said this will be "the only inaugural ball where guests can have their picture made with a 2500-pound Brahmin bull or sitting in the cockpit of a fighter jet."

The donating corporations included Ford, General Motors, major Washington law firms, Marriott Corporation, Enron, Conoco, Hunt Oil, Chevron, ExxonMobil, Southern Energy Company, American Airlines, major-league baseball companies, Coca-Cola, Pepsi, Philip Morris, U.S. Tobacco, Abbott Drug Laboratories, Bristol-Meyers Squibb, Pfizer, General Electric, AT&T, and Alcoa. The financial security and investment industry contributed over 2 million dollars.

Barron's Online wrote:

> The capital is filling up with pin-striped, Chamber of Commerce types, attracted by what promises to be the most pro-business, anti-regulatory administration since Ronald Reagan reigned. Bush has packed CEOs and industrial lobbyists on transition teams that are advising his new Cabinet secretaries and agency heads on pressing policy issues and new hires. The advisory team for nominee Gale Norton's Department of Interior is jammed with representatives of energy, mining and paper companies.[3]

As Steve Weiss from the Center for Responsive Politics observed, "The general public, which cannot give these large contributions, does not get access to the next president or his advisors. Money buys you access to the president and those who are shaping the policies."[4]

The world's most powerful corporation, one that literally controls the fate of the earth, is Lockheed Martin. As we have seen, this company, together with its smaller military corporate colleagues, is involved in the production of almost every single weapon and Star Wars system that we have examined. They are up to their necks in corporate donations to both presidential candidates, and congressional and senate candidates on both sides of politics. (Weapons-industry political action committees favored the Republicans to Democrats by a 2 to 1 margin in contributions. Since 1997, the four top missile contractors spent 4 million dollars in PAC contributions and 3 million dollars in soft-money contributions. They also spent 18 million dollars in lobbying—which is tax deductible.)[5]

Lockheed Martin was the top defense contractor for the year 2000, receiving 15.1 billion dollars of taxpayer funds. Boeing was next with 12 billion dollars, followed by Raytheon at 6.3 billion dollars.[6] As we know, Lockheed Martin employees sit on the boards of right-wing think tanks such as the Heritage Foundation and the Center for Policy Studies. But now that their man is ensconced in the White House, they are in the position to control domestic and international policies directly. These corporations are determined to build a multilayered Star Wars system, and to build every weapon they can conceive, whether America needs it or not.

If Bush proceeds with the full throttle, all systems green-and-go Star Wars, instead of the modest, modified 60-billion-dollar Clinton system, it could cost the nation 240 billion dollars over the years of construction. And while many of the expenditures would technically come under the rubric of "defense," as Bush noted in a speech in September 1999 before the Citadel military college in Charleston, South Carolina, when discussing "the need to bolster our unrivalled power," "I know the best defense can be a strong and swift offense," effectively offering a rubric for development of any weapon whatsoever.[7] We are heading rapidly toward a state of global disaster. A belligerent and ill-informed president sits in the White House (despite his perceived change of status since September 11, 2001), controlled by his corporate staff intent on extracting as much American tax money as they possibly can to build ever more exotic and dangerous weapons. Bush administration appointees are among the most hawkish and extreme in recent memory, and an alarming number of Bush's staff people have direct ties to Lockheed Martin.

The quartet of Vice President Cheney, Defense Secretary Rumsfeld, Secretary of State Colin Powell, and National Security Advisor Condoleezza Rice are now the most powerful people in the world. Believing as they do that America is the heart of the universe, that U.S. militarism must be used to protect American global business interests, that Russia is not to be trusted, and that China may need provoking into a new cold war arms race, they have embarked America upon a dangerous four-year journey.

Vice President Cheney, "a defacto leader of a somewhat ceremonial president," to quote the *Guardian* journalist Martin Kettle,[8] now occupies a position of great influence, orchestrating as he does the appointment of cabinet members, and directing the activities of the new president. As noted earlier, the vice president's wife, Lynn Cheney, is a former board member of Lockheed Martin.

Donald Rumsfeld, a former Republican congressman, former NATO ambassador, and former secretary of defense, maintains intimate ties to missile-defense advocates and anti–arms control proponents, and he is closely associated with Frank Gaffney's Center for Security Policy, the de-facto nerve center of the Star Wars lobby, as noted in Chapter Four. Rumsfeld also serves on the board of Empower America, which ran pro–Star Wars radio ads against an incumbent Nevada Democrat during the 1998 congressional elections.

His contrived Rumsfeld report of 1998 warned that America would be threatened by North Korean missiles within the next five years, although CIA estimates had placed that projected time frame at ten to fifteen years (this assuming that peacekeeping efforts to unite the Koreas and bring North Korea into the community of nations have failed),[9] and although, as U.S. intelligence analyst Robert Walpole said in testimony before Congress, the least likely way a foreign nation would deliver a nuclear weapon of mass destruction is a ballistic missile because it has a "return address." (On September 11, 2001, U.S. civilian planes were used as effective ballistic missiles.)

Shortly before his appointment as secretary of defense, Rumsfeld headed another Pentagon commission, that unveiled a report in January 2001 warning that America could face a "space Pearl Harbor." It advocated tighter security for American space systems and called for the appointment of an undersecretary of defense for space, intelligence, and information. It also called for increased military spending, estimating the cost to replace obsolete military satellites in the next decade at 50 billion dollars. Belligerent in tone, it said that the president should "have an option to deploy weapons in space to deter threats to, and, if necessary, defend against attacks on U.S. interests."[10]

At his Senate confirmation hearings Rumsfeld referred to the Antiballistic Missile treaty, the cornerstone of nuclear arms control, as "ancient history." He also questioned whether the U.S. could maintain its nuclear arsenal without nuclear testing. This testimony was supported by Senator Jesse Helms, head of the Senate foreign relations committee, when he said "The United States is no longer bound by the ABM treaty—that treaty expired when our treaty partner the Soviet Union ceased to exist." Helms went on to say "Personally, I do not think that a new kind of ABM treaty can be negotiated with Russia that would permit the kind of defenses that America needs and must have." [11] Helms had already antagonized Russia calling the country "an active proliferator" because of the transfer of sensitive technology to hostile states like Iran and North Korea. Russia's foreign ministry accused Rumsfeld and (deputy secretary of defense) Wolfowitz of behaving like cold war warriors who were trapped in a time warp. [12]

Rumsfeld is a forceful player who generally has his way against the most powerful opponents. As Gerald Ford's secretary of defense, he outmaneuvered Secretary of State Kissinger when Kissinger was in Moscow in a last-minute attempt to coax a SALT II arms-control agreement from the Soviets. Behind Kissinger's back, Rumsfeld convened a meeting of the national security council backed by the Joint Chiefs of Staff. After two hours of discussion, the Pentagon withdrew its support for SALT II. Rumsfeld was traveling and did not even attend the meeting. Ford was furious and SALT II became obsolete for that presidency. Kissinger calls him the most ruthless man he has ever known.

Rumsfeld's former colleagues describe him variously as a highly organized, highly political personality, and a master bureaucrat. [13] His outreach and influence is pervasive. Since 1992, he has been a member of the board of directors of the Tribune Company which, it boasts in its publicity statements, with "television, radio, newspapers and the internet, reaches nearly 80 percent of American households every day." [14]

Colin Powell, the new secretary of state, is an interesting enigma. Basically a company man, he worked his way up through the ranks of the bureaucracy, eventually becoming the first African American to be appointed chairman of the Joint Chiefs of Staff and subsequently the first African American secretary of state. However, he failed to protest the overt discrimination against blacks in Florida's vote-rigging, which gave Bush the presidency.

As an advisor in Vietnam during 1962 and 1963, unlike some others, he did not protest the destruction of villages and the killing of civilians. He had an early role in the investigation of the My Lai massacre, which he effectively covered up until it was exposed by other, more courageous men. He was involved in the Iran-Contra scandal while working with Defense Secretary Casper Weinberger.

Although a cautious person at heart, he was deeply involved in—and indeed responsible for—several military operations that flouted the international rule of law. In 1989, as chairman of the Joint Chiefs of Staff, he oversaw the invasion of Panama when an estimated 300 civilians were killed and buried by the U.S. military in secret graves. Three thousand more were seriously injured. America instigated this operation to capture Manuel Noriega, a man put into office by the CIA but who had ceased to please the American elite.

In his book, *Just Cause*, Powell enunciated his doctrine: "Use all the force necessary and do not apologize for going in big if that's what it takes." [15] Powell believes that American military force should only be used in overwhelming strength to achieve well-defined strategic interests, meaning that peacekeeping operations are not acceptable. [16]

He became a hero of Desert Storm when he warned the Iraqi army that "first we are going to cut it off, and then we are going to kill it." [17] Did he know that uranium weapons were used in that operation? If so, did he understand the medical implications of that operation, so clearly described in the military literature? If he did, he violated the fundamental principles of war. Innocent civilians are now threatened for the rest of time with malignancies and a damaged gene pool.

Powell describes Russia and China as countries that the U.S. would attempt to work with "not as potential enemies or adversaries, but not yet as strategic partners." By buying into this philosophy, he leaves the door open for more radical members of the administration to have their way. [18]

During his confirmation hearings, Powell said that the Bush administration would move full-speed ahead with a nationwide missile defense, [19] arguing that it was essential to build a "complete strategic framework" including defensive as well as offensive weapons. Taking the Rumsfeld line on the ABM treaty, he said "The framework that treaty was designed for was a framework that really isn't relevant now. We are moving forward with the capacity to develop a missile defense system, and the only way we can eventually move forward is to see the ABM treaty modified or eliminated or changed in some rather fundamental way." [20]

When Senators Joseph Biden and Lincoln Chafee said that the allies were skeptical about the NMD project, he brushed aside their concerns. "When people see something new come along they are terrified, but if it is the right thing to do, you do it anyway. . . . In the end of the day, it will benefit the world," he said.[21] Powell, however, says that if it was necessary to walk out of the ABM treaty, he would consult with the Russians and the allies. And in 1998 he joined the other Joint Chiefs of Staff by supporting ratification of the CTBT.[22]

Condoleezza Rice is at heart a right-wing ideologue who is dismissive of other countries. While having no direct Lockheed Martin connections, she fits in well with the White House ideology. She said that the trouble with Israel is that it is "so small," and that "Cuba is the road kill of history." [23] Strongly opposing the Comprehensive Test Ban Treaty, she wrote in *Foreign Affairs:*

> Since 1992, the United States has refrained unilaterally from testing nuclear weapons. It is an example to the rest of the world, yet does not tie its own hands "in perpetuity" if testing becomes necessary again. But in pursuit of a "norm" against the acquisition of nuclear weapons, the United States signed a treaty that was not verifiable, did not deal with the threat of the development of nuclear weapons by rogue states, and threatened the reliability of the nuclear stockpile. Legitimate congressional concerns about the substance of the treaty were ignored during negotiations.[24]

Other appointees mirror the corporate presidency:

As noted, Bruce Jackson, vice president of corporate strategy and development of Lockheed Martin, volunteered to be the overall chairman of the Bush foreign policy platform committee at the Republican convention, and it was he who wrote the Republican party's foreign policy platform.

Stephen J. Hadley, a partner in the Washington-based law firm Shea & Gardner, which represents Lockheed Martin, has been appointed deputy director of the National Security Council, working in the White House as Condoleezza Rice's chief deputy. An enthusiastic advocate of Star Wars, he is secretary of the committee to expand NATO and was also a member of the National Security Council staff of President Bush the first. Hadley also belongs to an eight-member foreign policy team formed during the Bush campaign, nicknamed the "Vulcans" after a statue representing the Roman god of fire and metalwork, commemorating the steel-making history in Birmingham, Alabama, Condoleezza Rice's hometown. Composed mostly of hawks, the group includes Rice and Hadley, and also Richard Armitage, Reagan's former assistant secretary of defense; Robert Blackwill, a member of Bush the first's National Security Council; Dov Zakheim, Reagan's former undersecretary of defense; Robert Zoellick, former undersecretary of defense for Bush; and Richard Perle, a man nicknamed "the prince of darkness" by his Pentagon colleagues during the Reagan administration when he was undersecretary of defense.[25, 26]

Another who is directing the Bush presidency toward a new cold war stance is Paul Wolfowitz, who headed the Paul Nitze Center for International Studies. Wolfowitz epitomizes the neoconservative wing of the Republican party cold war warriors. They still hate Russia, but were looking to China to fill the role of a new American threat on a global scale until terrorist activity recently took center stage.

Wolfowitz can take credit for the recent expansion of NATO; he authored a secret memorandum for the Pentagon, which leaked to the *New York Times* in 1992, warning that Yeltsin's Russia posed a grave potential threat to U.S. interests, and he advocated an all-out U.S.-led NATO war against Russia if it threatened the security of the newly independent Baltic republics. Although Russia did no such thing, Wolfowitz was installed as a neoconservative hero, and Clinton, ever compliant, expanded NATO into Czechoslovakia, Poland, and Hungary, much to Russia's discomfort and rage. (Now that the cold war is over, NATO has no tangible use, yet it continues to exist and is getting bigger. If Russia had been invited to become part of the NATO alliance, the act would have defused any cold war tensions that remained in Europe.) Wolfowitz and his accolytes believe that America must maintain its position as global superpower; no regional powers, such as China or Russia, must be allowed to develop, and American values and self-interests must reign supreme.

Richard Perle, who said on March 15, 1983, the fact that "nuclear winter that would wipe out all life on earth . . . is all the more reason to continue President Reagan's weapons buildup," is a friend of Wolfowitz. Perle is a hard-line ally of Israel, believing that there is no difference between the interests of the two countries. In 1996 he was simultaneously adviser to Dole's presidential bid and to Netanyahu's election campaign in Israel. During the Reagan days he often accused Secretary of State George Shultz of being too soft on Cuba, the Chinese, North Koreans, the Soviets, and Arabs.

Robert Zoellick, an ally of Wolfowitz and Perle, was White House deputy chief of staff to Bush the first. He supports NATO enlargement, uncritically supports Israel, and he regards Russia as an inherent adversary, not to be trusted or treated as a friend.[27]

John Bolton, undersecretary of state for arms control, nonproliferation, and international security is described by Senator Jesse Helms as "one of the best and wisest" nominations that Bush has made for a "senior foreign policy position." "Bolton is the kind of man with whom I would want to stand at Armageddon, for what the Bible describes as the final battle between good and evil in this world," Helms said at an American Enterprise Institute event. At Bolton's Senate confirmation hearing Helms said "John, I want you to take that ABM treaty and dump it in the same place we dumped our ABM cosigner, the Soviet Union—on the ash heap of history."

Bolton believes that the CTBT is dead, that Taiwan should have official diplomatic recognition separate from China, that the U.S. should stop paying dues to the United Nations, and that the U.S. should be indifferent to whether it ever has "normal" diplomatic relations with North Korea. With Bolton in control, not only will the ABM and CTB treaties be imperiled, but so will all the other arms control treaties, each of which took years to negotiate.[28]

Although he is currently enjoying record-breaking approval ratings in America, among the other 95 percent of the world's population there is a global fear of George W. Bush and his appointees:

> To describe Star Wars as criminally insane is to slander reputable psychopaths. It is inspired by the delusion that America can achieve absolute dominance, that she can fight without taking casualties, forget about deterrence and detonate nuclear weapons secure in the knowledge that her defensive missiles will shoot down any warheads launched in retaliation.
>
> —Nick Cohen, London *Observer*[29]

> The richer, stronger and more globally accountable America becomes, the more self-centered its politics grows. The end of the cold war should have brought great psychological dividends. Generous in global victory, free of paranoia and with wealth beyond imagining, here at last was its chance to become what it has always believed itself to be—the brave, the beautiful, the free and so on. . . . The high-flown rhetoric of the conventions is echoed in every high school valedictory speech, in every rotary and church, pledging allegiance to a constitution that has lost any vision of society beyond the pursuit of happiness. God's chosen people, uniquely blessed, nurture a self-image almost as deranged in its profound self-delusion as the old Soviet Union. The most advanced, knowledgeable, educated, psychoanalyzed, therapized nation on earth knows nothing of itself, irony-free and blind to the world around it.
>
> —Polly Toynbee, *The Guardian*[30]

Mikhail Gorbachev, the Soviet president who, more than any person on earth, helped to bring the cold war to an end, wrote a letter to

President Bush just after the Supreme Court made him president. He wrote:

> I hope, Mr. Bush, as the new American president, that you will give up any illusion that the twenty-first century can, or even should be the "American Century." Globalization is a given—but "American globalization" would be a mistake. . . . For ten years, U.S. foreign policy has been formulated as if it were the policy of a victor in war, the cold war. But at the highest reaches of U.S. policy making no one has grasped the fact that this could not be the basis for formulating post–cold war policy—from the standpoint of the old world, the post–cold war period ushered in hopes that are now fading. Over the past decade, the United States continued to operate along an ideological track identical to the one followed during the cold war . . . the expansion of NATO eastward, the handling of the Yugoslav crisis, the theory and practice of U.S. rearmament, including the utterly extravagant national missile defense system, which is based on the bizarre notion of "rogue states." . . . Isn't it amazing that disarmament moved further during the last phase of the cold war than during the period after its end? [31]

Russia is frightened of Star Wars. Because of the poor state of its weapons, Russia relies on a launch-on-warning policy. All 111 of Russia's operating satellites are on the brink of collapse, more than 70 percent are past their initial service lives, and 70 percent of them have military functions. [32] The deteriorating condition of the satellites and early-warning radars increases the possibility of false signals, and these conditions are compounded by the erosion of the Russian command and control system, possibly allowing a "rogue" commander to take control. We cannot assume that Russia has its weapons under strict control. The Bush people should realize that it is extremely unwise to threaten a wounded or inadequate nation, for they may respond in an unpredictable fashion.

In November 2000 Putin proposed a massive cut in the level of strategic weapons to 1000 or less, saying "there should be no pause in nuclear disarmament." He said a 1500 level could be reached by 2008, but only on the condition that the U.S. does not proceed with missile defense. Russia cannot afford its annual spending of 5.1 billion dollars on defense (compared with the U.S. expenditure of 310 billion dollars). To this end, Putin also approved a military reform program to cut his three million military personnel by 600,000.[33]

Because both sides recognized the inherent danger in the ongoing launch-on-warning posture, on December 16, 2000, Secretary of State Madeleine Albright and Russian Foreign Minister Igor Ivanov signed an agreement to strengthen cooperation on preventing accidental missile launches on both sides by expanding an early-warning center where both sides can exchange information.[34] However, the agreement—which still stands—will not cover missiles launched in combat, and either government can withhold advance information of certain space flights for national security reasons.[35]

Still, as a direct result of the U.S. election, Russia has changed its posture. Putin warned that the deployment of a national missile defense shield and NATO's continued expansion into Eastern Europe could "irreparably damage" global stability and the architecture of international relations.[36]

Thus, in January 2001, just after Bush was inaugurated, the Kremlin shelved its plans for radical cuts in its military structures. Soon thereafter Russia announced that it would double its defense spending over the next ten years if Washington decided to go ahead with its missile defense shield.[37]

During the same week, however, Putin wrote a letter to President Bush proposing broader Russian-American cooperation, and setting out the major issues on which he believes the two countries can cooperate. "When Russia and the U.S. act jointly or on parallel tracks, decisions meeting the interests of peace and international stability may be reached," he said, and affirmed that Russia wants warm relations with the United States. But Bush signaled that he will pay even less attention to Russian foreign policy concerns than did Clinton, who ignored Russia's protests about the expansion of NATO and the war against Yugoslavia.[38] However, at the November 2001 Crawford Ranch meeting in Texas between Bush and Putin, there was a post–September 11 magnanimity that pervaded the presidents' relationship, with Bush offering to reduce the U.S. strategic nuclear weapons arsenal down to between 1700 and 2200 within the next ten years. Putin did not give an immediate response.

Moscow analysts see Cheney, Rumsfeld, Powell, and Rice as hawks from a bygone era. "These are people who see themselves as victors of the cold war," according to Alexander Golts, a military commentator for the news magazine *Itogi.* "The Kremlin and the generals are flattered by that, because it reminds them of the days of the USSR when they were a great power. But the new American administration is making a very strong and negative impact on our military."[39]

Concerned about the missile shield, China and Russia hastily convened a meeting on January 13, 2001, at which they worked on a treaty to proclaim their friendship, while privately reassuring the U.S. that they still seek closer ties with them. Jonathon Pollack, chairman of the strategic research department at the Naval War College, says the treaty is a significant move in Sino-Russian ties and as such reflects Beijing's and Moscow's deep concerns about Bush and his people. James Mulvenon, a security expert at the Rand Corporation, echoed these sentiments: "The United States, through incompetence and ham-handed policy making, has effectively driven China and Russia together. . . . NMD is a perfect example. By not having a coordinated policy vis-à-vis the Europeans and the Russians, we let the Chinese play them off against us. There is an enormous resonance in both countries for blaming problems on American hegemony, and we have done nothing to drive a wedge between them.[40, 41]

The pact will almost certainly add fuel to the Wolfowitz clan stance. It will now be easy to convince the American people that China and Russia threaten the very existence of America with their newfound friendship and their combined nuclear arsenals. This dynamic will then reinforce exactly what the neoconservatives have been saying, and Star Wars will be legitimized.

CHINA AND THE BUSH ADMINISTRATION

What is China's response to Bush and Star Wars, apart from the Sino-Russian treaty, which at this stage is vague in its specific objectives?

China's view of America has taken a radical turn since 1998, when in its second white paper on national defense, it mentioned the United States ten times, each in a positive fashion. In September

2000, its third white paper mentions the U.S. thirteen times—all save two of the references are negative. China's attitude has been soured by events in recent years, including the expansion of NATO, the strengthening of the U.S.-Japan military relationship, a congressional report charging Chinese nationalists with two decades of espionage in the U.S., NMD, and the allied bombing of the Chinese embassy in Yugoslavia, which killed three of their journalists.[42] The bombing prompted serious internal debate about whether China should accelerate its military spending. However, the central committee decided to reaffirm their former emphasis on economic development.

American belligerence toward China is becoming uncomfortable. On a visit to Australia in July 2000, former secretary of defense William Cohen, having just left China, urged Australia to increase its military spending to ensure that its forces could support the U.S. if there were to be a war with China over Taiwan. Republican Tom DeLay, House majority whip, recently boasted of how he confronted the Chinese ambassador on *Meet the Press*. He grabbed the ambassador's hand as if to shake it, but instead squeezed it hard, yanked the ambassador close to him, and warned him not to underestimate the resolve of the American people. The ambassador, humiliated, left immediately.[43]

China is not a military threat to America. With a population of over 1.2 billion and a rapidly changing political arena moving from authoritarian communism to some form of free-enterprise capitalism, China's leaders have much to occupy their minds while providing food, education, and a decent standard of living for their people. The last thing that China needs is to divert money and attention to a new nuclear or conventional arms race in their region. But that is the dynamic that Bush is about to set up. If Congress approves the full Star Wars scenario, China will be forced to build more ballistic missiles to overcome America's missile defense. In fact, as noted previously, the U.S. intelligence agencies' report, "Foreign Responses to U.S. National Missile Defense Deployment," predicted just this.

But there is more at stake. The U.S. is about to deploy theater missile defense systems in Japan, South Korea, and possibly Taiwan, because TMD is legitimate under the ABM treaty. China will then be forced to build up her intermediate-range nuclear missile forces to "overload" the TMD system. Theoretically, these missiles could hit targets in India, an old enemy of China. The pro-nuclear regime in India will react badly to these developments and will be goaded into an ongoing nuclear arms race with China. Then what will nuclear Pakistan do? It will be pushed into an ongoing nuclear arms race against India, siding with its ally, China.[44]

However, since the American attack on Afghanistan, there is huge dissent in the streets of Pakistan amongst the Muslim fundamentalists who support the Taliban and Osama Bin Laden. These people also have a significant presence within the Pakistani military. There is a distinct prospect that if there were a civil war in Pakistan, they could gain the upper hand in the military and thereby control the twenty to thirty nuclear weapons that Pakistan has built over the past decade. This poses a terrifying prospect—arch enemies of a nuclear-armed India, themselves armed with nuclear weapons.

There is also Japan, a country with the third largest military in the world, with the world's most advanced technological base, a country with an aggressive past and huge stockpiles of pure plutonium, on the cusp of nuclearization. With a week's notice, Japan could construct nuclear weapons if it so decided. (Japan maintains the third largest military in the world because it can legally spend only 1 percent of its GNP on weapons, but it has a huge GNP.) China is well aware of these possibilities, and Japan is an old enemy of China. The nuclearization of Japan could then trigger a nuclear arms race between South Korea and Japan, two countries with deep enmities.

Taiwan is officially a part of China since Nixon's visit in the early seventies. However, animosity between China and Taiwan remains, and right-wing Republicans are enthusiastically adding fuel to this smoldering fire. In September 2000 the U.S. signed a 1.3 billion dollar arms deal with Taiwan, including the sale of 200 Amraam missiles, not to be made available unless China introduces a similar weapons system, an arrangement that is meant to signify America's pledge not to introduce new offensive military capacities into Asia.[45] But on April 1, 2001, an international incident induced a change in the Chinese-American relationship. A Chinese pilot collided with a U.S. spy plane off the coast of China, forcing the U.S. plane to land on Hainan, a Chinese island. The Chinese were furious that America was spying just off their coast and the U.S. was furious because the Chinese held the twenty-four-member crew for eleven days.

Despite the provocation and damage to U.S.-Chinese relations caused by this incident, the flights of the spy planes must continue, according to Secretary Rumsfeld.[46] This episode sharply increased tensions just before the Bush administration was to decide whether to send more military equipment to Taiwan. China was particularly concerned that Taiwan not obtain Aegis ships, which are an integral component of a theater missile defense system. Eventually, on April 24, 2001, the Bush administration announced that it would sell twelve P-3 Orion planes to enable Taiwan to patrol at sea and hunt for submarines, four Kidd-class destroyers that carry powerful sonar equipment to hunt for submarines and sub-hunting helicopters, and eight new diesel subs, to be made in Germany and the Netherlands. (However, these countries have announced their reluctance to assist the U.S. arming of Taiwan.) The Chinese find the submarines to be particularly provocative. For the moment, Bush has postponed the decision to equip Taiwan with Aegis ships and Patriot PAC-3 anti-missile batteries.

To make matters worse, two days after this decision was announced, President Bush declared that the United States would do "whatever it takes" to help Taiwan defend itself, including the use of military force. This statement was a distinct departure from the long-standing policy of American strategic ambiguity toward Taiwan—expressing a strong interest in that country's security while avoiding an outright promise to go to war in its defense.[47] Although Bush tried to backpedal in a subsequent interview, his statement was consistent with the hard-line Republican policy on China, whose platform states that "America will help Taiwan defend itself." Deputy Secretary of Defense Paul Wolfowitz and Deputy Secretary of State Richard Armitage have called for the strategic ambiguity to be abandoned completely.[48] Other nations were shocked and incensed about this change in strategy. Critical editorials abounded in the European and Australian press.

The Taiwanese themselves admit that they are close to China economically, with businesses on both sides involved in huge economic
deals. China has evolved into Taiwan's second-largest market for
trade and investment; 40 percent of Taiwan's foreign investment is in
China. Students cross the Taiwanese straights to go to Chinese medical schools and universities. It is the Taiwan military, like the United
States military, that is pushing for these weapons and influencing
foreign policy.[49]

As Taiwan becomes more militarized, China may conclude that
the U.S. is restoring a mutual defense pact with Taiwan, an agreement that fell by the wayside in 1979 when Washington normalized
diplomatic relations with Beijing and adopted a "one-China" policy,
recognizing the Chinese government as legitimate for Taiwan. With
TMD systems deployed in Japan, South Korea, Taiwan, and possibly
Australia, a compliant and peaceful U.S. ally, China will begin to feel
encircled by military hostility. (As an aside, TMD systems do not
pose as much of a threat to Russia as they do to China. Russia's
ICBMs are located deep within their continental interior, so interceptor rockets launched from coastal waters, as currently proposed, will
not achieve the velocity necessary to take out Russian missiles in
their boost phase.)

China is the Pentagon's premier villain, according to a study conducted by the Naval War College in Newport, Rhode Island, called
"Asia 2025." Since the fall of the Soviet Union, the major Pentagon
war games increasingly take place in Asia. According to the report,
the effort now is for the U.S. to "manage the rise of China as a great
power," and the Pentagon is concentrating on expanding the naval,
air, and space power in the Pacific region. They see China as "a force
for instability and a constant competitor."

The Pentagon is concerned with the emergence of China as the
greatest regional threat to U.S. interests, the lack of forward operating bases in Southeast Asia and South Asia if the U.S. is to remain a
key player in these regions, the emerging strategic potential of India,
and the need-at-all-costs to prevent a China-India alliance. They en-
vision five possible scenarios where China could be a threat, including an "unstable China" scenario, a "strong China," a "new South
Asian order," where India could either be an ally or opponent of

China, an "Asia realigns" scenario, or "the new Sino-Indian condominium" scenario.

There is a major conflict in the U.S. between engagement and containment of China. Instead of military confrontation, Clinton's policy was to engage China so that U.S. business interests could exploit the China market. He encouraged China's entry into the World Trade Organization so that it would end its protectionist trade policies, allowing U.S. corporations full access to Chinese resources. The Pentagon was unhappy with this approach, which strengthened China both economically and strategically. As Walden Bello says, the Asia 2025 study "speaks volumes about the Pentagon's grim determination to counter any significant threat to U.S. strategic hegemony in Asia.[50]

Another Pentagon study, "The 2001 Quadrennial Defense Review," also concentrates on China. While it continues to reiterate the U.S. policy of maintaining the ability to fight two conventional wars simultaneously, it states that the threat from Iraq and North Korea are fading (negating the Rumsfeld theory that legitimizes Star Wars). The review emphasizes the so-called China threat, stating that China should be the new focus of the U.S. military force structure, including its troop deployments, weapons procurement, research, and development. This policy ensures ever-increasing funding for the Pentagon's budget.

But China uses its Peoples Liberation Army not for international purposes, but to alleviate domestic problems such as floods and fires, to quell internal disputes, such as Xinjiang and Tibet, and for border disputes. Land forces are currently being reduced by hundreds of thousands. Even if Taiwan declares independence and America attempts to back Taiwan in its move, resulting in armed conflict, China has virtually no amphibious forces able to attack Taiwan.[51] It would prefer to spend its resources caring for the needs of its 1.3 billion people, and it has little interest in weapons construction. The risk of killing fellow Chinese and of provoking economic isolation and military failure would most likely result in China's peaceful wooing of Taiwan instead. As Dr. Nicholas Berry, senior analyst at the Center for Defense information, writes, "Americans who see China as the new imperialistic threat need to review the historical record. Unless history is meaningless as a predictor of events, China will not seek an

empire. As long as China's periphery is secure and no country is prepared to attack it, the PLA will carry out its internal and defensive
tasks, including putting pressure on Taiwan not to leave the fold." [52]

In warning the Bush administration not to include Taiwan in any
missile defense system, China urged the U.S. to desist from any arms
sales to that country. "If the United States is bent on its plan to include Taiwan in its TMD system, it will constitute a wanton interference and threat to Chinese sovereignty and security," it said, meaning
that if forced to by U.S. policy, it will arm itself appropriately to fight
a militarily aggressive Taiwan. This statement was issued only hours
after Colin Powell opined that China should not now be regarded as a
"strategic partner" as it had been during the Clinton administration. [53]

The air force is, at this moment, upgrading its bases in Guam and
on Wake Island in the Pacific to handle more B-1 and B-2 bombers.
They are repositioning cruise missiles in Guam, and American TMD
is being widely promoted throughout the region. The navy is expected to nearly double its presence in the Pacific within the next
few years. The U.S. has assigned over 230,000 military personnel, including the Pacific fleet, to the region. [54] Leaked internal documents
dated January 29, 1998, show that the U.S. naval security group command entered into a host-nation partnership at the joint-defense facility at Pine Gap in Australia, where they are currently monitoring
movements and telecommunications traffic of warships and naval
vessels from Pakistan, India, Indonesia, China, and North Korea.
China, the dominant country in the South China Sea, the Taiwan
Strait, and the Sea of Japan, is obviously of most interest to the U.S.
and intelligence officials. [55]

AMERICAN GLOBAL IMPERIALISM

Charmers Johnson, in a new book, *Blowback: The Costs and Consequences of the American Empire*, argues that instead of demobilizing
at the end of the cold war, "the U.S. imprudently committed itself to
maintaining a global empire." He believes that it is time to discuss
how the cold war helped to conceal an American imperial project,
and that America should by rights remove itself from South Korea

and from its military bases in Japan, while unilaterally drastically cutting its nuclear forces and declaring a no-first-use policy.

American historian Paul Kennedy calls U.S. global dominance "imperial overreach" and says that the maps of major U.S. force deployments around the world "look extraordinarily similar to the chain of fleet bases and garrisons possessed by that former great power, Great Britain, at the end of its strategic overreach.[56]

The British today are in a pickle.

Tony Blair worked well with Clinton, but he will be under particular pressure to cooperate with his new-look American allies, even while knowing that if he allows the Fylingdale radar station on the North York Moors National Park to be expanded for Star Wars, he will have a civil uprising on his hands.

Fylingdale neighbors realize that they will become one of the targets of America's mad plans. As retired geologist Peter Woods said, "If this installation became a target for hostile action, it would be like William the Conqueror all over again, who starved to death half the local population a millenium ago," on the North York Moors.

"Imagine us going to you and asking to put up a radar station in the middle of Yosemite National Park to protect Britain," Woods added. "Do you think the United States would just say, okay?"[57]

If Blair permits the Fylingdale station upgrade, plus another at Menwith Hill, he will be at odds with his European colleagues, and many within his own party. Since the summer of 2000, two white globes have been installed at Fylingdale, supposedly for tracking satellites.[58]

Inevitably these stations will be aggressively picketed by the Campaign for Nuclear Disarmament, Greenpeace, and the North Yorkshire branch of the Women's Institute, who are deeply concerned about the despoilation of the countryside. It will be Greenham Common all over again.*

France is an open opponent of NMD. During Bush's inauguration,

---

* Thousands of women set up camp at Greenham Common and staged protests during the eighties against the deployment of American cruise missiles on the Common; they prevailed and the missiles were removed.

French Defense Minister Alain Richard flew to Moscow for talks about the proposed U.S. NMD plan which Bush said would "provide protection for America's allies." [59]

French analyst Camille Grand said the NMD could stand for "no more disarmament." And French Foreign Minister Hubert Vedrine said that it is "not very serious" to think that states such as North Korea, Iran, Libya, or Iraq could threaten the world's only super-power, calling these threats microscopic or theoretical.[60]

According to Hugo Young of the *Guardian*, "A quiet turmoil of alarm has gripped the Foreign Office and the Ministry of Defense for months," in Britain. "They now face a Washington being peopled by voices that make a different analysis: scornful of Russia, arrogant about China, intolerant of European sensitivities, overwhelmingly impressed by the case for defending U.S. territory—and confident that the practical failure of NMD so far, like the untested capabilities of the boost-phase project, are mere blips on the relentless American path toward technological mastery."

If Blair decides to support NMD, Young says, it will create the deepest rupture with continental Europe.[61]

Greenland, a Danish protectorate, where another radar station at Thule will need upgrading, has said that the unproven concept of NMD will sow the seeds of global instability and pitch the country unwillingly into the center of a new cold war. The Thule station is also presently part of the U.S. early-warning system.[62]

Almost all European countries are adamantly opposed to any form of Star Wars, and are deeply concerned about the direction in which this new president is taking the world.

Meanwhile, Europe is uncomfortable about the way NATO is structured. During the Kosovo war, the Europeans had little say about how that conflict was conducted—America had sole access to most of the space-based information flow, deciding how and when the seventy-eight day operation would proceed.

Pre-September 11 Europe was fed up with its sycophantic position in relation to the U.S., which regularly ignored the United Nations and which intervened unilaterally in the Sudan, Afghanistan, and

Iraq without consulting its closest allies. When it did intervene with other nations, it took a military stand that allowed for no American casualties, which made it more a hindrance than a help. As the *Guardian* editorial said, *"Saving Private Ryan* has become the leitmotif of the whole operation."[63]

September 11 changed many of these dynamics. The whole world was appalled by the attacks upon America and a new international spirit of cooperation brought most nations of the world together to support America in its tragedy and time of need. Furthermore, new alliances were quickly formed to support the war in Afghanistan, and although much of the war was fought from the air causing many thousands of civilian casualties, eventually American troops were brought in at the end for "mopping up" operations.

Consequently, in November 2001, Europe decided to set up its own military and peacekeeping force, pledging 60,000 troops and its own equipment by 2003. The first European military initiative since the end of the cold war, it will involve additional military spending and will give the Europeans the ability to operate without the United States.

The United States is nervous that this EU (European Union) peacekeeping force may surpass and ultimately become more important than NATO—a move that Washington would strongly oppose.[64] Former secretary of defense William Cohen warned, "There will be no EU caucus in NATO. . . . If . . . they try to or are desirous of a separate operational planning capability, separate and distinct from NATO itself, then that is going to weaken ties between the U.S. and NATO and NATO and the EU."[65]

The Pentagon is not easily going to forego its European footing. On December 1, 2000, it released the strategy report for Europe and NATO, titled "Strengthening Transatlantic Security," which states that the U.S. will continue its reliance on deterrence as a cornerstone of security while maintaining a commitment to American nuclear forces in Europe. It calls for NATO enlargement, saying that "the U.S. military presence in Europe plays a critical role in protecting our economic interests."

It also states that, "overall the United States has embarked on its largest sustained increase in defense spending in fifteen years" and that they are planning the "execution of joint and multinational military operations in NBC (nuclear, biological, and chemical) environments. . . ." Referring to Russia, the report adds, "The transatlantic community cannot be truly secure if its enormous nuclear-armed neighbor, with its rich human and natural resources, withdraws behind a new curtain of hostility and authoritarian rule or collapses economically." (This provocative statement seems to go counter to President Putin's numerous conciliatory overtures to the United States and his overtures to rapidly reduce bilaterally the strategic arsenals.)

BUSINESS ARE US

The world has gone backward since 1987, when Reagan and Gorbachev sat in an intimate sitting room in a house in Reykjavik, Iceland, and almost agreed to eliminate nuclear weapons between the superpowers, an agreement that failed when Reagan refused to forgo his Star Wars project.

General Henry Shelton, the chairman of the Joint Chiefs of Staff, told Congress in September 2000 that the services would need significant increases in spending in the coming years, suggesting that this could consume a large part of the current budget surplus.[66] He endorsed a study from the congressional budget office that called for an increase in spending on new weapons from 60 billion dollars to 90 billion dollars annually. Bush has already pledged to spend 45 billion dollars more on the military over the next ten years, plus at least another 70 billion dollars on Star Wars.[67]

However, since the September 11, 2001 attack, the Pentagon and military-industrial complex have cynically used these terrible events to capitalize upon the trauma and despair of the American people and the Congress. Within days, Congress appropriated a 60-billion-dollar emergency spending package for reconstruction and combating terrorism. The greatest beneficiaries will be weapons manufacturers such as Raytheon and Lockheed Martin. Interestingly, among the very few companies that showed increased stock prices the week the market reopened on September 17 were Raytheon, up 37 percent, Alliant Tech Systems, up 23.5 percent, and Northrop Gromman, up 21.2 percent.

Star Wars corporations used this opportunity to push their wares on Capitol Hill with homilies such a "just because you have insurance against theft doesn't mean you shouldn't buy fire insurance." The democrats backed off their fight against NMD tests or other actions that would violate the ABM treaty in the wake of September 11. So compliant has the Congress become that Christopher Hellman from the Center for Defense Information suggested that military spending for 2002 could reach 375 billion dollars, a 66-billion-dollar increase over 2001, and some right-wing analysts such as Loren Thompson of the Lexington Institute suggested Congress may now be willing to push the Pentagon budget to 400 billion dollars per year, or more. The NMD program stands to benefit the most, followed by the scandal-plagued V22 Osprey aircraft made in Republican Representative Kurt Weldon's district in Pennsylvania, Lockheed Martin's F22 pushed by the Texas and Georgia delegations, Northrop Grumman's B2 pushed by Democratic Representative Norm Dicks from Washington and Republican Representative Randy "Duke" Cunningham from California at more than 2 billion dollars per plane. In the wake of the September 11 attacks the Bush administration is to accelerate weapons sales in the Middle East and South Asia, including Lockheed Martin F-16s to Oman and the United Arab Emirates, and other weapons systems to Egypt and Pakistan.[68, 69]

Under the banner *Business Are Us*, the Pentagon hosts a paper on their web site proclaiming that they are America's largest company, the next being Exxon with a budget of 165 billion dollars. With 5.1 million, the Pentagon is the nation's largest employer. It maintains 600 fixed facilities nationwide, with more than 40,000 properties and 18 million acres of land. It stations employees in 130 countries out of a total 178 of the world.[70] Its global presence is ubiquitous.

America is a nation that spends only six cents out of every dollar on educating its children and four cents on health care for every fifty cents it spends on the military-industrial complex.[71] Overall, the Pentagon's 310 billion dollars per year dwarfs the 44.5 billion dollars for the education department and 20.3 billion dollars for the National Institutes of Health.

Globally the annual military expenditure stands at 780 billion dollars. The total amount required to provide global health care, eliminate starvation and malnutrition, provide clean water and shelter for all, remove land mines, eliminate nuclear weapons, stop deforestation, prevent global warming, ozone depletion and acid rain, retire the paralyzing debt of developing nations, prevent soil erosion, produce safe, clean energy, stop overpopulation, and eliminate illiteracy is only one third that amount—237.5 billion dollars.[72]

In his farewell speech in January 1961, President Eisenhower warned, "In the councils of government, we must guard against the acquisition of unwarranted influence, whether sought or unsought, by the military-industrial complex. The potential for the disastrous rise of misplaced power exists and will persist. We must never let the weight of this combination endanger our liberties or democratic process."

This book illustrates in detail that these prophetic predictions have come to pass. We need to put aside our need for superiority over others, our need to be militarily powerful. America has excellent skills at conflict resolution. These must be deployed.

The Pentagon needs to be virtually dismantled. Amalgamating with the United Nations, its military expertise needs to be used quietly and efficiently for peacekeeping operations around the world. (Currently there are sixty-eight low-intensity wars in the world demanding attention.)[73] After the September 11 terrorist attack on the United States there was much discussion about what the response should be. I carefully advocated during my U.S. lecture tour over the next two weeks that the international community should work cooperatively together, including all the intelligence organizations— MI5, MI6, Mossad, the FBI, CIA, NSA—to identify, locate, and capture these international terrorists and bring them to trial before an international court of justice, as were their predecessors, the Nazis.

It is not necessary for America to proclaim itself the most powerful and the greatest nation on earth. It needs to *demonstrate* these qualities. As Edmund Burke said two centuries ago, "the only way evil flourishes is for good men to do nothing."

It is up to the women and men of the world to act. I would therefore like to address the men and women of America:

You belong to the most powerful nation on earth, an immensely wealthy country, populated by people who want to live their lives with compassion and integrity. You have a great and noble task ahead of you. Each of you can be as powerful as the most powerful person who ever lived. If you or your child were threatened with a lethal disease, you would do everything in your power to save that life. This is the analogy that you must now apply to the planet and in particular to your country.

America has the power and resources to reverse global warming, to save the ozone layer, to prevent chemical pollution, to stop deforestation, to curb the human overpopulation problem, and to prevent the rape of space. The money that America invests in killing must now be redirected urgently to the preservation of life. America must rise to its full moral and spiritual height to reach its intended destiny—the nation that saved the world.

In a similar vein, the people of Europe must resist the constant call from America to arm and re-arm. So too, the people of Canada, of Australia—and indeed all the people of the world. We cannot continue to behave as primitive animals killing for pleasure, killing for money, killing for religious imperatives, killing for greed and territorial imperative. Conflict resolution and peacekeeping must be our new priorities.

Even after the catastrophe of September 11, 2001, it is still inappropriate to rush off and kill thousands of innocent people for revenge. The only reaction by a civilized nation should be, as mentioned above, to work together with the international community to bring these criminals to justice. Never forget that thousands of nuclear weapons remain continuously on hair-trigger alert. Any disturbance of the international situation could trigger their launch and cast us all into the pall of conflagration and nuclear winter.

You cannot simultaneously prevent and prepare for war. The very prevention of war requires more faith, courage and resolution than are needed to prepare for war.

—Albert Einstein

APPENDIX A: MAJOR U.S. NUCLEAR-WEAPONS MAKERS

The companies below are all among the top ten Pentagon contractors for 2000. One of the ten, Litton Industries, has been bought out and integrated into Northrop Grumman. Nearly all of these firms are heavily involved in nuclear weapons work, including the U.S. missile defense program (Ground-Based Midcourse Defense Segment—GMDS—formerly National Missile Defense).

Boeing, Lockheed, TRW, and Raytheon, the four companies with the majority of missile-defense contracts, have spent over 40 million dollars on lobbying expenses and campaign contributions *from 1998 to 2001 alone* to guarantee that mega-billion-dollar Pentagon contracts for Star Wars and other weapons systems will keep coming. With firms like Boeing having 250,000 staff worldwide and Lockheed Martin operating plants in all 50 U.S. states, the weapons industry has tremendous political influence in Washington, D.C.

For data on companies selling weapons around the world, see the Federation of American Scientists Arms Sales Monitoring Project website: www.fas.org/asmp.

For another look at companies making nuclear weapons, see the Dirty Dozen list produced by Reaching Critical Will, a disarmament project of the Women's International League for Peace and Freedom, at www.reachingcriticalwill.org/dd/ddindex.html.

For information about companies profiteering from the bombing of Afghanistan and the "war on terrorism," see www.worldpolicy.org/projects/arms/updates/profiteers121701.html.

Lockheed Martin Corporation

2000 Pentagon contract awards: $15,000,000,000
1999 lobbying expenditures (inclusive of non-military products and services):
$4,160,000

2000 campaign contributions: $2,163,184 (to Democrats: 39%; to Republicans: 60%)

Headquarters:
Lockheed Martin Corporation
6801 Rockledge Drive
Bethesda, MD 20817
(301) 897-6000
www.lockheedmartin.com

Primary locations for missile-defense work:
Space Systems-Missiles & Space Operations
1111 Lockheed Martin Way
Sunnyvale, CA 94089
(408) 742-7151

Space Systems-Astronautics Operation
12999 Deer Creek Canyon Road
Littleton, CO 80127-5146
(303) 977-3000

Also doing missile defense work at Eagan, MN site.

Notes: Develops many components for missile defense; builds the Trident missile. Lockheed Martin and Boeing are by far the largest overseas arms dealers.

For Star Wars, Lockheed Martin (LM) designed the current booster system, including Payload Launch Vehicles, at sites in Sunnyvale, CA; Dallas, TX; and Orlando, FL. Also makes components of the Space-Based Infrared System (SBIRS) that provides the missile-defense system with early warning of missile launches against the U.S. The Airborne Laser program in Sunnyvale tests beams of laser energy to destroy theater ballistic missiles hundreds of miles away.

LM is also prime contractor for the Theater High Altitude Area Defense (THAAD) system—a ground-based system intended to destroy theater ballistic-missile threats to troops and military equipment. LM expects THAAD to be deployed in 2007.

LM was awarded a 589-million-dollar contract in 1999 for twelve more D5 nuclear missiles for Trident submarines. The government previously bought 372 D5s at nearly 60 million dollars each. Each Trident can destroy an entire continent with nuclear weapons.

In 2001, LM was awarded the biggest defense department contract in history to develop the F-35 high-tech fighter plane, expected to become the main attack plane for the Air Force, Navy, and Marines for decades to come. The contract, worth at least 200 billion dollars over many years, could grow to 400 billion dollars when foreign sales are added.

In 1999, LM won an Air Force contract valued at up to 1.5 billion dollars over fifteen years to modernize and integrate command systems of the North American Aerospace Defense Command (NORAD) in Colorado, as well as the command and control systems of the Colorado Springs, Colorado–based U.S. Space Command, the Air Force Space Command, and other sites in the United States and abroad. The upgrade will link some forty separate air, space, and missile-defense command and control systems into a network with new capabilities to handle space warfare, according to LM.

In addition, LM has a 47-million-dollar Air Force contract to upgrade the AN/FPS-117 radar that support the Atmospheric Early Warning System. These long-range surveillance radar systems are located at thirty-three sites from the far reaches of Canada and Alaska, as well as Iceland, Hawaii, and Puerto Rico, supported by an engineering facility at Hill Air Force Base in Utah.

LM makes the F-16 (along with Boeing) as well as the F-22, which, at more than 200 million dollars each, is the most expensive fighter plane ever built. At its plant in Grand Prairie, TX, LM is building the Patriot missile, which uses kinetic energy instead of a warhead to destroy enemy missiles. The U.S. Army may order over 1,000 Patriots, with foreign countries also expected to order them.

In the 1970's Lockheed Corporation (now Lockheed Martin) admitted to paying 22 million dollars in bribes to win overseas contracts. In 2001, LM paid a 4.25 million dollar settlement agreement between the U.S. Government and LM's Naval Electronics and Surveillance Systems Division. LM allegedly used Foreign Military Sales (FMS) funds illegally in a contract to modify sonar systems used by Egypt.

Management:
Vance Coffman, Chairman and Chief Executive Officer
2000 salary, including stock gains, bonuses, etc.: $3,959,000
Salary increase from 1999: 263%
5-year total: $10,382,000
(*Source:* Forbes, *May 14, 2001*)
Jeff Harris, President and General Manager, Missiles and Space Operations
    (Sunnyvale, CA)
Albert E. Smith, President, Space Systems-Astronautics Operations (Littleton, CO)

The Boeing Company

2000 Pentagon contract awards: $12,000,000,000
1999 lobbying expenditures (inclusive of non-military products and services):
    $8,020,000
2000 campaign contributions: $344,334 (to Democrats: 40%; to Republicans: 60%)

Headquarters:
Boeing World Headquarters
100 North Riverside Plaza

Chicago, IL 60606-1596
(312) 544-2000
www.boeing.com

Primary location for missile defense work:

Boeing Huntsville
499 Boeing Blvd.
Huntsville, AL 35806
(256) 461-2121

Boeing's other missile-defense facilities are located in Washington, D.C., Houston, Texas St. Louis, Missouri; Wichita, Kansas; Anaheim and Canoga Park, California; Kent, Washington; Colorado Springs, Colorado; Tucson, Arizona; Bedford, Massachusetts; and Ogden, Utah.

Notes: Prime contractor for missile defense, responsible for the development and integration of program components, including the Ground-Based Interceptor, X-Band Radar, Battle Management Command, Control and Communication systems (BMC3), Upgraded Early Warning Radar and interfaces to the Space-Based Infrared System Satellites. Seventy percent of U.S. missile defense testing is done at Boeing Huntsville. (TRW's missile-defense facility in Colorado Springs is another major test site.) In 2000, Boeing received a 6-billion-dollar missile-defense contract. The Redstone Arsenal, according to award-winning investigative reporter Karl Grossman, is "up to its neck in Star Wars work and sits alongside NASA's Marshall Space Flight Center which is developing a nuclear-propelled rocket for military and civilian operations."

In 2001, Boeing completed a 3-million-dollar missile-defense test silo at its airport plant in Huntsville, 90 feet underground. According to a company spokesperson, "A wide array of information is needed by Boeing . . . Engineers need to know what amount of stress the silo's concrete structure can withstand, and how silo doors will behave in sub-zero conditions. . . . We are going to have a special shroud built around the top of the silo, and then lower the temperatures to at least 30 degrees below zero. That's just to test the doors." Boeing is also building test silos at Vandenburg Air Force Base in California and two at Meck Island in the South Pacific. Boeing's Rocketdyne division in Canoga Park does research for hit-to-kill warheads for missile defense.

Boeing made joint direct-attack munitions, B-52 bombers, and B-1B Lancer long-range bombers used in the 2001 bombing of Afghanistan. Each Lancer carries up to eighty conventional bombs, thirty cluster bombs, and twenty-four guided "smart" bombs. B-52s also dropped 40 percent of the bombs on Iraq during the Gulf War (which killed an estimated 250,000 Iraqi civilians). Boeing and Lockheed are the largest U.S. arms exporters, with 60 percent of Boeing's sales made to other nations. They make F-16 planes for Israel, as well as the infamous V-22 Osprey aircraft, involved in accidents that have killed at least thirty U.S. military personnel.

Boeing leads the Airborne Laser (ABL) program (collaborating with Lockheed Martin and TRW). The ABL program is intended to put laser weapons on modified Boeing 747 freighter jets to detect and destroy theater ballistic missiles in their boost stages. Boeing provides the 747-400F aircraft and command-and-control computer system for this project.

In 1994, Boeing paid 75 million dollars in order to avoid criminal prosecution, which, at that time, was reportedly the largest non-criminal Pentagon payback case in government statements. The payment included 52 million dollars for overcharging computer-related work, overcharging on non-domestic government work, and 9 million dollars for hazardous-waste disposal costs. In 2000, the justice department sued Boeing for purportedly hiding a subcontractor's billing fraud of several million dollars. In 1999, Boeing paid 15 million dollars to settle a racial discrimination lawsuit on behalf of 12,000 present and 7,000 former African-American employees. Despite this record, the Pentagon still designated Boeing the prime missile-defense contractor.

Management:
Philip M. Condit, Chairman and Chief Executive Officer
2000 salary, including stock gains, bonuses, etc: $16,752,000
Salary increase from 1999: 11%
5-year total: $30,216,000
(*Source:* Forbes, *May 14, 2001*)
Michael M. Sears, Senior Vice President, President, Boeing Military Aircraft and
    Missile Systems Group
Harry C. Stonecipher, President, Chief Operating Officer, Vice Chairman

Raytheon Company

2000 Pentagon contract awards: $6,300,000,000
1999 lobbying expenditures (inclusive of non-military products and services):
    $1,800,000
2000 campaign contributions: $891,053 (to Democrats: 37%; to Republicans:
    62%)

Headquarters:
Raytheon Company
141 Spring Street
Lexington, MA 02421
(781) 862-6600
www.raytheon.com

Primary location for missile defense work:
Raytheon Missile Systems
1151 East Herman Road, Building 80707
P.O. Box 11337
Tucson, AZ 85706
(520) 794-3000

Notes: A major missile-defense provider—prime contractor for the Exoatmospheric Kill Vehicle (EKV), the intercept element of the Ground-Based Interceptor, intended to find and destroy its target with kinetic energy, or hit-to-kill technology. Along with Boeing, Raytheon will continue to construct and try out the EKV for possible use in Star Wars. They build the missile-defense program's X-Band Radar and Upgraded Early Warning Radar. Makes the radar sensor for the Theater High Area Altitude Defense (THAAD) system. Makes missiles for the Navy Theater-Wide program. Makes missiles for Navy Aegis destroyers to intercept long-range ballistic missiles fired from North Korea. Made 344 million dollars from Star Wars contracts in 1998–99 alone.

Maker of Tomahawk cruise missiles, launched from Navy ships and submarines to bomb Afghanistan in 2001 and Iraq in 1991. Produces Patriot missiles.

Raytheon paid 4 million dollars in 1994 to settle a government charge that the firm inflated an antimissile radar defense contract. In 1999, according to *Reuters,* Raytheon was forced to pay 3 million dollars to competitor AGES group and buy up 13 million dollars worth of AGES aircraft parts to resolve the claim that Raytheon hired a security company to spy on AGES and steal confidential documents. All this after the AGES Group was awarded a government contract formerly granted to Raytheon. There have been allegations that Raytheon's lobbyists may have paid off a Brazilian senator in 1995 to secure a 1.4-billion-dollar radar contract with Brazil.

Management:
Daniel P. Burnham, Chairman and Chief Executive Officer
2000 salary, including stock gains, bonuses, etc.: $3,813,000
Salary increase from 1999: 51%
5-year total: $9,300,000
(*Source:* Forbes, *May 14, 2001*)
Louise L. Francesconi, Vice President and Senior Vice President, Missile Systems

General Dynamics Corporation

2000 Pentagon contract awards: $4,100,000,000
1999 lobbying expenditures (inclusive of non-military products and services):
    $4,370,000
2000 campaign contributions: $1,187,205 (to Democrats: 40%; Republicans: 60%)

Headquarters:
General Dynamics
3190 Fairview Park Drive
Falls Church, Virginia 22042-4523
(703) 876-3000
www.generaldynamics.com
www.gdeb.com/about (Trident information)
www.gdds.com (other weapons)

Four major weapons-development sites:
General Dynamics Electric Boat (builds Trident submarines)
75 Eastern Point Road
Groton, CT 06340-4989
(860) 433-3000

Bangor Trident Site
General Dynamics Electric Boat
P.O. Box 6519
Silverdale, WA 98315-6519
(360) 598-5100

Kings Bay Trident Site
General Dynamics Electric Boat
1040 USS Georgia Avenue
Kings Bay, GA 31547
(912) 882-6551

General Dynamics Defense Systems
100 Plastics Avenue
Pittsfield, MA 01201
(413) 494-1110

Notes: At its large Electric Boat Division in Groton, Connecticut, General Dynamics produces the U.S. Navy's Trident and Seawolf nuclear submarines. One Trident is capable of incinerating an area the size of Russia. For the missile defense system, they are working on sea-based systems for the Navy's Aegis cruisers. 1999 profits of 880,000,000 dollars (a 141.0% increase from 1998). Sells many of its products overseas, including tanks to Egypt, Kuwait, Greece, Morocco, Oman, Thailand, and Taiwan.

Management:
Nicholas D. Chabraja, Chairman of the Board and Chief Executive Officer
2000 salary, including stock gains, bonuses, etc.: $10,435,000
Salary increase from 1999: 13%

5-year total: $31,755,000
(*Source:* Forbes, *May 14, 2001*)
Michael J. Mancuso, Senior Vice President and Chief Financial Officer
Michael W. Toner, President, Electric Boat Division

Northrop Grumman Corporation
(incorporated weapons giant Litton Industries in 2001)

2000 Pentagon contract awards: $3,100,000,000
1999 lobbying expenditures (inclusive of non-military products and services):
   $5,030,000
2000 campaign contributions: $602,930 (to Democrats: 42%; to Republicans:
   57%)

Headquarters:
Northrop Grumman Corporation
1840 Century Park East
Los Angeles, CA 90067-2199
(310) 553-6262
www.northgrum.com

Notes: In addition to its nuclear-weapons work, a major supplier of weapons that
bombed Yugoslavia and Afghanistan. Northrop Grumman (NG) makes the infamous B-2 Stealth bomber or "B-2 Spirit," which cost 2.2 billion dollars each. NG
has built 21 B-2s so far. Politicians like Senator Norm Dicks (D-Wa.) and Senator
Randy "Duke" Cunningham (R-Calif.) have been attempting to renew the Stealth
program by requesting funding for up to forty more planes.
   A smaller missile-defense subcontractor. Collaborating on the Space-Based Infrared System (SBIRS), designed to track missiles and relay data to destroy them before impact, with Lockheed Martin, Boeing, Litton TASC, Analex Corporation, and
the Space Dynamics Laboratory of Utah State University. NG is also involved in the
7-billion-dollar Airborne Laser program.

Management:
Kent Kresa, Chairman, President, and Chief Executive Officer
2000 salary, including stock gains, bonuses, etc.: $9,269,000
Salary increase from 1999: 63%
5-year total: $46,332,000
(*Source:* Forbes, *May 14, 2001*)
Ronald D. Sugar, President and Chief Operating Officer
Richard B. Waugh, Jr., Corporate Vice President and Chief Financial Officer

United Technologies Corporation

2000 Pentagon contract awards: $2,100,000,000
1999 lobbying expenditures (inclusive of non-military products and services):
    $4,660,000
2000 campaign contributions: $657,220 (to Democrats: 48%; to Republicans: 52%)

Headquarters:
United Technologies Corporation
One Financial Plaza
Hartford, CT 06103
(860) 728-7000
www.utc.com

Notes: United Technologies (UT) builds the Minuteman rocket motors that launch the missile defense tests. UT owns Pratt & Whitney, which makes military planes and other equipment. In 2001, P&W was awarded a 4-billion-dollar contract to develop its F135 engine for the Lockheed Martin Joint Strike Fighter (JSF) aircraft. Other UT companies involved in weapons work are Hamilton Sundstrand (makes parts for B-2, B-52s and other bomber and fighter planes) and Sikorsky (a leading helicopter maker).

Management:
George David, Chairman and Chief Executive Officer
2000 salary, including stock gains, bonuses, etc.: $18,384,000
Salary increase from 1999: 6%
5-year total: $66,196,000
(*Source:* Forbes, *May 14, 2001*)
Karl Krapek, UTC President and Chief Operating Officer

TRW Incorporated

2000 Pentagon contract awards: $2,000,000,000
1999 lobbying expenditures (inclusive of non-military products and services):
    $1,090,000
2000 campaign contributions: $496,819 (to Democrats: 21%; to Republicans: 79%)

Headquarters:
TRW Inc.
1900 Richmond Road
Cleveland, OH 44124-3760
(216) 291-7000
www.trw.com

Primary location for missile defense work:
TRW Space and Electronics Group
One Space Park
Redondo Beach, CA
(310) 812-4321

Notes: A major missile-defense contractor, TRW is the lead innovator of a central component of Star Wars: the Battle Management Command, Control, and Communications (BMC3) system, which links the computer systems that are supposed to differentiate between nuclear warheads and Mylar decoy balloons. In 2001, awarded a seven-year, 564-million-dollar contract for BMC3 products by prime contractor Boeing. TRW is also making spacecraft, Tactical High-Energy Lasers, Airborne Lasers, Space-Based Lasers, and target launch vehicles, and doing Theater Missile Defense work. TRW operates the Joint National Test Facility, a major missile-defense test site in Colorado Springs, Colorado that carries out realistic national and theater missile defense simulations (war games). Collaborating with Raytheon on the Space-Based Infrared System (SBIRS) Low program missile early warning system. TRW's site in Capistrano, California is building the megawatt-class Scud-killing laser.

As reported in the *New York Times* on March 7, 2001, former TRW senior engineer Nira Schwartz has come forward to reveal that TRW deliberately lied to the Pentagon about several missile-defense test-result failures. Dr. Schwartz says "It's not a defense of the United States. It's a conspiracy to allow them to milk the government. They are creating for themselves a job for life."

Dr. Schwartz was on TRW's antimissile team in 1995 and 1996. She says that in repeated tests the interceptors being designed failed, yet TRW maintained that the systems functioned properly. Dr. Schwartz consistently requested that her supervisor and associates tell the military and collaborating companies the truth about the results, but they told her "not to worry." Within days she was fired.

Management:
David M. Cote, Chairman and Chief Executive Officer
2000 salary, including stock gains, bonuses, etc.: $2,153,000
Salary increase from 1999: not applicable
5-year total: Not applicable. Replaced Joseph T. Gorman, whose 5-year total was
    $30,977,000.
(*Source:* Forbes, *May 14, 2001*)
Timothy W. Hannemann, Executive Vice President, General Manager, TRW
    Space and Electronics Group
Donald C. Winter, President and Chief Executive Officer, TRW Systems (missile
    defense)
Robert H. Swan, Executive Vice President, Chief Financial Officer

General Electric Company

2000 Pentagon contract awards: $1,600,000,000
1999 lobbying expenditures (inclusive of non-military products and services):
    $7,930,000
2000 campaign contributions: $304,750 (to Democrats: 42%; to Republicans: 58%)

Headquarters:
Corporate Headquarters
General Electric Company
3135 Easton Turnpike
Fairfield, CT 06431
(203) 373-2211
www.generalelectric.com

Notes: Owns the NBC network. Formerly a major nuclear-weapons maker. Still designs nuclear power plants. General Electric Aircraft Engines (GEAE) is the world's leading manufacturer of military aircraft jet engines, including those powering Airborne Laser aircraft. In 2001, the U.S. Navy awarded GEAE a contract of over 35 million dollars for 100 engines for Navy Hornet aircraft. GE has a long record as an arms dealer, selling to Israel, Chile, South Africa, South Korea, Greece, Turkey, Egypt, Bahrain, Australia, Canada, Finland, Kuwait, Malaysia, Singapore, Spain, Sweden, Switzerland, and Japan, among others.

Management:
Jeffrey R. Immelt, Chairman of the Board and Chief Executive Officer
2000 salary, including stock gains, bonuses, etc.: not applicable. Immelt replaced
    Jack Welch, who made $76,425,000 in 2000 and whose five-year total was
    $324,789,000.
(*Source:* Forbes, *May 14, 2001*)
Dennis D. Dammerman, Vice Chairman of the Board and Executive Officer

Science Applications International Corporation

2000 Pentagon contract awards: $15,100,000,000
1999 lobbying expenditures (inclusive of non-military products and services):
    $1,495,000
2000 campaign contributions: $640,060 (to Democrats: 36%; to Republicans: 63%)

Headquarters:
10260 Campus Point Drive
San Diego, CA 92121

(858) 826-6000
www.saic.com

Notes: A major DOD and DOE nuclear-weapons consultant and contractor. Supports the U.S. Navy Space and Naval Warfare Systems. In 2001, according to a company press release, SAIC secured a contract for "the U.S. Army Space and Missile Defense Command (SMDC) to support the Ballistic Missile Defense Organization's (BMDO) Wide Bandwidth Information Infrastructure (WBII) program and apply advanced information technology (IT) to missile-defense ground-test facilities. Under this contract, the SAIC team will create a network for geographically distributed ground test facilities for both the Theater High Altitude Area Defense (THAAD) and Navy Theater Wide (NTW) missile defense programs. For the NTW program, the Aegis Weapons System Combat Systems Engineering Development Sites (CSEDS) in Moorestown, New Jersey, and the Standard Missile-III SIL in Tucson, Arizona will be linked using networking and virtual private network (VPN) technology." SAIC and engineering giant Bechtel recently won a 3.1-billion-dollar contract to support the department of energy's civilian radioactive-waste management program at Yucca Mountain in Nevada.

Management:
J. R. Beyster, President and Chief Executive Officer
2000 salary, including stock gains, bonuses, etc.: not applicable
D.P. Andrews, Corporate Executive Vice President, Federal Business
Thomas E. Darcy, Executive Vice President and Chief Financial Officer
Sources: Lobbying expenditure and campaign contribution information from:

The Center for Responsive Politics
1101 14th St., NW, Suite 1030
Washington, DC 20005-5635
(202) 857-0044
www.opensecrets.org/lobbyists/98lookup.htm
info@crp.org; webmaster @crp.org

Other data sources include: MotherJones.com U.S. Arms Sales page; Bruce Gagnon/Global Network Against Weapons and Nuclear Power in Space; Steven Saples; The Real Rogues Behind Star Wars by Rachel Ries, Rachel Glick, Tim Nafziger, Mark Swier, and Kevin Martin.

OTHER U.S. COMPANIES WORKING ON NUCLEAR WEAPONS (A PARTIAL LIST)

Honeywell Inc.
2000 E. Bannister Road
Kansas City, MO 64131
350th Highway
(816) 737-4200

Notes: In October, 2000, the U.S. department of energy awarded a five-year, 1.8-billion-dollar contract to Honeywell Inc. to continue operating its southeast Kansas City nuclear weapons parts plant. The site makes electronic, mechanical, and metal components to keep existing nuclear weapons in operating order, employs about 3,000 people, and is adding another 250 workers.

Also active in the research and development, testing, production, maintenance, and retirement of atomic bombs are Westinghouse Electric Company (warhead assembly), Fluor Daniel Corp., Bechtel National, Inc., BWX Technologies Inc., and Mason & Hanger-Silas Mason Company, Inc.
Source: Stephen Schwartz, Bulletin of the Atomic Scientists

OTHER U.S. COMPANIES INVOLVED IN MISSILE DEFENSE (A PARTIAL LIST)

Logicon Software, Computer Sciences Corporation, Alliant Techsystems, Alliant Missile Products, GenCorp (Aerojet Missile and Space Propulsion Unit—150 million dollars in contracts in 2001)

U.S. NUCLEAR WEAPONS LABORATORIES

Lawrence Livermore National Laboratory
7000 East Avenue
Livermore, CA 94550-9234
(925) 422-1100
www.llnl.gov
llnlweb@llnl.gov
Contractor: University of California Board of Regents for the U.S. department of energy. Major nuclear weapons work includes the massive Stockpile Stewardship and Management Program and the National Ignition Facility. According to Tri Valley CARES, the Lab is planning to take over the testing of plutonium bomb cores for the U.S. arsenal; is seeking a permit from the California department of toxic sub-

stances control for a new 32-million-dollar radioactive waste treatment facility without an Environmental Impact Report; and is scheduled to receive plutonium shipments from Rocky Flats (former nuclear-weapons plant in Colorado).
Director: Bruce Tarter

Sandia National Laboratories
1515 Eubank SE
Albuquerque, NM 87123 (main facility)
(505) 845-0011
7011 East Avenue
Livermore, CA 94550
(925) 294-3000
www.sandia.gov
gperri@sandia.gov (public affairs office)
Contractor: Sandia Corporation, a wholly-owned subsidiary of Lockheed Martin Corporation, for the U.S. department of energy. Headquarters in Albuquerque with a smaller laboratory in Livermore. According to their website, "designs all non-nuclear components for the nation's nuclear weapons."
Director: C. Paul Robinson

Los Alamos National Laboratory
1663 Central Avenue, MS A117
Los Alamos, NM 87545
(800) 508-4400; (505) 665-4400
www.lanl.gov
cro@lanl.gov (public affairs office)
Contractor: University of California Board of Regents for the National Nuclear Security Administration. "[T]he Laboratory continues to ensure the safety and reliability of the U.S. nuclear weapons stockpile" according to their website.
Director: John C. Browne

Oak Ridge National Laboratory
One Bethel Valley Road
Oak Ridge, TN 37831
(865) 574-4163
www.ornl.gov
mclaughlinmz@ornl.gov (public affairs office)
Contractors: Lockheed Martin, Bechtel National, Westinghouse Electric, and others. Produces nuclear-weapon components to support the design laboratories and the Nevada Test Site. See additional information below regarding the planned National Security Complex.
Director: William J. Madia

Nevada Test Site
c/o U.S. Department of Energy
Nevada Operations Office
Office of Public Affairs and Information
P.O. Box 98518
Las Vegas, NV 89193-8518
(702) 295-0944
www.nv.doe.gov
carter@nv.doe.gov (public affairs office)
Contractors: Lockheed Martin, Bechtel National, and others. The Nevada Test Site, where nuclear weapons have been tested since the 1960's, is located about 65 miles northwest of the city of Las Vegas, and is surrounded on three sides by the Nellis Air Force Range.
Source: Brookings Institution, Tri Valley CARES

For more information on the laboratories and who is managing the U.S. department of energy nuclear weapons complex, see the Brookings Institution website www.brook.edu/fp/projects/nucwcost/sites.htm.

HUGE NEW NUCLEAR-WEAPONS COMPLEX IN THE WORKS

Still grounded in a Cold War mentality, the U.S. department of energy in late 1998 announced plans for a new, patriotically-titled "National Security Complex" in Oak Ridge, Tennessee. Oak Ridge is presently home to the Y-12 Plant, the last remaining full-scale operating nuclear-weapons factory in the U.S., and the Oak Ridge National Laboratory, which designs nuclear-weapons parts. Three Tennessee Valley Authority commercial nuclear reactors—Watts Bar Unit 1 (near Spring City, TN) and Sequoyah Units 1 and 2 (at Soddy Daisy, TN) —have been chosen as the "preferred" sites to manufacture tritium for U.S. nuclear weapons. The decision breaches the longstanding policy of not producing bomb material in civilian nuclear power plants. According to Robert Tiller of Physicians for Social Responsibility, "Our leaders are upset that Iraq might use civilian facilities to produce components for weapons of mass destruction, but the United States is now committed to do that very thing—turning a civilian reactor into a bomb facility."

The DOE Environmental Impact Statement for Oak Ridge describes the first step in building a new 4-billion-dollar bomb plant, allowing the U.S. government to do 10 times more nuclear-weapons work than current levels and to start production of new nuclear weapons.

Sources: William Hartung, Brookings Institution; Stephen Schwartz, Charles D. Ferguson, Bulletin of the Atomic Scientists; Oak Ridge Environmental Peace Alliance; Ralph Nader, Associated Press

APPENDIX B: U.S. NUCLEAR-WEAPONS CONTROL CENTERS AND GOVERNMENT AUTHORITIES

CHEYENNE MOUNTAIN
    OPERATIONS CENTER (CMOC)
Cheyenne Mountain Air Force Station
1 NORAD Road, Suite 101-213
Cheyenne Mountain AFS, CO 80914-
    6066
Located on the south side of Colorado
    Springs, CO
(719) 474-2238; (719) 474-2240
www.cheyennemountain.af.mil/cmoc

The computer surveillance center for nuclear war, headquarters of the early warning system. According to their website, "CMOC serves as the command center for both North American Aerospace Defense (NORAD) and United States Space Command (US-SPACECOM). NORAD is the central collection and coordination center for a worldwide system of satellites, radars, and sensors that provide unambiguous, timely, and accurate air, space, missile, and nuclear detonation warning and attack assessments." In addition, according to the *Washington Times* (3/29/01), "The U.S. Space Command recently became the military unit in charge of preparing for cyber-battle, or what the Pentagon calls 'computer network defense' and its offensive counterpart, 'computer network attack.' " CMOC is the expected command center of any future U.S. missile defense system.

Director: General Ralph E. Eberhart, United States Air Force, Commander in Chief, North American Aerospace Defense Command

UNITED STATES STRATEGIC
    COMMAND (STRATCOM)
U.S. Air Force's Strategic Air
    Command (SAC)
Offutt Air Force Base, Nebraska
Next to the city of Bellevue and just
    south of Omaha
www.stratcom.af.mil
(402) 294-5961 (Public Affairs Office)

The command and control center for all U.S. nuclear warheads. According to STRATCOM's website, the Command's mission is "to deter military attack on the United States and its allies, and should deterrence fail, employ forces so as to achieve national objectives. The Command has responsibility for all U.S. Air Force and U.S. Navy strategic nuclear forces supporting the national security objective of strategic deterrence." STRATCOM provides "intelli-

gence on countries and other entities possessing or seeking weapons of mass destruction" and develops "a Single Integrated Operational Plan that fully satisfies national guidance."
Director: Admiral Richard W. Mies, Commander in Chief, United States Strategic Command

PROJECT ELF
Clam Lake, WI 54517
No listed number; see directions to site below

Relatively unknown to the general public, Project ELF (Extremely Low Frequency Communication System) controls the U.S. Navy's Trident submarine first-strike communication system for nuclear war.

According to Nukewatch, "The Project ELF center is an essential part of the Navy's offensive nuclear-war plan, a one-way communications trigger for its nuclear-armed Trident and Fast-Attack submarines. It is designed to coordinate a massive coordinated multi-submarine attack by submarine-launched ballistic nuclear missiles. Each sub carries twenty-four extremely accurate 'Trident II' missiles with up to 192 thermonuclear warheads. Combined, the Tridents threaten the equivalent of over 80,000 Hiroshima-sized bomb blasts. About half the Tridents subs are at sea at any one time, with their warheads continually on 'alert' launch status.

"The Trident submarine fleet and its ELF activation constitute the costliest and deadliest weapon system in history. Total long-term costs for the Trident fleet are estimated at 155 billion dol-

lars, with each of eighteen subs costing 1.9 billion dollars."

Project ELF location: From WI Hwy 77, go south 4 miles on County GG. Turn right on fire road 173 and go 2.9 miles. Then turn right again on fire road 176 and go .2 mile. The Project ELF front gate is on the right.
Source: Nukewatch

Two watchdog groups for more information: Nukewatch / Coalition to Stop Project ELF and Loaves & Fishes Catholic Worker. (See the antinuclear group list.)

JOINT DEFENSE SPACE
   RESEARCH FACILITY
   (PINE GAP)
Near Alice Springs, Australia

A controversial Central Intelligence Agency (CIA) satellite-tracking station, Pine Gap is heavily involved in U.S. nuclear war-fighting readiness. The southern hemisphere adjunct to NORAD in Colorado, Pine Gap's space-based missile early warning and monitoring system is designed to confirm an attack on the U.S. and launch nuclear war.

Two of its ground antennae are part of the U.S. Defense Satellite Communications System. These antennae connect to geostationary satellites which detect tactical and intermediate range missiles, as well as intercontinental ballistic missiles. The data is relayed immediately to NORAD.

Employing nearly 1,000 people, mainly from the CIA and the National Reconnaissance Office, Pine Gap is one of the world's largest satellite ground control stations, with spy satellites that circle the globe. What little data is released to the public suggests that Pine Gap conducts massive espionage with these electronic eavesdropping satellites, intercepting telephone, radio, data links, and other communications. The Australian government's 1994 Defense White Paper reaffirms support both for U.S. nuclear weapons and Pine Gap's part in policing Asia and the Pacific to secure U.S. and Australian strategic and economic interests.

Pine Gap may also be used as a frontline base for a planned U.S. National Missile Defense tracking program, called SBIRS (Space-Based Infra-Red System) designed to be operational by 2004. *Flight International* magazine has disclosed that the U.S. and Australia plan not only to jointly run this aspect of the missile-defense system, but to construct a new test range in Western Australia. North of Broome, the range would allow the U.S. Navy to test ship-based antimissile systems. Simulated ballistic missiles would be launched from Australia, and—if the tests succeeded—quickly be shot down by the U.S. Navy.

Popular Australian Prime Minister Gough Whitlam, it is widely believed, was deposed in 1975 because of his plans to announce in Parliament that Pine Gap was run by the CIA and the CIA were extremely reluctant to have this information released.

Pine Gap and about thirty other sites make up the joint U.S.-Australia facilities. During a May 1992 visit, U.S. Defense Secretary (now Vice President) Dick Cheney confirmed that the U.S. bases in Australia had been used in the Gulf War. In 1991, U.S. newspapers reported that Pine Gap was instrumental in the tracking of guidance and trajectory of U.S. Patriot missiles

The U.S. is developing a combination of satellite and laser technologies that goes far beyond what was unleashed against Iraq in 1991. Plans to militarize and control space are outlined in a document called "Vision for 2020." The plan would require the development of ground-based antisatellite weapons (ASATs), space-based ASATs, and space-based earth strike weapons. These systems are controlled and coordinated by ground bases such as those in Pine Gap, Australia, the Marshall Islands and other countries.

Sources: John Pike, Federation of American Scientists Intelligence Resource Program; Jennifer Thompson; Ross Dowe; Duncan Campbell; Zohl de Ishtar; Andrew Clark, The Sunday Age

PRESIDENT GEORGE W. BUSH
President of the United States of America and Commander in Chief of the U.S. Armed Forces
The White House
1600 Pennsylvania Avenue
Washington, DC 20500
(202) 456-1414
fax: (202) 456-2561
president@whitehouse.gov

As Commander in Chief, he is in charge of nuclear weapons and nuclear war.

THE PENTAGON
700 Army Navy Drive (visitor entrance)
Arlington, VA 22202
(703) 545-6700

To visit:
Director, Pentagon Tours
Room 1E776, 1400 Defense Pentagon
Washington, DC 20301-1400
(703) 695-1776
www.defenselink.mil/pubs/pentagon
   and www.dtic.mil/ref/html/
   welcome/wlcm.htm
tourschd.pa@sd.mil

The headquarters of the U.S. Department of Defense

DONALD H. RUMSFELD
Secretary of Defense
1000 Defense Pentagon
Washington, DC 20301-1000
(703) 692-7100
DOD comment line: (703) 697-5737
web site to send an e-mail:
   www.defenselink.mil/faq/comment.
   html#Form

Ardent proponent of missile defense and war in space.

PAUL WOLFOWITZ
Deputy Secretary of Defense
1010 Defense Pentagon
Washington, DC 20301-1010
(703) 692-7150
DOD comment line: (703) 697-5737
web site to send an e-mail:
   www.defenselink.mil/faq/comment.
   html#Form

JOHN BOLTON
Undersecretary of State for Arms
   Control and International Security
Office of the Undersecretary of State
   for Arms Control and International

Security and Senior Advisor to the
President and the Secretary of State
for Arms Control, Nonproliferation,
and Disarmament
Department of State
2201 C Street NW, Room 7208
Washington, DC 20520
(202) 647-1522

A key advisor for the president's nuclear-weapons policy. John Bolton's extreme right-wing views and opposition to nuclear disarmament inspired the *Boston Globe* to label Bolton, "the Armageddon Nominee." There is concern that his outlook on nuclear weapons policy and foreign relations would increase the likelihood of nuclear war.

SPENCER ABRAHAM
Energy Secretary
U.S. Department of Energy
1000 Independence Ave., SW
Room 7A-257
Washington, DC 20585
(202) 586 6210; (800) dial-DOE
www.energy.gov
the.secretary@doe.gov

Manages the U.S. department of energy, which controls nuclear-weapons development. Abraham actively supports missile defense. A former Michigan Senator, he voted to eliminate up to 90 percent of the toxic chemicals industry must report, undermining a community's right to know. He also consistently voted for the "Mobile Chernobyl" bill to transport irradiated reactor fuel to Yucca Mountain, 65 miles from Las Vegas.

APPENDIX C: LOCATIONS OF THE MAJORITY OF USABLE U.S. NUCLEAR WEAPONS

Most U.S. nuclear weapons are found at the locations below, including weapons for both strategic and tactical systems.

1. NAVAL WEAPONS
Naval Base, Kings Bay, Georgia
Naval Base, Bangor, Washington
(Kings Bay and Bangor together house the eighteen U.S. Trident submarines that carry the C-4 and D-5 missiles.)

2. AIR FORCE WEAPONS
Nellis Air Force Base (AFB), Las Vegas, Nevada
Whiteman AFB, Knob Knoster, Missouri
Barksdale AFB, Shreveport, Louisiana
Minot AFB, Minot, North Dakota (has 150 missiles in silo field)
Malstrom AFB, Great Falls, Montana (has 200 missiles in silo field as well as storing old ICBMs)
F. E. Warren AFB, Cheyenne, Wyoming (has 200 missiles—150 MM III's and 50 MX—in silo field shared with Colorado and Nebraska)
Kirtland AFB, Albuquerque, New Mexico

3. U.S. NUCLEAR WARHEADS OVERSEAS
According to Admiral Eugene Carroll, Center for Defense Information, "there are an estimated 150 to 200 U.S. tactical nuclear bombs (total) on as many as seven NATO bases in Europe. These are what remain of the so-called 'nuclear umbrella' of 7,000 U.S. nuclear weapons present in Europe for use by NATO during the Cold War." For more information, see the websites listed above.

For locations of all nuclear weapons worldwide, including Russian and Chinese weapons, see www.nrdc.org/nuclear/tkstock/p53-94.pdf (current as of 1/3/02—requires Adobe Acrobat Reader).
Sources: Center for Defense Information; Nukewatch; Stephen Schwartz, Bulletin of the Atomic Scientists*; Natural Resources Defense Council; the Brookings Institution; and Bill Sulzman*

STORAGE SITES FOR NUCLEAR WEAPONS MATERIALS
Pantex Plant
P.O. Box 30020
Amarillo, TX
(806) 477-3000
www.pantex.com
Storage location for a large amount of material recovered from weapons disas-

sembled since 1992 in the form of so-called nuclear pits (triggers).

Department of Energy
Westinghouse Savannah River
    Company Site
Aiken, South Carolina
(803) 725-6211; (803) 725-3011
http://sro.srs.gov
Storage location for disassembled secondaries for thermonuclear weapons. Has produced nuclear materials since 1951.
Source: Center for Defense Information

KEY MISSILE DEFENSE TESTING
AND RESEARCH SITES
Redstone Arsenal
U.S. Army Strategic Space and Missile
    Defense Command
106 Wynn Drive
Huntsville, AL 35807
(256) 955-5369; (256) 876-2151
www.redstone.army.mil
See more information under "Boeing" in the nuclear-weapons-company list.

Joint National Test Facility
730 Irwin Avenue
Schriever AFB, CO 80912-7300
(719) 567-9202
http://www.jntf.osd.mil/
jntf.info@jntf.osd.mil
Along with Redstone, a major missile defense test facility. According to their web site, "The primary project currently hosted by the JNTF-DC is Wargame 2000, a real-time, interactive, discrete event, command-and-control missile defense simulation. Wargame 2000 is intended to provide a simulated combat environment that will allow war-fighting commanders,

their staffs, and the acquisition community to examine missile and air defense concepts of operation (CONOPS)." Operated by TRW in collaboration with Boeing.

Vandenberg Air Force Base
Visitor Center, Building Number
    1796
Vandenberg AFB, CA 93437
On Highway 1, 55 miles north of Santa
    Barbara, CA
(805) 606-7662
www.vafb.af.mil
A "launch site" for missile defense tests. See http://mocc.vafb.af.mil/launchsched.asp for the nuclear-weapons test schedule.

Space Command Headquarters
Peterson Air Force Base
Directorate of Public Affairs
Headquarters, U.S. Space Command
250 S. Peterson Blvd, Suite 116
Peterson AFB, CO 80914-3190
(719) 554-6889
www.cheyennemountain.af.mi
See more information in the nuclear weapons control center list.

Patrick Air Force Base/Cape Canaveral
Public Affairs
45 SW/PA
1201 Edward H. White II Street
Patrick AFB, FL 32925
(321) 494-1110
Located south of Cocoa Beach, Florida The Cape physically tests the missiles and Patrick administers/directs them.

Los Angeles Air Force Base
The Space and Missile Systems Center

Office of Public Affairs
2420 Vela Way Suite 1467
El Segundo, CA 90245
(310) 363-0030
www.losangeles.af.mil
Directs the space-based laser program.

Kirtland Air Force Base
Public Affairs
1680 Texas Street SE
Kirtland AFB, NM 87117
(505) 846-0011 (operator)
(505) 846-5500 (Defense Threat
   Reduction Agency)
www.kirtland.af.mil
Home to the Defense Nuclear Weapons
School and The Nuclear Weapons
Product Support Center.

Missile Test Center
NASA Stennis Space Center
Stennis Space Center, MI 39529
(800) 237-1821
www.ssc.nasa.gov
Testing for missile defense conducted
by Lockheed.

Note: Fort Greely and Kodiak Island in
Alaska are slated to be part of a vast Pacific "test bed" meant to allow for more
realistic intercept tests. At present, the
only integrated tests of interceptors designed to shoot down long-range missiles are launched from a U.S. test range
in the Kwajalein Atoll of the Republic
of the Marshall Islands. Thule, Greenland is the site of a radar station that
will be retrofitted if the missile-
defense program goes ahead. (Denmark, which controls Greenland, will
have to permit the upgrade.) Shemya
Island in the Alaskan Aleutians is the
location for a proposed missile-defense
battle-management radar station and
100 interceptors. Radar in the U.S. (including at Cape Cod, Massachusetts and
Beale Air Force Base, California) and
Great Britain are scheduled for Star
Wars upgrades. The Pine Gap CIA base
in Australia may become a key site for
missile-defense activity.

*Source: Global   Network   Against
Weapons and Nuclear Power in Space*

What follows is by no means an exhaustive list. There are many local groups and general-focus organizations that are also committed to nuclear disarmament.

For an extensive internet list of antinuclear groups with links to their web sites, see the web page of Proposition One, http://prop1.org/prop1/azantink.htm.

Alliance for Nuclear Accountability
1801 18th Street, NW, Suite 9-2
Washington, DC 20009
(202) 833-4668
and
1914 N. 34th St, Suite 407
Seattle, WA 98103
(206) 547-3175
www.ananuclear.org
ananuclear@earthlink.net
A national network of organizations working on issues of nuclear weapons production and waste cleanup.

Antiwar.com
520 S. Murphy Avenue, #202
Sunnyvale, CA 94086
www.antiwar.com
egarris@antiwar.com
Web site updated daily with extensive international news coverage culled from major and alternative media. Devoted to noninterventionism. Regular readers are pacifists, leftists, "greens,"

and independents, as well as many on the Right who oppose imperialism.

ARC Ecology
833 Market Street, Suite 1107
San Francisco, CA 94103
(415) 495-1786
http://arc.home.igc.org/
Focuses on the connection between military activities and pollution. Among many issues ARC brings to the forefront is that today the U.S. military produces more hazardous waste annually than the five largest international chemical companies combined.

Back from the Brink
6856 Eastern Avenue, Suite 324
Washington, DC 20012
(202) 545-1001
www.backfromthebrink.org
www.dontblowit.org
The Back from the Brink Campaign is associated with the DontBlowIt.org

campaign, both working to take nuclear weapons off hair-trigger alert.

British American Security Information
   Council (BASIC)
1012 14th Street, NW, Suite 900
Washington, DC 20005
(202) 347-8340
and
Lafone House
11-13 Leathermarket Street
London, SE1 3 HN
England
020 7407 2977
www.basicint.org
basicus@basicint.org
basicuk@basicint.org
BASIC is an independent research organization that analyzes government policies and promotes public awareness of defense, disarmament, military strategy, and nuclear policies in order to foster informed debate.

Bulletin of the Atomic Scientists
   (Educational Foundation for
   Nuclear Science)
6042 S. Kimbark Avenue
Chicago, IL 60637
(773) 702-2555
www.thebulletin.org
bulletin@thebulletin.org
Covers international security and nuclear policy issues in an authoritative, thoughtful, and nontechnical style that is accessible to anyone with an interest in international affairs. Known worldwide as the keeper of the minutes-to-midnight "Doomsday Clock."

Campaign for Nuclear Disarmament
   (U.K.)
162 Holloway Road
London N7 8DQ

England
020 7700 2393
www.cnduk.org
enquiries@cnduk.org
Campaigns nonviolently to rid the world of nuclear weapons and other weapons of mass destruction, including changing government policies to eliminate British nuclear weapons. Several chapters in the United Kingdom and Ireland. Largest U.K. peace group.

Center for Defense Information
1779 Massachusetts Avenue, NW
Washington, DC 20036-2109
(202) 332-0600
www.cdi.org
info@cdi.org
Retired military officers and experienced civilians working together to analyze military spending, policies, and weapons systems, and inform the public with unbiased facts and valid alternatives. Publishes *The Defense Monitor*. No weapons contractor funding. See the military spending clock in action at www.cdi.org/msc/clock.html (with the U.S. spending $589,802 a minute).

Center for Economic Conversion
222 View Street
Mountain View, CA 94041
(650) 968-8798
www.conversion.org
 cec@igc.org
Committed to helping build an economy that meets social needs and works in harmony with the environment.

Coalition to Reduce Nuclear Dangers
10 Maryland Avenue NE, Suite 505
Washington, DC 20002
(202) 546-0795
www.crnd.org
coalition@clw.org

Coalition to Reduce Nuclear Dangers was founded in 1995 to coordinate the largest and most active arms control and disarmament groups in a common effort to strengthen national and international security by reducing the threats posed by nuclear weapons and prevent new nuclear threats from emerging. 17 member groups.

Council for a Livable World
110 Maryland Avenue, NE, #409
Washington, DC 20002
(202) 543-4100
www.clw.org
clw@clw.org
The Council for a Livable World, the Council for a Livable World Education Fund, and PeacePAC are arms control groups committed to ridding the world of weapons of mass destruction and eliminating wasteful military spending. The Council and PeacePAC are also political lobbies that endorse political candidates.

Earth Island Institute
300 Broadway, Suite 28
San Francisco, CA 94133
(415) 788-3666
www.earthisland.org
earthisland@earthisland.org
Founded by veteran environmentalist David Brower, EII is involved in over 30 environmental projects worldwide to preserve and restore the natural world. *Earth Island Journal* (the first magazine on tree-free paper) often reports on nuclear weapons issues.

The Ex-USSR Antinuclear Campaign (ANC)
c/o Socio-Ecological Union
    International

P.O. Box 211
121019 Moscow, Russia
7 095 298 3087
7 095 921 7161
http://iisd1.iisd.ca/50comm/
    commdb/desc/d06.htm
anc@cci.glasnet.ru
and
Antinuclear Campaign
c/o ECODEFENSE!
Moskovsky prospekt 120-34
236006 Kaliningrad, Russia.
7 011 243 7286
ecodefense@glas.apc.org
Active Russian antinuclear groups.

Federation of American Scientists
307 Massachusetts Avenue, NE
Washington, DC 20002
(202) 546-3300
www.fas.org
fas@fas.org
Monitors nuclear weapons, radioactive waste, and arms sales.

Friends Committee on National
    Legislation
245 Second Street, NE
Washington, DC, 20002-5795
(202) 547-6000
(800) 630-1330 (in the U.S.)
www.fcnl.org
fcnl@fcnl.org
A Quaker lobby in the public interest, committed to a world free of war and the threat of war.

Global Network Against Weapons and
    Nuclear Power in Space
P.O. Box 90083
Gainesville, FL 32607
(352) 337-9274
www.space4peace.org
globalnet@mindspring.com

A major group coordinating efforts to stop the missile defense program. Also working to keep space free of weapons and nuclear power. Sponsors conferences and actions at test sites. Coordinates activities with U.S. and international groups. Web site is updated frequently and has many links and protest calendars.

Global Security Institute
1801 Bush Street
San Francisco, CA 94109
(415) 775-6760
www.gsinstitute.org
info@gsinstitute.org
Works with politicians and the public to eliminate nuclear weapons. Founded by Senator Alan Cranston (1914–2000).

Grandmothers for Peace International
9444 Medstead Way
Elk Grove, CA 95758
(916) 684-8744
www.grandmothersforpeace.org
wiednerb@aol.com
Activist group of women who realize that if things do not change, their grandchildren could be part of the last generation on earth. Members visit elected officials, circulate petitions, march, protest, give speeches, publish an international newsletter, and do civil disobedience (including being arrested). Several chapters nationwide.

Greenpeace
702 H Street, NW
Washington, DC 20001
(800) 326-0959
www.greenpeace.org
greenpeace.usa@wdc.greenpeace.org
Worldwide environmental and peace group with offices on most continents.

Greenpeace's campaign for a nuclear-free future includes educational programs and protest actions (highlighted on web site). Actively working to stop missile defense.

Greens / Green Party USA
P.O. Box 1134
Lawrence, MA 01842
(978) 682-4353
www.greenparty.org
gpusa@greens.org
and
The Association of State Green Parties (ASGP)
P.O. Box 18452
Washington, DC 20036
(202) 232-0335
www.greenparties.org
capeconn@rcn.com
Political party and movement with many state chapters and local affiliates. Included in their political platform and values is the abolition of nuclear weapons and nonviolent conflict resolution. Aligned with Green Parties throughout the world.

Indigenous Environmental Network
P.O. Box 485
Bemidji, MN 56601
(218) 751-4967
www.ienearth.org/hotspots.
    html (nuclear campaign)
ien@igc.org
An alliance of grassroots indigenous peoples working to protect the sacredness of Mother Earth from contamination and exploitation by strengthening, maintaining, and respecting traditional teachings and natural laws.

Institute for Common Sense in the Nuclear Age (ICSNA)

3250 Wilshire Blvd., Suite 1400
Los Angeles, CA 90010-1438
(213) 386-4901
www.nuclearcommonsense.org
info@nuclearcommonsense.org
Founded by Dr. Helen Caldicott, ICSNA's mission is to produce a massive and effective public education campaign via the media within the United States about the dangerous nuclear policies of the Bush administration. ICSNA experts representing the military, science, medicine, politics, and academia will appear on television and radio, and write articles and opinion pieces about the missile defense program, the militarization of space, and a revival of the nuclear power industry. ICSNA, a 501(c)(3) non-profit, is now fundraising its initial five-year budget. Donations are tax-deductible.

International Action Center
39 West 14th Street, #206
New York, NY 10011
(212) 633-6646
www.iacenter.org
www.actionsf.org
iacenter@action-mail.org
and
2489 Mission Street., #28
San Francisco, CA 94110
(415) 821-6545
iac@actionsf.org
and
1247 E Street, SE
Washington, DC 20003
(202) 543-2777
iacenterdc@yahoo.com
Founded by Ramsey Clark, former U.S. attorney general, IAC has been a leading organizer of opposition (including massive protests in New York, Wash-

ington, and San Francisco) against U.S. military intervention, such as the attacks on Iraq, Kosovo, and Afghanistan. IAC's mission also links militarism and corporate greed with struggles against racism and oppression throughout the world. Web site receives over 1 million hits a day.

International A.N.S.W.E.R. (Act Now to Stop War & End Racism)
National Office:
39 West 14th Street, #206
New York, NY 10011
(212) 633-6646
Washington DC Office:
1247 E Street, SE
Washington, DC 20003
(202) 543-2777
www.internationalanswer.org
info@internationalanswer.org
Coordinates actions to build an active antiwar movement internationally. Web site has calendar of worldwide events.

International Physicians for the Prevention of Nuclear War (IPPNW)
727 Massachusetts Avenue
Cambridge, MA 02139
(617) 868-5050
www.ippnw.org
ippnwbos@ippnw.org
A nonpartisan global federation of medical organizations dedicated to research, education, and advocacy relevant to the prevention of nuclear war. 1985 Nobel Peace Prize winner. Initiated from the work of Physicians for Social Responsibility under the leadership of Dr. Helen Caldicott.

Lawyers' Committee on Nuclear Policy
(LCNP)
211 East 43rd Street
New York, NY 10017
(212) 818-1861
www.lcnp.org
lcnp@aol.com
Works on many global initiatives to rid
the world of nuclear weapons.

Military Toxics Project
P.O. Box 558
Lewiston, ME 04243
(877) 783-5091 (toll free)
www.miltoxproj.org
Committed to uniting activists, organizations, and communities to clean up
military pollution and prevent toxic
and radioactive pollution caused by
military activities, including depleted
uranium.

Mothers Alert
c/o Citizens Energy Council
P.O. Box U
Hewitt, NJ 07421
www.mothersalert.org
mothersalert@yahoo.com
Dedicated to providing information on
the links between increased radiation
in the environment and health. Active
in many campaigns to stop nuclear
power, including the Tooth Fairy project, showing very high levels of strontium 90 in baby teeth.

Nevada Desert Experience
P.O. Box 46645
Las Vegas, NV 89114-6645
(702) 646-4814
www.nevadadesertexperience.org
nde@igc.org; sallight1@earthlink.net
Calls for ending the destruction and for

repairing the damage caused by U.S.
and U.K. nuclear testing on Western
Shoshone land at the Nevada Test Site.
Sponsors gatherings. Also working to
stop shipments of radioactive waste to
the Site, 60 miles from Las Vegas.

Nuclear Age Peace Foundation/
Abolition 2000
PMB 121, 1187 Coast Village Road,
Suite 1
Santa Barbara, CA 93108-2794
(805) 965-3443
www.wagingpeace.org
www.abolition2000.org
wagingpeace@napf.org
admin@abolition2000.org
Committed to the abolition of all nuclear weapons and other weapons of
mass destruction and to promoting
peaceful conflict resolution.

Nuclear Control Institute
1000 Connecticut Avenue, NW, Suite 410
Washington, DC 20036
(202) 822-8444
www.nci.org
nci@mailback.com
Monitors nuclear activities worldwide and pursues strategies to halt nuclear arms, particularly eliminating
atom-bomb materials—plutonium and
uranium—from nuclear power and research programs.

Nuclear Disarmament Partnership
(NDP)
1875 Connecticut Avenue, NW,
Suite 1012
Washington, DC 20009
(202) 667-4260 ext. 240
www.disarmament.org
kcrandall@disarmament.org

A joint effort of Peace Action, Physicians for Social Responsibility, 20/20 Vision, Women's Action for New Directions, and Abolition 2000 to promote effective nuclear-disarmament measures by linking education and action between U.S. citizen advocates for disarmament and Washington, DC policy makers. Congressional Action Days, online fact sheets, and other programs.

Nuclear Information Resource Service
1424 16th Street, NW, # 404
Washington, DC 20036
(202) 328-0002
www.nirs.org
nirsnet@nirs.org
Conducts many campaigns against nuclear power and radioactivity.

Peace Action
1819 H Street, NW, #420
Washington, DC 20006
(202) 862-9740
www.peace-action.org
pdeccy@peace-action
The largest grassroots peace and disarmament organization in the U.S., committed to the abolition of nuclear weapons and redirection of excessive Pentagon spending to domestic investment. 27 state chapters.

Physicians for Social Responsibility
1875 Connecticut Ave, NW, Suite 1012
Washington, DC 20009
(202) 667.4260
www.psr.org
psrnatl@psr.org
Works to create a world free of nuclear weapons, global environmental pollution, and gun violence. Over 30 chap-

ters in the U.S. Under the direction of past president Dr. Helen Caldicott, membership expanded to over 20,000.

Project Abolition
109 East Clinton Street, Suite 10
Goshen, IN 46528
(219) 535-1110
www.projectabolition.org
kmartin@fourthfreedom.org
amillar@fourthfreedom.org
kwood@igc.org (field coordinator)
Founded in 1999 to increase public awareness of nuclear danger and build grassroots support in the United States for the reduction and elimination of nuclear weapons. Very active against the missile defense program.

Proposition One Committee
P.O. Box 27217
Washington, DC 20038
(202) 462-0757
www.prop1.org
prop1@prop1.org
A grassroots voter initiative movement for disarmament of nuclear weapons and the conversion of the arms industries to human and environmental needs.

Shundahai Network
P.O. Box 6360
Pahrump, NV 89041
(775) 537-6088
www.shundahai.org
shundahai@shundahai.org
Formed at the Nevada Test Site in 1994 by long-term nuclear disarmament activists, at the request of Corbin Harney, a Western Shoshone spiritual leader. International network of activists and organizations integrating the environ-

mental, peace and justice, and indigenous land rights communities. Affinity groups: Western Shoshone Defense Project, (702) 468-0230, and Western Shoshone National Council, (702) 879-5203.

Tri-Valley CAREs (Communities
    Against a Radioactive Environment)
2582 Old First Street
Livermore, CA 94550
(925) 443-7148
www.igc.org/tvc
marylia@earthlink.net
Founded in 1983 by local citizens concerned that nuclear weapons work at the Lawrence Livermore and Sandia National Laboratories was poisoning their communities.

TUC Radio
P.O. Box 410009
San Francisco, CA 94141
(415) 861-6962
www.tucradio.org
tuc@tucradio.org
Produces weekly national radio program on planetary well-being and globalization heard on over 100 stations. Archive of over 400 programs—many feature environmental and antinuclear themes.

Union of Concerned Scientists
2 Brattle Square
Cambridge, MA 02238
(617) 547-5552
www.ucsusa.org/security/oweapons.
    html
www.thebulletin.org
ucs@ucsusa.org
Working toward changes in U.S. policy to allow deep cuts in nuclear forces and to reduce the alert status of nuclear

missiles. Also has global food, environment and clean energy programs. Publishes *Bulletin of the Atomic Scientists*.

The Video Project
P.O. Box 77188
San Francisco, CA 94107
1-800-4-PLANET (1-800-475-2638)
www.videoproject.org
video@videoproject.net
Distributes the largest collection of nuclear disarmament-oriented videos to schools, groups, and individuals. Also offers many environmental videos. Run by Act Now Productions.

Washington Peace Center
1801 Columbia Road, NW, Suite 104
(202) 234-2000
www.washingtonpeacecenter.org
wpc@igc.org
Has played a significant role in the antinuclear movements of the 1970s and was a key player in the Central America and Middle East solidarity movements of the 1980s. Today, the Peace Center plays a critical role in organizing opposition to U.S. militarism in Iraq, Afghanistan, and elsewhere. Also addresses organizing for economic and social justice (nationally and internationally) toward establishing structures and relationships that are nonviolent, nonhierarchical, humane, and just.

Western States Legal Foundation
1504 Franklin Street, Suite 202
Oakland, CA 94612
(510) 839-5877
wslf@earthlink.net
A non-profit, public interest organization which monitors, analyzes, and challenges nuclear weapons programs at the Lawrence Livermore, Los

Alamos, and Sandia National Laboratories, and the Nevada Test Site.

Women Against Military Madness
(WAMM)
310 East 38th Street, Suite 225
Minneapolis, MN 55409
(612) 827-5364
www.worldwidewamm.org
wamm@mtn.org
A nonviolent feminist organization working to dismantle systems of militarism and global oppression.

Women's Action for New Directions
691 Massachusetts Avenue
Arlington, MA 02476
(781) 643-6740
www.wand.org
info@wand.org
Mission: To empower women to act politically to reduce militarism and violence and to redirect excessive military spending to human and environmental needs. Weekly e-mail political action alert bulletin to members, as well as a quarterly newsletter. Supports women political candidates who support WAND objectives. Over 30 U.S. chapters. Founded by Dr. Helen Caldicott. For WAND's resources on missile defense, go to: www.no-starwars.org.

Women's International League for
Peace and Freedom (WILPF)
1213 Race Street
Philadelphia, PA 19107
(215) 563-7110
www.wilpf.org/disarm/disarm.html
wilpf@wilpf.org
Working to achieve through peaceful means world disarmament, full rights for women, racial and economic justice, and an end to all forms of violence.

World Policy Institute / Arms Trade
Resource Center (ATRC)
New School University
66 Fifth Avenue, 9th floor
New York, NY 10011
(212) 229-5808
www.worldpolicy.org/wpi/
wpiprojects.html#arms
berrigaf@newschool.edu
ATRC does original research, public education, and policy advocacy on the problem of conventional arms proliferation. Many projects focused on nuclear weapons, global arms sales, stopping terrorism, etc.

FOUNDATIONS THAT DONATE TO ANTINUCLEAR CAUSES

Ploughshares Fund
Fort Mason Center
Bldg. B, Suite 330
San Francisco, CA 94123
(415) 775-2244
www.ploughshares.org
ploughshares@ploughshares.org
A public grantmaking foundation that supports initiatives for stopping the spread of weapons of war, from nuclear arms to land mines. Funds over 130 programs, many of them focused on reducing the nuclear threat.

W. Alton Jones Foundation
232 East High Street
Charlottesville, VA 22902-5718
(804) 295-2134
www.wajones.org/programs/secure
secure@wajones.org
The Secure World Program seeks to build a secure world, free from the nuclear threat. Funds over 190 programs.

Antinuclear Civil Resistance Groups in the United States and Great Britian

In the nonviolent tradition of Martin Luther King, Jr., Mahatma Gandhi, and Rosa Parks, these groups work to end the nuclear threat by incorporating civil resistance to consciously disrupt the nuclear war machine. Defending their actions under international law, many activists risk arrest and jail sentences to prevent the crime against all humanity that is a nuclear holocaust. General antinuclear groups also engage in civil resistance as the circumstances merit.

Members of many religious faiths, including indigenous peoples, Christians, Muslims, Jews, and Buddhists, have come together to oppose nuclear weapons and work for their elimination.

Many Catholic Worker group houses in the U.S. support local and national resistance in addition to their tradition of hospitality to the poor. Houses with a legacy of antinuclear activism are included here.

The work of Rosalie Bertells, Roman Catholic nun, scientist, and internationally recognized expert on low-level radiation, has documented how more than 1.3 billion people have been killed, sickened, or maimed by nuclearism over the past 55 years, and how pollution released from nuclear weapons operations has drastically changed the global environment and endangers all life forms.

Plowshares (or Ploughshares) groups are faith-based activists who, in the spirit of Bible passage, *Isaiah* 2:4, are willing to hammer on launch computers and pour their blood on missile silos and pray until arrested and be sent to prison, in some cases for long periods of time. For information about the continuing Plowshares actions, see www. plowsharesactions.org.

Complete contact information as to addresses, telephone numbers or web sites were in some instances not available at press time.

[Katya Komisaruk; Jack Cohen-Joppa, The Nuclear Resister; Bonnie Urfer; Bruce Gagnon, Global Network Against Weapons and Nuclear Power in Space; Ground Zero Center for Non-violent Action, and many others helped compile this list.]

Aldermaston Women's Peace Camp
07808 553778 (U.K. mobile)
www.gn.apc.org/aldermastonwpc
Conducts a monthly peace camp at
AWE Aldermaston in Berkshire, England. A women-only campaign, committed to stop the production of
Britain's nuclear weapons at AWE Aldermaston, and to see the site shut
down and safely decommissioned.

Alliant Action
(651) 698-9352; (651) 698-2810
www.circlevision.org/
    alliantaction.html#top
alliantaction@circlevision.org
info@circlevision.org
Focus: Weekly vigils at Minnesota's
largest military contractor and war
merchant Alliant Techsystems (affili-
ated with Lockheed Martin), doing
missile defense work in Eagan, MN.

Brandywine Peace Community
P.O. Box 81
Swarthmore, PA 19081
(610) 544-1818
www.geocities.com/brandywine
    peace/index.htm
brandywine@juno.com
Focus: Lockheed Martin, the world's
largest weapons corporation and the
major U.S. nuclear weapons contractor.

Buddhist Peace Fellowship
P.O. Box 4650
Berkeley, CA 94704
(510) 655-6169
www.bpf.org
bpf@bpf.org
Many Dharma centers and local practice groups campaign against nuclear
weapons and nuclear waste, including

actions at weapons locations and the
Nevada Test Site.

Campaign for the Accountability of
    American Bases (CAAB)
8 Park Row
Otley, West Yorkshire LS21 1HQ
England
+44 (0)1943 466405
www.caab.org.uk
anniandlindis@caab.org.uk
A campaign opposed to weapons of
mass destruction in general and nuclear weapons, in particular the U.S.
missile defense system. Focus: American bases in the U.K. and abroad.

Christian Campaign for Nuclear
    Disarmament
cnd@gn.apc.org

Citizen Weapons Inspections
www.nonviolence.org/nukeresister/
    nr112/citizeninspections.html
Perspective: Without a recognized
means to enforce international law
against weapons of mass destruction,
individuals are responsible for identify-
ing the sites and elements of weapons
that represent crimes against humanity. Web site includes coalition contact
information.

Citizens for Peace in Space
P.O. Box 915
Colorado Springs, CO 80901
(719) 389-0644
Focus: U.S. Space Command (Colorado
Springs, CO). Very active in stopping
missile defense.

Citizens Awareness Network
(413) 339-5781; (802) 387-4050

Des Moines Catholic Worker
P.O. Box 4551
Des Moines, IA 50306

Dorothy Day Catholic Worker
503 Rock Creek Church Road, NW
Washington, DC 20010
(202) 882-9649

Faslane Peace Camp
Shandon, Helensburgh G84 8NT
Scotland
01436 820901(U.K.); +44 1436 820901
   (international)
http://ds.dial.pipex.com/cndscot/
   camp/index.htm
www.hull.ac.uk/php/ggsdah/faslane/
   Fashome.htm
cndscot@dial.pipex.com
faslanepeacecamp@hotmail.com
Focus: Stopping the Trident submarine,
Britain's weapon of mass destruction, at
the Scottish site chosen for the U.K.'s
Polaris nuclear defense system.

Fellowship of Reconciliation
P.O. Box 271
Nyack, NY 10960
(914) 358-4601
www.forusa.org

Global Network Against Weapons and
   Nuclear Power in Space
[see page 191]

Ground Zero Center for Nonviolent
   Action
16159 Clear Creek Road, NW
Poulsbo, WA 98370
(360) 779-4672; (360) 377-2586
www.gzcenter.org
info@gzcenter.org
Focus: Bangor Submarine Base, the Pacific home for Trident submarines, and

witnessing to and resisting all nuclear
weapons.

Healing Global Wounds
P.O. Box 420
Tecopa, CA 92389
(760) 852-4175
and
P.O. Box 13
Boulder Creek, CA 95006
(408) 338-0147
hgw@scruznet.com
Focus: Nuclear weapons testing and its
impact on Native Americans.

Jonah House
Baltimore, MD
(410) 233-6238
disarmnow@erols.com
Focus: Plowshares activism against nuclear weapons.

Livermore Conversion Project
P.O. Box 31835
Oakland, CA 94604
(510) 663-8065
Focus: Lawrence Livermore National
Laboratory.

Loaves & Fishes Catholic Worker
1614 Jefferson Street
Duluth, MN 55812
(218) 728-0629
Focus: Project ELF in Wisconsin (often
works with Nukewatch and a coalition
of groups).

Los Alamos Study Group
212 East March Street, Suite 10
Santa Fe, NM 87501
(505) 982-7747
info@lasg.org
Focus: Los Alamos National Laboratory.

National War Tax Resistance
  Coordinating Committee
P.O. Box 6512
Ithaca, NY 14851
(800) 269-7464
nwtrcc@nwtrcc.org

National Trident Resistance Network
(203) 777-3849
skobasa@snet.net

New Hampshire Peace Action
P.O. Box 771
Concord, NH 03302
(603) 228-0559

No Nukes Pennsylvania
(717) 260-0700

Norfolk Catholic Worker
1321 West 38th Street
Norfolk, VA 23508
(757) 423-5420

Nuclear Free Great Lakes
c/o Citizens Action Coalition of
  Indiana
2015 Western Ave, #101
South Bend, IN 46629
(219) 232-7905

The Nuclear Resister (magazine)
P.O. Box 43383
Tucson, AZ 85733
(520) 323-8697
www.nonviolence.org/nukeresister
nukeresister@igc.org
Information about and support for im-
prisoned antinuclear and antiwar activists.

Nukewatch / Coalition to Stop Project
  ELF
P.O. Box 649

Luck, WI 54853
(715) 472-4185
www.nukewatch.org
nukewtch@lakeland.ws
Focus: Project ELF, the launching system for Trident nuclear submarines.
Collaboration of several antinuclear
groups.

Oak Ridge Environmental Peace
  Alliance (OREPA)
P.O. Box 5743
Oak Ridge, TN 37831
(865) 483-8202
www.stopthebombs.org
orep@earthlink.net
Focus: Oak Ridge Y-12 nuclear weapons
plant.

Peace Action New Mexico
226 Fiesta Street, Suite F
Santa Fe, NM 87501
(505) 989-4812
lanlaction@igc.org
Focus: Los Alamos National Laboratory.

Peace Park Antinuclear Vigil
http://prop1.org [click on "Peace
  Park"]
Outside the White House 24 hours a
day since June 3, 1981.

Raytheon Peacemakers
c/o Martha Gagliardi & Hattie Nestel
P.O. Box 248
Athol, MA 01331
(978) 249-9400
mgagliardi@arrsd.mec.edu
Focus: Weapons giant Raytheon.

St. Francis Catholic Worker
(573) 443-0096
sfhcw913@aol.com

St. Martin De Porres Catholic Worker
House
26 Clark Street
Hartford, CT 06120
(860) 724-7066
cdoucot@erols.com

Trident Ploughshares 2000 (U.K.)
42-46 Bethel Street
Norwich NR2 1NR
United Kingdom
01324 880744
www.tridentploughshares.org
tp2000@gn.apc.org
Focus: Trident submarines in the U.K.

Vandenberg Action Coalition
(831) 421-9794
www.geocities.com/vafb_m19
peter@rcnv.org
pnut119@hotmail.com

Focus: Vandenburg AFB (missile defense & ICBM test launches). Very active in stopping missile defense.

War Resisters League
339 Lafayette Street
New York, NY 10012
(212) 228-0450
www.warresisters.org
wrl@igc.apc.org
Advocates Gandhian nonviolence to create a democratic society free of war and oppression. Publishes *The Nonviolent Activist* (readable on-line). Over 40 local chapters. Organizes yearly "Day Without the Pentagon" nationwide to educate about the impact of a weapons economy. YouthPeace campaign counters militarism and the culture of violence it perpetuates.

NOTES

Introduction

1. Situation Reports, STATFOR.com (September 11, 2001)
2. "Pentagon Recommends the use of Nuclear Weapons," *Japan Today* (September 19, 2001)
3. Jeffrey St. Clair, "Trigger Happy, Bush Administration Hawks Want to Deploy 'Mini-nukes' Against Osama Bin Laden," www.inthesetimes.com/issue/25/26/news2.shtm
4. Dana Milbank, "U.S. Pressed on Nuclear Response, A Policy of Less Ambiguity, More Pointed Threat Is Urged," *The Washington Post* (October 5, 2001)
5. Wes Vernon, "Father of Neutron Bomb: Use it on Osama," www.af.mil/vision (September 25, 2001)
6. James Carroll, "Bombing with Blindfolds On" *The Boston Globe* (November 11, 2001)
7. Nigel Chamberlain and Dave Andrews, "Thermobaric Warfare," www.cnduk.org/briefing/thermo.htm (January 11, 2001)
8. Andrew Maykuth and Jonathan S. Landay, "US Intensfies Attacks with BLU-82s, Knight Ridder Newspapers (November 6, 2001)
9. "Backgrounder on Russian Fuel Air Explosives (Vacuum Bombs)," Human Rights Watch, www.hrw.org/press/2000/02/chech0215b (February 2000)
10. Tim Weiner, "U.S. Bombs Strike 3 Villages and Reportedly Kill Scores," *The New York Times* (December 1, 2001)
11. "Protocol 1, Relating to the Protection of Victims of International Armed Conflicts, Article 51"
12. Geov Parrish, "Where the Bodies Are," www.workingforchange.com (October 22, 2001)
13. "Unexploded Cluster Bombs Pose Threat to Civilians, Dawn, Pakistan," Centre for Research on Globilisation, www.globalresearch.ca/articles/DAW111B (November 15, 2001)
14. Amy Waldman, "Food Drops Go Awry, Damaging Houses," *The New York Times* (November 21, 2001)
15. "Unexploded Cluster Bombs Pose Threat to Civilians"
16. USAF, www.aviationzone.com/facts/ac130
17. "International Action Center Factsheet: The Truth About the U.S. War in Afghanistan," [www.iacenter.org] *Toronto Globe and Mail* (November 3, 2001)
18. Michael R. Gordon, "U.S. Hope to Break the Taliban with Pounding From the Air," *The New York Times* (October 17, 2001)
19. Thom Shanker and Stephen Lee Myers, "U.S. Sends in Special Plane with Heavy Guns," *The New York Times* (October 16, 2001)

20. "Bunker Busters Brought Into Use," *The Daily Camera,* Camera Wire Services; and Raymond Whitaker, "Attack on Afghanistan: Washington's Fearsome Arsenal," *The Independent* (November 4, 2001)
21. Dr. Helen Caldicott, *Missile Envy* (New York: William Morrow, 1984)
22. "Afghan War Will Shape Future U.S. Military Structure," www.stratfor.com (November 23, 2001)
23. Dr. Farrukh Saleem, "Stop the Bombing Please," *JANG,* Pakistan, www.jang.com.pk/thenews/index (November 4, 2001)
24. Professor Marc Herold, "A Dossier on Civilian Victims of United States' Aerial Bombing of Afghanistan," www.cursor.org/stories/civilian_deaths.htm (December 6, 2001)
25. Bill Nichols and Peter Eisler, "The Threat of Nuclear Terror Is Slim But Real," *USA Today* (November 28, 2001)
26. Ibid.
27. Louis Charbonneau, "Experts Warn of Low Grade Nuclear Terror Attack," *Reuters* (November 2, 2001)
28. Matthew Wald, "Reactors and Their Fuel are Among the Flanks U.S. Needs to Shore Up," *The New York Times* (November 4, 2001)
29. Dr Helen Caldicott, *Nuclear Madness* (New York: W.W. Norton, 1994)
30. Michael Grunwald and Peter Behr, "Are Nuclear Plants Secure?" *The Washington Post* (November 3, 2001)
31. Matthew Wald, "Agency Weighs Buying Drug to Protect Against Radiation-Induced Ailments," *The New York Times* (November 29, 2001)
32. Efward Luttwak, "New Fears, New Alliance," *The New York Times* (October 2, 2001)
33. Barbara Slavin, "Pentagon Builds Case to Bomb Iraq," *USA Today* (November 11, 2001)
34. "Iraq Says to Consider Return of Weapons Monitoring," *Reuters* (November 21, 2001)
35. Elaine Scolino and Alison Mitchell, "Calls for New Push into Iraq Gain Power in Washington," *The New York Times* (December 3, 2001)
36. Anton La Guardia, "Iraq 'Not Linked to September 11,' " *The Telegraph* (November 11, 2001)
37. Barbara Slavin, "Pentagon Builds Case to Bomb Iraq," *USA Today* (November 19, 2001)
38. Jason Vest, "Beyond Osama: The Pentagon's Battle with Powell Heats Up," *The Village Voice* (November 20, 2001)
39. Sandra Sobieraj, "U.S. to Pursue Missile Test Plans," The Associated Press (November 16, 2001)
40. Jim Wurst, "U.S. Supports Weapons Cut While Opposing International Agreements," *News World Communications Inc.* (November 14, 2001)
41. "N-Testing to Resume?" Opinion/Editorial, www.downwinders.org
42. Jim Wurst, "A Call to Arms Control," *The Washington Times* (November 12, 2001)
43. "Action on Threat Reduction," andrew@californianpeaceaction.org (November 9, 2001)
44. Ibid.
45. William D. Hartung, "Bush's War on Terrorism: Who Will Pay and Who Will Benefit?" www.motherjones.com (September 27, 2001)

46. William D. Hartung, "The War Dividend," www.motherjones.com (September 28, 2001)

47. John Pilger, "The Truths They Never Tell Us," *The New Statesman* (November 26, 2001)

48. James Dao, "U.S. is Expecting to Spend $1 Billion a Month on War," *The New York Times* (November 12, 2001)

49. Frida Berrigan, "The War Profiteers: How Are Weapons Manufacturers Faring in the War," World Policy Institute (December 17, 2001)

50. "The Military Budget Up, Up, and Away," Arms Trade Resource (December 20, 2001)

51. Michael R. Gordon, "U.S. Arsenal: Treaties vs. Nontreaties," *The New York Times* (November 14, 2001)

52. Simon Tisdall, "How the Future was Shanghaied," *The Guardian* (October 21, 2001)

Chapter One: The Tragedy of Wasted Opportunities

1. Robert S. Norris and William M. Arkin, "Global Nuclear Stockpiles, 1945–2000" *Bulletin of the Atomic Scientists* (March/April 2000)

2. William D. Hartung, "Quick on the Trigger," *The Progressive Report* (November 2000)

3. Janne E. Nolan, *An Elusive Consensus: Nuclear Weapons and American Security After the Cold War* (Washington, DC: The Brookings Institution Press, 1999)

4. Robert S. Norris and William M. Arkin, "U.S. Nuclear Forces, 2000," *Bulletin of the Atomic Scientists* (May/June 2000)

5. Robert S. Norris and William M. Arkin, "Russian Nuclear Forces, 2000," *Bulletin of the Atomic Scientists* (July/August, 2000)

6. Personal communication with Admiral Eugene Carroll, Center for Defense Information, Washington, D.C.

7. *Peace Action: People for Nuclear Disarmament,* Australia (August/September 2000)

8. Bruce Blair, "U.S. Expanding Nuclear Targets," *The Guardian* (June 16, 2000)

9. Ibid.

10. Andrew Lichterman and Jacqueline Cabasso, *Faustian Bargain 2000—why "stockpile stewardship" is fundamentally incompatible with the process of nuclear disarmament,* Western States Legal Foundation (5108395387)

11. Jacqueline Cabasso, "The Role of National Legislations and International Legal Instruments," *Proceedings of the International Symposium, Science, Ethique & Society, Federation Mondiale Des Travailleurs Scientifiques* (Case 404-93514 Montreuil, Cedex)

12. William D. Hartung and Frida Berrigan, "Lockheed Martin and the GOP: Profiteering and Pork Barrel Politics with a Purpose," www.worldpolicy.org/projects/arms

13. William D. Hartung, "Stop Throwing Money at the Arms Trade Resource Center," (October 12, 2000)

Chapter Two: The Reality of Nuclear War

1. "1MT Surface Blast: Pressure Damage," *The American Experience,* WGBH/PBS Online

2. Dr. Helen Caldicott, *Missile Envy, Revised Edition* (New York: Bantam Books, 1986)

3. Stephen A. Fetter and Kosta Tsipis, "Catastrophic Releases of Radioactivity," *Scientific American*, vol. 244, no. 4 (April 1981)

4. Caldicott

5. R. P. Turco, A. B. Toon, T. P. Ackerman, J. B. Pollack, C. Sagan, "The Climatic Effects of Nuclear War," *Scientific American* (August 1984)

6. Dean Babst, "Nuclear Winter," www.geocities.com/mothersalert/nuclearwinter.html

7. Ibid.

8. Bruce G. Blair, Harold A. Feiveson, and Frank N. von Hippel, "Taking Nuclear Weapons off Hair Trigger Alert," *Scientific American* (November 1999)

9. Ibid.

10. Ibid.

11. James Risen, "Computer Ills Meant U.S. Couldn't Read Its Spy Photos," *The New York Times* (April 12, 2000)

Chapter Three: It's a Mad, Mad World: Nuclear Scientists and the Pentagon Play with Deadly Gadgets

1. David Pasztor, "Building a Better Bomb," *San Francisco Weekly* (May 27, 1998)

2. Normon Solomon, "Los Alamos Spin," *San Francisco Bay Guardian* (June 28, 2000)

3. Ibid.

4. R. P. Turco, A. B. Toon, T. P. Ackerman, J. B. Pollack, C. Sagan, "The Climatic Effects of Nuclear War," *Scientific American* (August 1984)

5. David Beers, "The Bomb Tribe," *Mother Jones* (March/April 1995)

6. Dr. Andreas Toupadakis, "Personal Responsibility for World Peace," University of Notre Dame Conference on Averting Nuclear Anarchy: The Current Crisis in Arms Control (March 31, 2000)

7. Raphael Aron, *Cults Too Good to Be True* (New York: HarperCollins, 1999)

8. Ibid.

9. Beers

10. Hugh Gusterson, *Nuclear Rites: A Weapons Laboratory at the End of the Cold War* (Berkeley, CA: University of California Press, 1996)

11. Ibid.

12. Ibid.

13. Ibid.

14. Ibid.

15. Ibid.

16. Ibid.

17. William M. Arkin, "The Last Word," *The Bulletin of the Atomic Scientists* (September/October 2000)

18. Gusterson

19. Ibid.

20. Ibid.

21. Much of the material for this section was obtained from a study conducted by Janne E. Nolan in the book *An Elusive Consensus: Nuclear Weapons and American Security After the Cold War* (Washington, DC: Brookings Institution Press, 1999)

22. Ibid.
23. Ibid.
24. Ibid.
25. Ibid.
26. Ibid.
27. Ibid.
28. Ibid.
29. Ibid.
30. Ibid.
31. Ibid.
32. Ibid.
33. Ibid.
34. Ibid.
35. Ibid.
36. Ibid.
37. Ibid.
38. Ibid.
39. Ibid.
40. Ibid.
41. Ibid.
42. Ibid.
43. Ibid.
44. Ibid.
45. Ibid.
46. Ibid.

Chapter Four: Corporate Madness and the Death Merchants

1. Dr. Helen Caldicott, *If You Love This Planet* (New York: W.W. Norton, 1992)
2. Ibid.
3. Ibid.
4. William Greider, "Waking Up the Global Elite," *The Nation* (October 2, 2000)
5. The Heritage Foundation 1999 Annual Report, 214 Massachusetts Avenue, NE, Washington, DC, 20002
6. Caldicott
7. William D. Hartung, World Policy Institute, "The Military-Industrial Complex Revisited: How Weapons Makers Are Shaping U.S. Foreign and Military Policies," *The Progressive Response*, Vol. 3, No. 23 (July 2, 1999)
8. The CATO Institute 1998 Annual Report, 1000 Massachusetts Avenue, NW, Washington, DC, 20001
9. Leslie Wayne, "After High-Pressure Years, Contractors Tone Down Missile Defense Lobbying," *The New York Times* (June 13, 2000)
10. Ibid.
11. Hartung
12. Ibid.
13. Ibid.

14. Ibid.
15. Steven Lee Meyers, "Pentagon Says North Korea Is Still a Dangerous Military Threat," *The New York Times* (September 22, 2000)
16. Bill Mesler, "Why the Pentagon Hates Peace in Korea," *The Progressive Response* (September 2000)
17. Hartung
18. Howard French, "Seoul Fears U.S. Is Chilly About Détente with North," *The New York Times* (March 23, 2001)
19. Hartung
20. Ibid.
21. Frida Berrigan, Michelle Ciarrocca, and William Hartung, "Lockheed Martin: All-Purpose Merchant of Death," *ATRC Update*, Part III, Arms Trade and Resource Center, (212) 229-5808, ext. 106, (June 26, 2000)
22. "Smart Shopping by the Pentagon," *The New York Times* (October 31, 2001)
23. William D. Hartung, "Saint Augustine's Rules—Norman Augustine and the Future of the American Defense Industry," *World Policy*, Volume XIII, Number 2, (Summer 1996)
24. Ibid.
25. Ibid.
26. Ibid.
27. Ibid.
28. Ibid.
29. Norman Kempster, "New Anti-terror Cabinet Agency Urged; Defense; The Plan Calls for an Overhaul of the Government's Approach to Security and Predicts an Attack on American Soil Within 25 Years," *Los Angeles Times* (February 1, 2001)
30. Ibid.
31. Berrigan, et al.
32. Ibid.
33. Hartung
34. Ibid.
35. Hartung, "The Military-Industrial Complex Revisited"
36. Ibid.
37. William D. Hartung and Frida Berrigan, "Lott and Lockheed: Partners in Influence Peddling," hartung@newschool.edu (July 31, 2000)
38. Ibid.
39. William D. Hartung, "Lawmakers, Guns and Money," World Policy Institute (September 23, 2000)
40. Dana Milbank, "On the Outside Looking In as Tom DeLay Whips Up Some Fundraisers," *The Washington Post* (August 2, 2000)
41. Charles Lewis, " 'Reformer With Results'? Don't Count on It," an investigative report for the Center for Public Integrity (August 8, 2000)
42. Hartung and Berrigan, "Lott and Lockheed: Partners in Influence Peddling"
43. Ibid.
44. Lewis
45. William D. Hartung, "Moderate or Militant: Will the Real Dick Cheney Please Stand Up?" World Policy Institute and Arms Trade Resource Center, hartung@newschool.edu
46. Personal communication with Admiral Eugene Carroll, Center for Defense Information

47. Lowell Bergman, Diana B. Henriques, Richard A. Oppel, Jr., and Michael Moss, "Mixed Reviews for Cheney in Chief Executive Role at Halliburton," *The New York Times* (August 24, 2000)

48. Gretchen Morgenson, "The Stock Option and the Stump, Cheney's Retirement Package, Some Uncharted Territory," *The New York Times* (August 18, 2000)

49. William D. Hartung, "Blue Dogs, Pork and 'Morality': The Arms Industry's Buyout of the Democratic Party," Arms Trade Resource Center, hartung@newschool.edu (August 11, 2000)

50. John Isaacs "Senator Lieberman: On the Right of the Democratic Party on National Security Issues," Council for a Livable World, jdi@clw.org (August 7, 2000)

51. Hartung, "Blue Dogs, Pork and 'Morality' "

52. "Lockheed Martin: All-Purpose Merchant of Death," World Policy Institute Issue Brief (July 2000)

53. Hartung, "The Military-Industrial Complex Revisited"

54. Ibid.

55. Aaron Rothenburger, "Arms Makers' Cozy Relationship with the Government" in "Action Atlas on U.S. Arms," *Mother Jones,* motherjones.com (1999)

56. Geov Parrish, "General Electric, U.S. Arms Exporters," *Mother Jones,* Mojowire

57. Ibid.

58. Alice Slater, "The Global War System," *Abolition 2000* web site

59. Pamina Firchow and Tamar Gabelnick, "Uncle Sam: Arms Merchant to the World," *San Francisco Examiner* (September 8, 2000)

60. Firchow, et al.

61. Geov Parrish, "Lockheed Martin, U.S. Arms Exporters," *Mother Jones,* Mojowire

Chapter Five: Manhattan II

1. Nuclear Non-Proliferation Treaty, 1995

2. "Stockpile Stewardship and Management Program," Department of Energy, Defense Programs (February 29, 1996)

3. Ibid.

4. Dr. Robert Civiak, "Managing the U.S. Nuclear Weapons Stockpile," Tri-Valley CAREs (July 2000)

5. David Pasztor, "Building a Better Bomb," *San Francisco Weekly* (May 27, 1998)

6. Ibid.

7. Pasztor

8. Ibid.

9. Civiak

10. Senior Airman Adam Stump, 354th Fighter Wing Public Affairs, "B-2 Successfully Drops Improved Bunker Buster Bomb," *Air Force News Service* (March 26, 1998)

11. Andrew Lichterman and Jacqueline Cabasso, "Faustian Bargain 2000: Why 'Stockpile Stewardship' Is Fundamentally Incompatible with the Process of Nuclear Disarmament," Western States Legal Foundation, 1440 Broadway, Suite 500, Oakland, CA 94612 (May 2000)

12. Ibid.

13. Ibid.

14. Ibid.

15. Steve Goldstein, "Bill Would Give Push to 'Mini-Nuke,'" *The Philadelphia Inquirer* (October 16, 2000)

16. Dana Milbank, "U.S. Pressed on Nuclear Response," *The Washington Post* (October 5, 2001)

17. Ibid.

18. Wes Vernon, "Father of Neutron Bomb: Use It on Osama," www.af.mil/vision (September 25, 2001)

19. Civiak

20. Lichterman and Cabasso

21. Christopher E. Paine and Dr. Matthew McKinzie, "When Peer Review Fails: The Roots of the National Ignition Facility (NIF) Debate," Natural Resources and Defense Council (www.nrdc.org/nuclear/nif2/findings.asp)

22. James Glanz, "Laser Project Is Delayed and Over Budget," *The New York Times* (August 19, 2000)

23. "National Ignition Facility Amendment," susangordon@earthlink.net (June 24, 2000)

24. Richard Boone, "'Stockpile Stewardship' of Nuclear Weapons: the Deal to Subsidize Nuclear Weaponeers," *Facing Reality*, Project for Participatory Democracy (March 1998)

25. Greg Mello, "Subcritical Tests," Western States Legal Foundation (February 10, 2000)

26. Civiak

27. Walter Pincus, "Virtual Nuclear Arms Tests," *The Washington Post* (July 22, 2000)

28. Boone

29. M. G. McKinzie, T. B. Cochran, C. E. Paine, "Explosive Alliances: Nuclear Weapons Simulation Research at American Universities," NRDC Nuclear Program (January 1998)

30. William Broad, "Los Alamos Scientist's Book Creates a New Controversy," *The New York Times* (August 5, 2001)

31. McKinzie, et al., "Explosive Alliances"

32. Ibid.

33. Ibid.

34. Ibid.

35. Ibid.

36. Ibid.

37. Boone

38. Matthew L. Wald, "Nuclear Sites May Be Toxic in Perpetuity, Report Finds," *The New York Times* (August 8, 2000)

39. H. Joseph Hebert, "Nuke Sites May Not Be Rid of Contaminants," AP (August 8, 2000)

40. Ibid.

41. "Study: Levels of Waste Unknown," AP (October 27, 2000)

42. Matthew L. Wald, "U.S. Raises Estimate of Plutonium Spilled Making Arms," *The New York Times* (October 21, 2000)

43. Ibid.

44. Mary Manning, "Nuclear Tests Released More Harmful Elements Than Admitted Before," *Las Vegas Sun* (October 23, 2000)

45. Robert Alveraz, "Nuclear Wildfires," *The Nation* (September 18/25, 2001, Vol. 271, No. 8, p 30, 2000)

46. Personal communication with Robert Alveraz

47. Judith Graham, "U.S. Hot to Fireproof Nuclear Sites, Western Fires Spark Fear of Catastrophe," *Chicago Tribune* (October 25, 2000)

48. "Gap Questions Government Assurances on Hanford Fire," Government Accountability Project, www.whistleblower.org/www/hanfire.htm (July 20, 2000)

49. Graham

50. Alveraz

51. Judith Graham, "U.S. Hot to Fireproof Nuclear Sites, Western Fires Spark Fear of Catastrophe," *Chicago Tribune* (October 25, 2000)

52. Alveraz

53. Manning

Chapter Six: Star Wars: The Story of National Missile Defense Systems

1. "National Missile Defense," Union of Concerned Scientists Fact Sheet, "The Safeguard Experience" (February 1999)

2. Francis Fitzgerald, *Way Out There in the Blue* (New York: Simon and Schuster, 2000)

3. Ibid.

4. Ibid.

5. Ibid.

6. Ibid.

7. Robert Aldridge, "Son of Star Wars: A Background Paper on National Missile Defense," Pacific Life Research Center (August 15, 2000)

8. Ibid.

9. Ibid.

10. Theodore Postol, "The Target Is Russia," *The Bulletin of the Atomic Scientists* (March/April 2000)

11. Ibid.

12. Andrew Marshall, "U.S. Spies Inflate Risk from 'Rogue' States," *Independent Digital (UK) LTD* (June 11, 2000)

13. Ibid.

14. Fitzgerald

15. Aldridge

16. John Isaacs, "A Political Decision," *The Bulletin of the Atomic Scientists* (March/April 2000)

17. Steven Lee Myers, "U.S. Missile Plan Could Reportedly Provoke China," *The New York Times* (August 10, 2000)

18. President Bush's speech on missile defense, CNN.com (May 1, 2001)

19. Jack Spencer and Michael Scardaville, "In Defense of Development of Missiles," *The Miami Herald* (October 17, 2000)

20. Steve LaMontagne, "Missile Defense Encourages Proliferation," *Washington Times* (October 22, 2000)

21. John Isaac, "A Political Decision," *The Bulletin of the Atomic Scientists* (March/April, 2000)

22. AFP, "Senate Overwhelmingly Passes U.S. Defense Authorization Bill" (October 2, 2001)

23. Karl Grossman, *Weapons in Space* (New York: Seven Stories Press, 2001)

24. Karl Grossman, "Master of Space," *The Progressive Report* (January 2000)

25. Burton Richter, "It Doesn't Take Rocket Science," *The Washington Post* (July 23, 2000)

26. Dr. Helen Caldicott, *Missile Envy* (New York: Bantam, 1986)

27. Bruce Gagnon, "New Names for Star Wars Systems," globalnet@mindspring.com (August 16, 2001)

28. Much of this section is derived from the excellent work by Bob Aldridge, who became one of my mentors in the early 1980s after I read his book *Counterforce Syndrome.*

29. "Theater Missile Defense," Union of Concerned Scientists, Appendix 2, from the UCS Fact Sheet

30. Charles Pena, "From the Sea: National Missile Defense Is Neither Cheap Nor Easy," CATO Institute (September 6, 2000)

31. Rodney Jones, "Taking National Missile Defense to Sea: A Critique of Sea-based and Boost Phase Proposals," Council for a Livable World (October 2000)

32. Aldridge

33. Ibid.

34. Mary McGrory, "Star Wars: Calling a Bomb a Bomb," *The Washington Post* (July 13, 2000)

35. William Broad, "Ex-Employee Says Contractor Faked Results of Missile Tests," *The New York Times* (March 7, 2000)

36. Ibid.

37. Jim Wolf, "FBI Probing TRW for Missile Defense Related Fraud," Reuters (September 11, 2000)

38. David Abel, "Tiff Between White House, MIT Professor Gets Personal," *The Boston Globe* (September 8, 2000)

39. David Wright and Theodore Postol, "Missile Defense System Won't Work," *The Boston Globe* (May 11, 2000)

40. "BMDO Plans Next NMD Integrated Ground Test in Early 2001," *Inside Missile Defense* (September 20, 2000)

41. Stan Crock, "The Dodgy Science of Missile Defense," *Business Week* (August 17, 2000)

42. David Wood, "Missile Defense Would Take President—and Maybe Humans—Out of the Loop," *The Seattle Times* (July 19, 2000)

43. Ibid.

44. Crock

45. David Morgan, "Ballistic Missile Defense: A Submission to the Standing Committee on National Defense and Veterans Affairs," House of Commons, Ottawa, Canada (April 5, 2000)

46. Nick Cohen, "Protection Racket. It Matters Not Whether It's Bush or Gore. We'll Still Have Son of Star Wars Foisted on U.S.," *The Observer* (November 12, 2000)

47. Robert Alveraz, "Nuclear Wildfires," *The Nation* (September 18/25, 2001)

48. "Warhead Elimination," Union of Concerned Scientists Briefing (July 11, 2000)

49. Michael R. Gordon, "U.S. Arsenal: Treaties vs. Nontreaties," *The New York Times* (November 14, 2001)

50. David E. Sanger, "Before and After Bush and Putin's Banter: No Agreement on Missile Defense," *The New York Times* (November 16, 2001)

51. "Warhead Elimination"

52. "ABM Talking Points," *Bulletin of the Atomic Scientists* (January 20, 2000)

53. "China Warns Future U.S. President Over Missile Shield," AFP (November 2, 2000)

54. John Isaacs, "A Political Decision," *Bulletin of the Atomic Scientists* (March/April, 2000)

55. Nigel Chamberlain, "CND's Response to Paul Brown" *The Guardian* (April 5, 2000)

56. Richard Norton-Taylor, "Son of Star Wars British Ministers Are Going Along Meekly with Washington's Grandiose and Dangerous Plans," *The Guardian* (April 15, 2000)

57. Christopher Lockwood, "Westminster Backlash Over 'Son of Star Wars,'" *Telegraph* (August 3, 2000)

58. Hugo Young, "The Planned American Missile Shield May Not Even Work Properly," *The Guardian* (February 1, 2000)

59. Theodore Postol, "The Target Is Russia," *Bulletin of the Atomic Scientists* (March/April, 2000)

60. Ibid.

61. Robert Suro, "Key Missile Defense Radar Planned for Remote Island," *The Washington Post* (May 7, 2000)

62. Srdja Trifkovic, "The Coming National Missile Defense Scandal," The Rockford Institute (June 21, 2000)

Chapter Seven: Space: The Next American Empire

1. William B. Scott, "USSC Prepares for Future Combat Missions in Space," *Aviation Week & Space Technology* (August 5, 1996)

2. "Implementing Our Vision for Space Control," Speech by General Richard B. Meyers, United States Space Foundation, Colorado Springs (April 7, 1999)

3. Keith Hall, speech to National Space Club (September 15, 1997)

4. Halford J. Mackinder, "The Geographical Pivot of History," *Geographical Journal* (1904)

5. Karl Grossman, *Weapons in Space* (New York: Seven Stories Press, 2001)

6. "Vision for 2020," U.S. Space Command, Director of Plans (February 1997)

7. Bruce Gagnon, "Space Domination: Pyramid to the Heavens," www.globenet.free-online.co.uk (July 16, 2000)

8. Grossman

9. Gagnon

10. "Space Force Is an Idea Whose Time May Have Come," editorial, *Florida Today* (March 14, 2000)

11. "The Investment in Space," *Air Force Association Organization Magazine* (February 2000)

12. Paul Hoversten, "The Best Defense May Be a Better Map," *The Washington Post* (February 19, 2000)

13. "The Warfighters Edge: First Hyperspectral Images from Space," *Spacewar*, Kirtland Air Force Base (September 8, 2000)

14. Bruce Gagnon, "Pentagon Funds Global 3-D Mapping Mission," www.spacedaily.com/spacecast/news/milspace-00c.html (January 31, 2000)
15. "White House Supports Air Force Vision on Spacelift Partnership," Air Force press release (February 9, 2000)
16. Bruce Gagnon, "Global Network Against Weapons & Nuclear Power in Space"
17. Tech. Sgt. Stefan Alford, "AOC Declared Official Weapons System," www.af.mil/news/Sept2000 (September 12, 2000)
18. Army Captain Deanna Bague, "Joint Services Conduct Modern Day War Games," *Air Force News* (June 21, 2000)
19. "Megawatt Laser Test Brings Space Based Lasers One Step Closer," *Space Daily* (April 26, 2000)
20. Grossman
21. U.S. Air Force Advisory Board, "New World Vistas: Air and Space Power for the 21st Century," *Space Technology Volume* (1996)
22. Mike Moore, "Unintended Consequences," *Bulletin of the Atomic Scientists* (January/February 2000)
23. Bill Sweetman, "Securing Space for the Military," *Jane's Defense Weekly*
24. Ellen Messmer, "US Army Kick-Starts Cyberwar Machine," *CNN-Technology* (November 22, 2000)
25. Richard J. Newman, "The New Space Race," *US News and World Report* (November 8, 1999)
26. James Oberg, "NASA Knew Mars Polar Lander Doomed," UPI (March 21, 2000)
27. John Noble Wilford, "NASA Sending 2 Rovers to Mars in Twin Trips Landing in 2004," *The New York Times* (August 11, 2000)
28. John Noble Wilford, "Shaken NASA Offers New Plan for Mars Exploration Missions," *The New York Times* (October 27, 2000)
29. Jerome Groopman, "Medicine on Mars: How Sick Can You Get During Three Years in Deep Space?" *The New Yorker* (February 14, 2000)
30. Barry E. DiGregorio, "Rethinking Mars Sample Return," *Space News* (1997)
31. Leonard David, "NASA Urged to Create Facility for Mars Samples," *Space News* (March 31–April 6, 1997)
32. Brian Berger, "NASA Considers Building Mars-Sample Quarantine Facility," *Space News* (April 12, 1999)
33. Keay Davidson, "NASA, Slightly Humbled, Dreams On," *San Francisco Examiner* (January 23, 2000)
34. Leonard David, "Business Sees Cash Among the Constellations," *Space.com* (January 9, 2000)
35. Jackie Alan Giuliano, *Healing Our World: Weekly Comment,* "The Migration Begins: The International Space Station,", 2000 Lycos, Inc., registered trademark of Carnegie Mellon University (September 2000)
36. "International Space Station: Missions Accomplished and Continued Assembly, and Background," www.boeing.com (November 7, 2000)
37. George Musser and Mark Alpert, "How to go to Mars," *Scientific American* (March 2000)
38. Karl Grossman, "U.S. Plans to Wage War in Space," presentation in Toronto, Canada (October 2000)
39. Paul Hoversten, "Nuclear-powered Probes in the Plans for Mars," *Space.com*

40. "DRAFT Programmatic Environmental Impact Statement for Accomplishing Expanded Civilian Nuclear Energy Research and Development and Isotope Production Missions in the United States, Including the Role of the Fast Flux Test Facility," Summary, United States Department of Energy, Office of Nuclear Energy, Science and Technology, Washington DC (July 2000)

41. AP, "Lab Contamination rises," *The Denver Post* (July 30, 1996); Reuters, "Workers exposed to plutonium at U.S. Lab" (March 17, 2000)

42. Grossman

43. Dave Dooling, "Nuclear Power: The Future of Space Flight," *Space.com* (July 22, 2000)

44. "U.S. Launch Vehicles Claimed Harmful to Ozone Layer," *Moscow Aviatsiya Rosmonavtika* (December 6, 1989)

45. William J. Broad, "NASA Moves to End Longtime Reliance on Big Spacecraft," *The New York Times* (September 16, 1991)

46. Sharon Ebner, "Solid Fuel Critics Say Ozone Is in Danger," Mississippi *Sun Herald* (March 17, 1990)

47. Karl Grossman, "The Pentagon Prepares to 'Master Space,'" *Network* (July/August 2000)

Chapter Eight: Nuclear War in the Gulf and Kosovo

1. Nicholas Arons, "A Few Vignettes from Iraq," *The Guardian, Iraq Notebook* (Volume 7, 2000)

2. John Pilger, "War Against the Children," *The Guardian, Iraq Notebook* (Volume 7, 2000)

3. Joby Warrick, "Maps Reveal Scattering of Ky. Plutonium," *The Washington Post* (October 1, 2000)

4. Dr. Helen Caldicott, *Nuclear Madness* (New York: W. W. Norton, 1994)

5. Dr. Asaf Durakovic, "Medical Consequences of Internal Contamination with Depleted Uranium," *Metal of Dishonor*, International Action Center, NY (1999)

6. Caldicott

7. Dolores Lymburner, "Another Human Experiment," *Metal of Dishonor*, International Action Center, NY (1999)

8. Ibid.

9. "Former Head of Pentagon's Depleted Uranium Project Condemns Environmental Contamination of Vieques, Puerto Rico, an Island Close to 10,000 U.S. Citizens," www.viequeslibre.org (June 14, 2000)

10. Rob Edwards, "Dangerous Work," *New Scientist* (July 8, 2000)

11. Thomas Williams, "Depleted Uranium in NATO Bases Raises Health Issues," *Hartford Courant* (May 20, 1999)

12. Matthew L. Wald, "Nuclear Sites May Be Toxic in Perpetuity," *The New York Times* (August 8, 2000)

13. Personal communication with Dr. Hari Sharma

14. Federally Sponsored Research on Persian Gulf Veterans' Illnesses, Annual Report to the Congress of the Research Working Group of the Persian Gulf Veterans Coordinating Board (April 1997)

15. Dr. Melissa McDiarmid, Transcript of March 25, 1998 VA.DoD teleconference on the D.U. Program

16. Cat Euler, "The Consequences of Depleted Uranium Ammunitions," Campaign for Depleted Uranium (July 6, 2000)

17. Sara Flounders, "The Struggle for an Independent Inquiry," *Metal of Dishonor*, International Action Center, NY (1999)

18. Siegwart-Horst Gunther, "How Depleted Uranium Shell Residues Poison Iraq, Kuwait and Saudi Arabia," *Metal of Dishonor*, International Action Center, NY (1999)

19. Dan Fahey, "Depleted Uranium Weapons: Lessons from the 1991 Gulf War, A Postwar Disaster for Environment and Health," Laka Foundation (May 1999)

20. Ibid.

21. Ibid.

22. Gunther

23. Euler

24. Environmental News Service, "Children Most at Risk from Depleted Uranium" (April 26, 2001)

25. Cherry Norton, "Health Danger that Divides Medical Opinion," *Independent News* (October 4, 1999)

26. Fahey

27. Ibid.

28. Ibid.

29. Cat Euler, "Depleted Uranium Exposures to Civilians and Military Personnel," Paper presented at the 14th Low Level Radiation and Health Conference in Reading (July 14, 2000)

30. Lilliam Irizarry, "Puerto Rico Wants Uranium Probe," AP (January 11, 2001)

31. Max Sinclair and Jared Israel, "DU Used—in Somalia and Germany," *Der Spiegel* (January 23, 2001)

32. John Catalinotto and Sarah Flounders, "Is the Israeli Military Using Depleted-Uranium Weapons Against the Palestinians?" International Action Center, NY (November 27, 2000)

33. "Depleted Uranium Weapons," Issue Brief, Physicians for Social Responsibility (July 1999)

34. "European Countries Announce Balkans Syndrome Tests for Military Personnel," SGT (January 10, 2001)

35. "Radiation Fears Widen in Balkan Peace Force," *London Telegraph* (December 31, 2000)

36. Marlise Simons, "Radiation from Bombing Alarms Europe," *The New York Times* (January 7, 2001)

37. Burt Herman, "Uranium Use in Kosovo War Suspected as Veterans Fall Ill," *The Sydney Morning Herald* (January 9, 2001)

38. Kim Sengupta, "MoD 'Monitoring' Health Checks on Kosovo Soldiers," news@antic.org (December 28, 2000)

39. Patricia Reaney, "Scientists Doubt Uranium Weapons Cancer Link," *The New York Times* (January 9, 2001)

40. BBC News, "Depleted Uranium Threatens Balkan Cancer Epidemic" (July 30, 1999)

41. The Committee for National Solidarity, UNEP, Geneva (January 16, 2001)

Chapter Nine: The Lockheed Martin Presidency
and the Star Wars Administration

1. M. W. Gruzy, "Viewpoints: Fighting Fictional Foes," *St. Louis Post-Dispatch* (January 17, 2001)
2. Russell Mokhiber and Robert Weissman, "Corporate Conservative, Corporate President," *Focus on the Corporation* (January 11–18, 2001)
3. Diedre Griswold, "As Economic Storm Gathers, CEOs & Bush Meet in Secret," *Workers World Newspaper* (January 18, 2000)
4. Jerry White and Paul Scherrer, "Washington Inaugural Celebrations: Corporate America Welcomes Bush," *WSWS: News and Analysis: North America: U.S. Politics* (January 20, 2001)
5. William D. Hartung and Michelle Ciarrocca, "Reviving Star Wars," *The Baltimore Sun* (January 21, 2001)
6. United States Department of Defense press advisory (January 24, 2001)
7. Sean Gonsalves, "Star Wars: The Sequel," *The Cape Cod Times* (December 26, 2000)
8. Martin Kettle, "Bush Team Is Back with a Vengeance," *The Guardian Weekly* (January 4–10, 2001)
9. William D. Hartung, "Rumsfeld: An Ideologue on Missile Defense," World Policy Institute, www.foreignpolicy-infocus.org/papers/rumsfeld
10. Jean-Michel Stoullig, "Rumsfeld Commission Warns against 'Space Pearl Harbor,' " AFP (January 11, 2001)
11. Tabassum Zakaria, "Helms Says U.S. not Bound by ABM Treaty" *globalnet@mindspring.com* (January 11, 2000)
12. "Rumsfeld in Cold War Time Warp, Says Angry Moscow," Reuters (March 20, 2001)
13. Elaine Sciolino and Eric Schmitt, "In Defense Post, Infighter Known for Working the Means to his End," *The New York Times* (January 8, 2001)
14. Karl Grossman, globalnet@mindspring.com
15. David Corn, "Questions for Powell," *The Nation* (January 8, 2001)
16. Jane Perlez, "A Soldier Statesman Who Has Advocated a Blend of Strength and Caution," *The New York Times* (December 17, 2000)
17. Robert Parry, "From Vietnam to Florida's Disenfranchisement of Black Voters: Unheroic Moments in Secretary of State Nominee Colin Powell's Career," *Between the Lines* (December 25, 2000)
18. Ian Brodie, "Powell Insists Defense Rests on 'Star Wars,' " *London Times* (December 18, 2000)
19. Barry Schweid, "Powell Pushes for Missile Defense," AP (January 17, 2001)
20. David Storey, "Powell Endorses U.S. Missile Defense," Reuters (January 17, 2001)
21. Schweid
22. Ibid.
23. Kettle
24. Daryl Kimball, "N-Testing Update," dkimball@clw.org (December 19, 2000)
25. Karl Grossman, "Aerospace Executives on Bush Star Wars Team," globalnet@mindspring.com (December 24, 2000)
26. Serge Trifkovic, "President Bush's Foreign Affairs," www.rockfordinstitute.org/NewsST121500 (December 15, 2000)

27. Ibid.

28. "The Armageddon Nominee," *The Boston Globe* (April 2, 2001)

29. Nick Cohen, "Protection Racket," *The Observer* (November 12, 2000)

30. Polly Toynbee, "Special Report: The U.S. Elections," *The Guardian* (August 22, 2000)

31. Mikhail Gorbachev, "Mr. Bush, the World Doesn't Want to Be American," *International Herald Tribune* (December 30, 2000)

32. Simon Saradzhyan, "Russian Strategic Missile Force Stripped of Oversight for Two Space Forces," *Space News* (January 25, 2001)

33. Vladimir Isachenkov, "Putin Proposes Deeper Nuclear Cuts," AP (November 13, 2000)

34. "U.S., Russia Sign Missile Agreement," AP (December 16, 2000)

35. Space Wire, "Former Military Commanders Oppose U.S.-Russian Launch Notification Agreement," AFP (December 12, 2000)

36. AFP, "Putin Warns U.S. Against Missile Defense Buildup, Enlarging NATO" (January 26, 2001)

37. "Russia Threatens to Take Arms Race to Space," *London Times* (January 25, 2001)

38. Michael Wines "In Letter to Bush, Putin Urges Wider U.S.-Russian Cooperation," *The New York Times* (January 25, 2001)

39. Ian Traynor, "Russia Halts Military Cuts as Hawks Take over in U.S.," *The Guardian* (January 18, 2001)

40. Erik Eckholm, "Power of U.S. Draws China and Russia to Amity Pact" *The New York Times* (January 14, 2001)

41. John Pomfret, "Beijing and Moscow to Sign Pact, Stronger Ties Sought to Check U.S. Influence" *The Washington Post* (January 13, 2001)

42. John Pomfret, "U.S. Now a 'Threat' in China's Eyes," *The Washington Post* (November 15, 2000)

43. Bruce Gagnon, globalnet@mindspring.com

44. Achin Vanaik, "How Much of a Reprieve?" *The Hindu* (September 27, 2000)

45. "Missile Sale to Taiwan Has Unusual Clause," AP (September 30, 2000)

46. Robert Burns, "U.S. Military Chiefs Recommend Plan to Resume Surveillance Flights," AP (April 17, 2001)

47. Michael O'Hanlon, "A Need for Ambiguity" *The New York Times* (April 27, 2001)

48. Gay Alcorn, "Bush Backpedals on Taiwan" *The Sydney Morning Herald* (April 27, 2001)

49. William Foreman, "U.S. Weapons Would Be Little Help if China Gets Serious," *The Sydney Morning Herald* (April 27, 2001)

50. Walden Bello, "Asia 2025: The Pentagon Prepares for Asian Wars," www.focusweb.org (October 17, 2000)

51. Jon Basil Utley, "20 Facts About China (Rarely Reported to Conservatives)," www.againstbombing.com/chinapoints.html

52. Dr. Nicholas Berry, "Is China an Aggressive Power?" *The Defense Monitor* (2000)

53. AFP, "China Warns U.S. to Keep Taiwan out of Any Missile Defense Plans" (January 18, 2001)

54. Bruce Gagnon, globalnet@mindspring.com

55. "U.S. Secretly Monitors Asian Navies from Australia," AP (January 27, 2001)

56. Paul Monk, "Dragon's Tail," *The Australian's Review of Books* (November 2000)

57. Ellen Hale, "Radar Picks up 'Star Wars;' Rumor in England, Uneasiness at Key Site," *USA Today* (January 24, 2001)

58. Andy Beckett "Special Report: George Bush's America," *The Guardian* (April 20, 2001)

59. Julie Hyland, "Bush Commitment to U.S. National Defense Causes International Protests," www.wsws.org (January 24, 2001)

60. "Allies Ponder Response to Bush on Missile Defense," Reuters (January 25, 2001)

61. Hugo Young, "A Special Relationship Under Fire from Missile Defense," *The Guardian* (December 21)

62. "Bush Upsets Danish Opposition Over Missile Defense Station," AFP (January 24, 2001)

63. "Leader," *The Guardian* (January 4, 2001)

64. Michael Gordon, "EU to Go It Alone with New Army," *The New York Times* and *The Sydney Morning Herald* (November 22, 2001)

65. Ian Blach, "U.S. Warns Europe Against Building Own Defense Force," *The Guardian* and *The Sydney Morning Herald* (December 6, 2001)

66. Steven Lee Myers, "A Call to Put the Budget Surplus to Use for the Military," *The New York Times* (September 28, 2000)

67. Simon Tisdall, "Bush Plan for Fortress America Hawks Say Threats Justify Defense Boost," *The Guardian* (January 13, 2001)

68. William D. Hartung, "The War Dividend," *motherjones.com* (September 28, 2001)

69. William D. Hartung, "Bush's War on Terrorism: Who Will Pay and Who Will Benefit?" *motherjones.com* (September 27, 2001)

70. www.defenselink.mil/pubs/dod101/largest/html

71. Gustav Niebuhr, "A Mission to Redirect Money Used for Defense," *The New York Times* (October 3, 2000)

72. "What the World Wants," The World Game Institute, wgi@worldgame.org

73. "Bush's Defense Advisors Faced by 68 Conflicts Worldwide: Report," AFP (January 2, 2001)

Appendix A: Major U.S. Nuclear-Weapons Makers

1. Kevin Martin, Rachel Glick, Rachel Ries, Tim Nafziger, and Mark Swier, "The Real Rogues Behind Star Wars," *Z magazine*, www.thirdworldtraveler.com/Corporations/Real_Rogues.html (September 2000)

2. Ibid.

3. Ibid.

4. Ibid.

5. Ibid.

6. Ibid.

7. Ibid.

8. Ibid.

9. Ibid.

10. Ibid.

11. Ibid.

INDEX